Population projections

Population projections by sex,
age and marital status for
United Kingdom and constituent
countries from mid-1977

Prepared by the Government Actuary
in consultation with
the Registrars General

Series PP2 no.9

London : Her Majesty's Stationery Office

ISBN 0 11 690699 5

Acknowledgements

The Government Actuary, in consultation
with the three Registrars General, has
responsibility for the production of
the national projections and for the
assumptions regarding the future on
which they are based. The Government
Actuary wishes to acknowledge the
co-operation of the Registrars
General and also the contribution of
the Office of Population Censuses and
Surveys in preparing the booklet for
publication.

Contents

		Page
1	Introduction	1
2	Method of projection	3
3	Base population	4
4	Mortality	6
5	Migration	9
6	Fertility	11
7	Projections by marital condition	13
8	Results of the projections	16
9	References	20

Appendix Tables

I	England and Wales	(a - e see below)	22
II	Wales	(a - c ")	36
III	Scotland	(a - c, e ")	46
IV	Great Britain	(a - d ")	58
V	Northern Ireland	(a - c, e ")	70
VI	United Kingdom	(a - d ")	82

a   Actual and projected Total population as at mid-year, by sex and age-groups, 1951, 1961, 1971 to 2017

b   Annual changes in projected Total population 1977 to 2017

c   Projected Total population as at mid-year, by sex and single ages 1977 to 1989, 1991 - 2017

d   Projected Total population as at mid-year, by sex, age and marital condition 1977 - 2017

e   Mortality rates by sex and single ages, 1977 - 2017

Introduction

Purpose

The primary purpose of the national projections is to provide an estimate of the future population of the United Kingdom (and of its constituent countries), and of its composition by sex and age, as a common framework for use in national planning in a number of different fields. A single principal projection is made each year on a set of assumptions which seems most appropriate on the basis of the statistical evidence available at the time. The fact that a single principal projection is made, and not a variety of projections on different sets of assumptions, has led some commentators to conclude that the projection is a 'forecast' or 'prediction' of the future course of events. It fulfils this role, however, only to a limited extent, because it is not possible to make exact predictions of changes in the behaviour of individuals or the structure of society; indeed changes can take place which were previously quite unforeseen. Also in some circumstances the publication of a projection can itself influence future events, for knowledge of the long term implications of current trends may lead to changes in the attitudes and behaviour of individuals and society in general, and in Government policies, so as to invalidate the assumptions on which the projection was based.

In spite of the uncertainties, it has been considered more suitable to produce a single 'official' set of projections for common use to provide consistency between the many users of the projections. Neither the amount of detail given in this booklet, nor the sophistication of some of the techniques used, should deflect the reader from constantly bearing in mind that any set of projections is based on a particular set of assumptions which are almost certain to prove incorrect to a greater or lesser degree, even though at the time they were adopted they were judged to be the best that could be made.

However in planning for the future it is often necessary to examine the consequences of making differing assumptions about births, deaths and migration. The effects of varying the fertility assumptions together with some comments on the effect of varying the mortality and migration assumptions were the subject of some discussions in the penultimate section of the previous booklet in this series.[1]

Projections of the population of the United Kingdom and of its constituent countries by sex and age have been made by the Government Actuary's Department since the 1920s. One of the main uses of the earlier projections was in connection with long term financial estimates under the Contributory Pensions Acts and other schemes of social insurance. Projections made since the war, however, have been increasingly used in all areas of government planning. Since 1955 new projections have been made every year and, through publication by the Central Statistical Office and by the Registrars General, have been made generally available. The present booklet is one of an annual series, started in 1970, which gives detailed results of the projections for the United Kingdom, for Great Britain and for each of the constituent countries separately, together with a description of the methods employed and of the assumptions on which the projections are based.

For the mid-1977 based projections only minor changes have been made to the assumptions underlying the mid-1976 based principal projection. As a result, the population projections presented in this booklet differ only marginally from the principal projections in the 1976 based set. Some users may find that they do not need to revise analyses and estimates based on the previous set of projections.

Other publications

The projections are published in summary form in the *Annual Abstract of Statistics* and in *Social Trends* in the year following the base year of the projections, and those for the UK in one of the issues of the *Monthly Digest of Statistics* appearing earlier in the year. Summaries of the projections for England and Wales, Great Britain and the United Kingdom appear in an OPCS Monitor (Series PP2). The projection for Wales also appears in the same series and in the *Digest of Welsh Statistics* in the year following the base year. Projections for Scotland appear in the *Registrar General's Quarterly Return*, in the *Annual Report, Part II*, and in the *Scottish Abstract of Statistics*. For Northern Ireland publication is in that country's *Digest of Statistics* in the September issue in the year following the base year. Relevant articles also appear in *Population Trends*, the quarterly journal of the Office of Population Censuses and Surveys.

Further information

Reasons of space have precluded the publication of all the projected figures available; for example Appendix Tables 1(c) - VI(c) only give numbers by age and sex at five-yearly intervals from 1991 onwards. Figures for years not covered by the table (up to the year 2015) may be obtained from the Government Actuary's Department (22 Kingsway, London WC2B 61E, telephone 01-242 6828).

In addition to the national projections which are the subject of this booklet, regional projections are prepared and published by the Office of Population Censuses and Surveys by the General Register Office for Scotland, and by the Welsh Office.

Method of projection

Component method

Separate projections were made for England and Wales combined, for Wales alone, for Scotland and for Northern Ireland, in each case on bases agreed with the appropriate Registrar General. The projections for Great Britain are the sum of the projections for England and Wales combined and for Scotland; those for the United Kingdom add the projection for Northern Ireland to that for Great Britain.

The projections for each of the countries were made by what is known as the component method. The basic principle is that the number of persons of a given age and sex who will be in the population one year after the starting date of the projections is the number a year younger in the starting population, less deaths in the year, plus or minus migrants. To obtain the children under age 1 one must take the survivors of births assumed to occur during the year, adjusted for migration. Given the starting population and assumptions regarding births, deaths and migration the process can be repeated indefinitely. Algebraically the formula used is:

$$ {}^{n}P_{x} = {}^{n-1}P_{x-1} (1 - {}^{n-1}q_{x-\frac{1}{2}}) \pm {}^{n}M_{x} $$

where ${}^{n}P_{x}$ = number of persons at mid-year n aged x last birthday;

${}^{n}M_{x}$ = net number of migrants in the period mid-year (n-1) to mid-year n who would be aged x last birthday at mid-year n;

${}^{n-1}q_{x-\frac{1}{2}}$ = probability of death within a year for a person aged (x-1) last birthday at mid-year (n-1).

The mortality of migrants between the date of the migration and mid-year n is small and has been ignored.

Births

The number of births in a future year is obtained by applying fertility rates to the total number of women in the population for each age between 15 and 45.

The formula used is:

$$ {}^{n}B = \sum_{x=15}^{x=44} \frac{1}{2} ({}^{n-1}P_{x}^{f} + {}^{n}P_{x}^{f}) {}^{n}f_{x} $$

where ${}^{n}B$ = number of live births in period mid-year (n-1) to mid-year n;

${}^{n}P_{x}^{f}$ = number of women at mid-year n aged x last birthday;

and ${}^{n}f_{x}$ = fertility rate for births in the period mid-year (n-1) to mid-year n to women aged x last birthday at childbirth.

The total number of births is then divided by sex in a constant ratio.

To obtain for each sex the number of survivors of babies born during the year the formula used is:

$$ {}^{n}P_{0} = {}^{n}B (1 - {}^{n-1}_{\frac{1}{2}}q_{0}) \pm {}^{n}M_{0} $$

where ${}^{n-1}_{\frac{1}{2}}q_{0}$ = probability that a baby of that sex born in the period mid-year (n-1) to mid-year n will die before the end of that period;

and ${}^{n}M_{0}$ = net number of migrants of that sex in the same period who are under age 1 at mid-year n.

The four elements entering into the calculations are thus: the base population; mortality; migration; fertility. These are considered in turn.

Base Population

Definitions

The projections are based on the estimates of the Total population at mid-1977 made by the Registrars General The Total population is defined as the Civilian population plus all members of HM forces stationed at home and abroad. This is in contrast with the Home population which is defined as the Civilian population plus members of the armed forces, both UK and allied, stationed in the country. The Total population, which excludes some persons whose stay in the country is only temporary and includes some whose absence is also only temporary, provides a better base than the Home population for a projection involving estimates of the numbers of births, deaths and survivors in the population in future years. It is nevertheless necessary to bear in mind the difference in definition between Home and Total population when using the projections and when, for instance, making comparisons with most of the tables in publications such as *Population Trends*.

Estimates

The estimates of the population at mid-1977 used in this booklet with the exception of those for marital condition are part of the new series of population estimates which have been recalculated for each year back to mid-1971. Thus the estimates for mid-1977 are not directly comparable with estimates for previous years used as the base population in earlier projection booklets. The marital condition estimates used in this booklet are however based on the old series of estimates as the recalculated series for marital condition was not available at the time of preparation of the mid-1977 based projections. More information about the new estimates can be obtained from *Population Trends* 10, 11 and 12 and also from the OPCS Monitors in the PP1 series.

The estimates of the Total population at mid-1977 in five-year age-groups are given in Table 1. Figures for individual ages and by marital status are given in the Appendices.

Table 1 Estimated Total population at mid-1977

thousands

Age last birthday	England and Wales	Wales	Scotland	Great Britain	Northern Ireland	United Kingdom
Males						
0-4	1,579	90	174	1,753	67	1,820
5-9	1,946	110	217	2,163	76	2,239
10-14	2,076	117	236	2,312	81	2,393
15-19	1,932	106	227	2,159	73	2,232
20-24	1,765	96	199	1,964	59	2,023
25-29	1,777	97	185	1,962	51	2,013
30-34	1,744	95	171	1,916	51	1,966
35-39	1,437	79	147	1,583	42	1,626
40-44	1,399	77	144	1,543	39	1,582
45-49	1,422	81	146	1,568	38	1,606
50-54	1,458	84	147	1,605	38	1,643
55-59	1,397	81	136	1,533	37	1,570
60-64	1,258	73	122	1,381	32	1,413
65-69	1,128	65	111	1,239	28	1,266
70-74	835	48	80	915	20	935
75-79	482	28	45	527	13	540
80-84	225	13	20	246	6	251
85 & over	117	6	11	127	2	130
All ages	23,977	1,346	2,518	26,496	753	27,248
Females						
0-4	1,491	84	164	1,655	63	1,718
5-9	1,840	103	206	2,045	71	2,117
10-14	1,971	110	224	2,195	75	2,270
15-19	1,831	104	215	2,046	69	2,115
20-24	1,666	94	190	1,857	56	1,913
25-29	1,747	98	181	1,928	48	1,975
30-34	1,706	94	167	1,873	49	1,922
35-39	1,394	76	149	1,543	42	1,585
40-44	1,354	74	149	1,503	41	1,544
45-49	1,422	80	154	1,577	41	1,618
50-54	1,496	87	157	1,653	41	1,694
55-59	1,500	89	155	1,655	39	1,694
60-64	1,421	83	148	1,569	37	1,605
65-69	1,388	81	144	1,532	36	1,567
70-74	1,190	69	122	1,312	29	1,341
75-79	883	51	89	971	21	993
80-84	537	30	51	588	12	600
85 & over	361	20	31	392	6	399
All ages	25,198	1,427	2,696	27,894	776	28,670
Persons	49,175	2,773	5,214	54,390	1,529	55,918

Mortality

Past trends

The course of mortality rates over the thirty years since the end of the Second World War has been broadly similar in England and Wales, Scotland and Northern Ireland. There has been a general pattern of improving mortality but the rate of improvement has tended to slow down in recent years after the fairly dramatic changes of the immediate post-war period. The rate of improvement has also varied considerably between different age-groups and has affected males and females to differing extents. The general features of recent trends are illustrated in broad age-groups in Figure 1. Further details are given in the published studies of mortality trends by Martin and Daykin[2,3] and in the recent OPCS study *Trends in mortality 1951-1975*[4], which also gives details of trends in rates of mortality by cause of death.

Assumptions made

Although mortality rates have shown clearly defined trends over quite long periods, there have also been substantial fluctuations from year to year, sometimes as a result of climatic factors or because of the prevalence of particular illnesses. In 1976 an influenza epidemic in the early part of the year gave rise to significantly higher mortality at the older ages than in the preceding few years. In the same period infant mortality fell to a lower level than ever recorded. For the mid-1976 based projection the three years 1973, 1974 and 1975 were used to provide a measure of the level of mortality. A period shorter than three years may be unrepresentative because of annual fluctuations and a longer period might begin to mask the underlying trend. The experience of these three years is still thought to provide an average in line with the long term trend. Therefore the mid-1976 assumptions for mid-77 to mid-78 have been adopted for the base year in the current projections.

As in previous projections it has been assumed that mortality rates at the various ages will decrease in geometrical progression, ie by constant proportions each year, for the forty years of the projection period. The proportions appropriate for each age were reviewed for the previous (mid-1976 based) projections on the basis of work, commissioned specially for this purpose, by Dr W F Scott[5], who studied the trends of mortality by medical causes of death. A brief summary of the results of these studies was given in the previous booklet in this series[1]. The same factors have again been adopted for these new projections; they are shown in Table 2 together with the rates of mortality which have been assumed for 1977-78, the first year of the projection. Appendix Tables Ie, IIIe and Ve give the mortality rates, incorporating the improvement factors, assumed for the years 1991-92 and 2011-12.

Expectation of life

If mortality rates in the United Kingdom were to remain constant at the assumed mid-1977 level, the expectation of life at birth for a male would be 69.1 years and for a female 75.2 years; however the assumed improvement in mortality would extend this expectation by about two years for a baby born in 1977 to 71.3 years for a male and 77.5 for a female. (These estimates are calculated on the basis that the rates of improvement assumed for the 40 year period of the projections would continue to apply thereafter.)

Figure 1 Age-standardised death rates by age-group, actual and projected Great Britain, 1931–2017

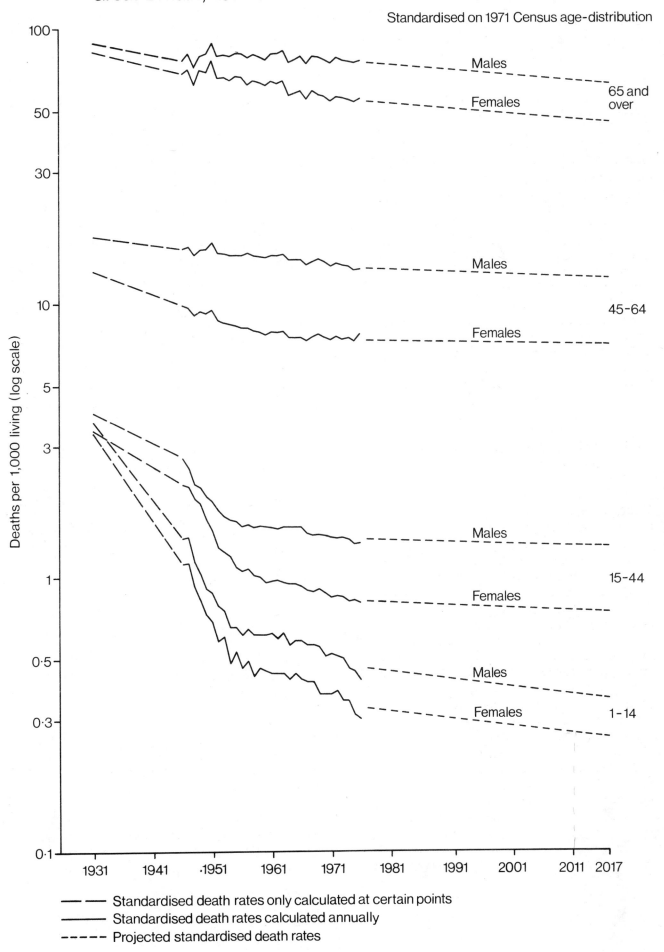

Standardised on 1971 Census age-distribution

65 and over

45-64

15-44

1-14

Deaths per 1,000 living (log scale)

Males
Females

Males
Females

Males
Females

Males
Females

— — Standardised death rates only calculated at certain points
——— Standardised death rates calculated annually
- - - - Projected standardised death rates

Table 2 Mortality rates** assumed for the base year, mid-1977 to mid-1978, and rates of improvement

Age last birthday	England and Wales	Scotland	Northern Ireland	Percentage improvement in 40 years†	Equivalent annual improvement factor†
Males					
0*	0.01815	0.01969	0.02702	25	0.9928
2	0.00064	0.00081	0.00082	25	0.9928
7	0.00033	0.00043	0.00046	25	0.9928
12	0.00033	0.00036	0.00056	25	0.9928
17	0.00112	0.00110	0.00172	0	1.0000
22	0.00097	0.00113	0.00209	12	0.9968
27	0.00086	0.00107	0.00188	17	0.9954
32	0.00106	0.00142	0.00192	10	0.9974
37	0.00159	0.00237	0.00246	10	0.9974
42	0.00294	0.00404	0.00380	0	1.0000
47	0.00546	0.00686	0.00685	0	1.0000
52	0.00957	0.01158	0.01130	0	1.0000
57	0.01564	0.01878	0.01806	6	0.9985
62	0.02503	0.02969	0.02859	15	0.9959
67	0.04117	0.04581	0.04432	20	0.9944
72	0.06597	0.07009	0.06731	17	0.9954
77	0.09840	0.10500	0.10301	15	0.9959
82	0.14382	0.15303	0.15667	13	0.9965
87	0.20660	0.21823	0.25090	13	0.9965
Females					
0*	0.01488	0.01544	0.02833	25	0.9928
2	0.00049	0.00053	0.00064	25	0.9928
7	0.00023	0.00026	0.00022	25	0.9928
12	0.00020	0.00020	0.00020	25	0.9928
17	0.00040	0.00046	0.00060	0	1.0000
22	0.00041	0.00040	0.00048	14	0.9962
27	0.00048	0.00054	0.00046	25	0.9928
32	0.00067	0.00087	0.00081	25	0.9928
37	0.00114	0.00151	0.00142	10	0.9974
42	0.00204	0.00255	0.00229	1	0.9997
47	0.00350	0.00415	0.00371	0	1.0000
52	0.00540	0.00669	0.00590	0	1.0000
57	0.00824	0.01033	0.00945	3	0.9992
62	0.01261	0.01551	0.01481	10	0.9974
67	0.02030	0.02402	0.02394	14	0.9962
72	0.03436	0.03886	0.04019	16	0.9957
77	0.05915	0.06516	0.06908	17	0.9954
82	0.10125	0.10692	0.11697	18	0.9951
87	0.15844	0.17163	0.18748	19	0.9947

** Deaths per person in age/sex group
* Probability that a baby born in the year preceding 1 July 1978 will not survive that date
† The improvement factors apply to each country

Migration

Past trends

The United Kingdom, and each of its constituent countries, has traditionally been a net exporter of population; the inflow of persons coming from abroad has usually been exceeded by the outflow of persons leaving the United Kingdom. In only two periods has this pattern been reversed. The first was in the 1930s when there was a considerable inflow of refugees from the rest of Europe and when an economic slump in the main receiving countries reduced - and even reversed - the net outflow to those countries. The second was in a few few years around 1960 when there was a substantial inflow of overseas Commonwealth citizens. This inflow was subsequently reduced by legislation, notably the Commonwealth Immigrants Act 1962. The late 1960s saw a return to the traditional pattern for the United Kingdom as a whole, of a net loss of population by migration, which has been virtually maintained ever since.

Assumptions

This brief summary of past experience indicates some of the difficulties encountered in formulating assumptions concerning future migration. Not only is the level of net migration liable to fluctuate from year to year but there can also be sudden changes in trends as a result of economic conditions or legislative action both within and outside the United Kingdom. The future inflow of Commonwealth citizens has been assessed on the basis of UK Government policy and the political and economic situation in other countries early in 1978. In the case of UK citizens (and intra-UK movement), migration is a response to many social and economic factors, and the assumptions draw heavily on recent experience. The historical picture of the UK as a net exporter of population has influenced the long term overall assumption that some 40 thousand more people a year will leave the United Kingdom than will enter it.

This total number of migrants assumed must be subdivided by age and sex so that the net numbers at each age for each sex may be incorporated in the projection process described earlier in this booklet. As the age/sex structures tend to differ for the varying categories of migrant it is necessary to consider the composition of the assumed total net outflow from the United Kingdom (and constituent countries) in terms of the components relating to Aliens, Commonwealth citizens, United Kingdom citizens and intra-British Isles movement. The age/sex structures assumed for the different streams are based largely on the experience of the recent past shown by figures in the International Passenger Survey, by the 1971 Census and by other available sources.

These structures follow the pattern that might be expected, namely that New Commonwealth citizens immigrating and United Kingdom citizens emigrating are more likely to be permanent settlers (many of them married with families), whereas the other categories are comprised of a large proportion of persons for whom migration, initially at least, may only be contemplated as a short term venture (and these tend to be single and slightly younger).

Details of the net outward flows assumed are shown in Table 3. On the basis of recent trends and what is thought most likely for the future it was assumed that there would be a net outflow from the United Kingdom of 30 thousand persons in 1977-78, increasing to 40 thousand persons per annum from mid-1982.

For the United Kingdom as a whole an overall net loss of 368 thousand persons by migration is assumed for the decade mid-1977 to mid-1987, comprising a net outflow of children aged 0-14 (158 thousand), a net inflow of persons in the age-group 15-24 years (160 thousand) and a net outflow of persons over age 25 (370 thousand including 14 thousand aged 65 and over) - in all a net loss of 195 thousand males and 173 thousand females. In the longer term the assumed age/sex pattern is broadly similar.

The assumed long term total migration from the United Kingdom is the same as in the previous projection. England and Wales is now expected to lose 5 thousand fewer persons by migration each year and Scotland 5 thousand more.

Table 3   Actual and assumed net migration

thousands

Mid-year to mid-year	England and Wales	Wales	Scotland	Great Britain	Northern Ireland	United Kingdom
Persons						
1971-72	- 4.8	+ 5.9	- 27.6	- 32.4	- 11.8	- 44.2
1972-73	+ 18.9	+ 10.8	- 10.7	+ 8.2	- 12.8	- 4.6
1973-74	- 64.5	+ 7.4	- 2.0	- 66.5	- 10.2	- 76.7
1974-75	- 44.2	+ 5.9	- 19.0	- 63.2	- 8.7	- 71.9
1975-76	- 15.0	+ 4.7	- 4.8	- 19.8	- 8.9	- 28.7
1976-77	- 17.3	+ 2.6	- 9.8	- 27.1	- 8.2	- 35.3
1977-78	- 11.0	+ 4.0	- 10.0	- 21.0	- 9.0	- 30.0
1978-79	- 11.0	+ 4.0	- 10.0	- 21.0	- 9.0	- 30.0
1979-80	- 14.0	+ 4.0	- 10.0	- 24.0	- 9.0	- 33.0
1980-81	- 17.0	+ 4.0	- 10.0	- 27.0	- 9.0	- 36.0
1981-82	- 20.0	+ 4.0	- 10.0	- 30.0	- 9.0	- 39.0
1982-83 and after	- 21.0	+ 4.0	- 10.0	- 31.0	- 9.0	- 40.0
Males						
1977-78	- 5.6	+ 2.0	- 5.8	- 11.3	- 4.5	- 15.8
1978-79	- 5.3	+ 2.0	- 5.8	- 11.1	- 4.5	- 15.6
1979-80	- 7.1	+ 2.0	- 5.8	- 12.8	- 4.5	- 17.3
1980-81	- 8.8	+ 2.0	- 5.8	- 14.6	- 4.5	- 19.1
1981-82	- 10.5	+ 2.0	- 5.8	- 16.3	- 4.5	- 20.8
1982-83 and after	- 11.0	+ 2.0	- 5.8	- 16.8	- 4.5	- 21.3
Females						
1977-78	- 5.4	+ 2.0	- 4.2	- 9.7	- 4.5	- 14.2
1978-79	- 5.7	+ 2.0	- 4.2	- 9.9	- 4.5	- 14.4
1979-80	- 6.9	+ 2.0	- 4.2	- 11.2	- 4.5	- 15.7
1980-81	- 8.2	+ 2.0	- 4.2	- 12.4	- 4.5	- 16.9
1981-82	- 9.5	+ 2.0	- 4.2	- 13.7	- 4.5	- 18.2
1982-83 and after	- 10.0	+ 2.0	- 4.2	- 14.2	- 4.5	- 18.7

Fertility

Recent trends

The number of live births in the United Kingdom in 1977, at 657 thousand, was about 2¾ per cent lower than in the previous year, reflecting a continuation of the downward trend which has persisted since 1964. Individual quarters, however, have shown a departure from the trend, with decreases of 7½, 4 and ½ per cent respectively in the March, June and September quarters, compared with the same quarters a year earlier, followed by an increase of over 1½ per cent in the December quarter. Provisional data shows that 164 thousand live births occurred in the March quarter of 1978, a figure about 1 per cent higher than that for the corresponding quarter of 1977. All the constituent countries of the United Kingdom have experienced a similar departure from the preceding downward trend. When seasonally adjusted the overall number of births per quarter has remained relatively stable for the last 18 months.

A fuller description of past trends in period and generation fertility was given in the previous booklet in this series. Readers are referred also to the *Demographic Review 1977*[6].

Assumptions

The additional evidence which has become available since the mid-1976 based population projections were prepared does not give any firm grounds for revising the broad pattern of the fertility assumptions which were made then for the principal projection. A further fall in the total period fertility rate* below the 1977 level, however, now seems less likely. For the mid-1977 based projections fertility rates have been assumed to remain constant until 1980 at the level reached at the turn of 1977-78. For 1981 onwards the same fertility rates have been used as in the previous set of projections. The higher fertility rates in the period mid-1977 to mid-1981 result in 58 thousand more births in the United Kingdom than in last year's projection.

Table 4 for England and Wales and Table 5 for Scotland show the total period fertility rates since 1965 and those assumed for the future, together with the projected numbers of annual births. Fertility in Wales is assumed to bear a similar relationship to that in England and Wales as in the mid-1976 based projections. For Northern Ireland a constant total period fertility rate of 2.6 children per woman has been assumed from 1979 onwards. A discussion of the basis for the assumptions was given in *Population projections 1976-2016*.[1]

---

* *The total period fertility rate is the average number of live born children which would result if women experienced the assumed age-specific fertility rates as they passed through their reproductive period.*

Table 4 Total period fertility rates (TPFR) and numbers of live births
(thousands) in each calendar year 1965-1991, England and Wales

Year	TPFR	Live births	Year	TPFR	Live births
Actual			**Projected**		
1965	2.86	863	1978	1.69	576
1966	2.76	850	1979	1.69	579
1967	2.66	832	1980	1.69	583
1968	2.58	819	1981	1.70	592
1969	2.48	798	1982	1.78	627
1970	2.41	784	1983	1.88	671
1971	2.38	783	1984	1.99	719
1972	2.19	725	1985	2.06	754
1973	2.02	676	1986	2.09	774
1974	1.90	640	1987	2.10	785
1975	1.79	603	1988	2.10	791
1976	1.72	584	1989	2.10	794
1977*	1.67	569	1990	2.10	794
			1991	2.10	792

* *Provisional*

Table 5 Total period fertility rates (TPFR) and numbers of live births
(thousands) in each calendar year 1965-1991, Scotland

Year	TPFR	Live births	Year	TPFR	Live births
Actual			**Projected**		
1965	2.99	100.7	1978	1.71	63.0
1966	2.88	96.5	1979	1.71	63.7
1967	2.87	96.2	1980	1.71	64.4
1968	2.82	94.8	1981	1.77	67.4
1969	2.68	90.3	1982	1.85	71.4
1970	2.57	87.3	1983	1.96	76.5
1971	2.54	86.7	1984	2.07	81.7
1972	2.28	78.6	1985	2.14	85.3
1973	2.13	74.4	1986	2.17	87.2
1974	1.97	70.1	1987	2.18	88.0
1975	1.90	67.9	1988	2.18	88.2
1976	1.79	64.9	1989	2.18	88.2
1977*	1.70	62.2	1990	2.18	87.8
			1991	2.18	87.0

* *Provisional*

Projections by marital condition

Purpose

For many purposes estimates of the future population are required in more detail than a simple split by age and sex, and projections subdivided between married and not married have been shown in the seven previous booklets of this series. New projections by marital condition have been made on the basis of the marriage and other assumptions described below.

Estimates

The projections are based on provisional estimates of the population by marital condition. The estimates were made by applying the marital condition structure for 1976 (given in the 1976 based projections booklet) to the 1977 estimate of Total population. Any errors in the provisional estimates for 1977 are likely to be small and their effect on the projection is negligible in relation to the uncertainty about future patterns of marriage and divorce referred to in the next paragraph.

Past trends and assumptions for the future

Patterns of marriage and divorce have been changing significantly throughout the post -war period and have, in particular, been markedly affected by developments in divorce and family law such as the Divorce Law Reform Act 1969 and the Family Law Reform Act 1970. In determining the rates to be assumed for the future in the projections, account was taken of the trends over the past fifteen years, bearing in mind the particular factors associated with major changes in the trends. As in the previous projections, it has been assumed that recent trends will continue for two or three years. In the longer term changes in the social and economic environment could affect marriage and divorce in a variety of ways but such changes must be regarded as essentially unpredictable and for the purposes of these projections marriage and divorce rates have been assumed to remain constant from 1980 onwards, at the level assumed in the mid-1976 projection. The main features of past rates of first marriage, divorce and remarriage, divorce and remarriage of divorced persons and the assumptions for the future for England and Wales are illustrated in Figures 2(a)-(f).

Mortality rates vary according to marital status; data analysed for the reports of the Government Actuary on the English and Scottish Life Tables have been used to determine rates appropriate to married, single and other persons separately which are consistent with the mortality rates by sex and age that were used in the main projection.

Results

Particulars of the projected numbers and the proportions married in the population for selected future years are given in Appendix Tables Id, IVd, and VId. Further details concerning the not-married group, and figures for other years, are available from the Government Actuary's Department.

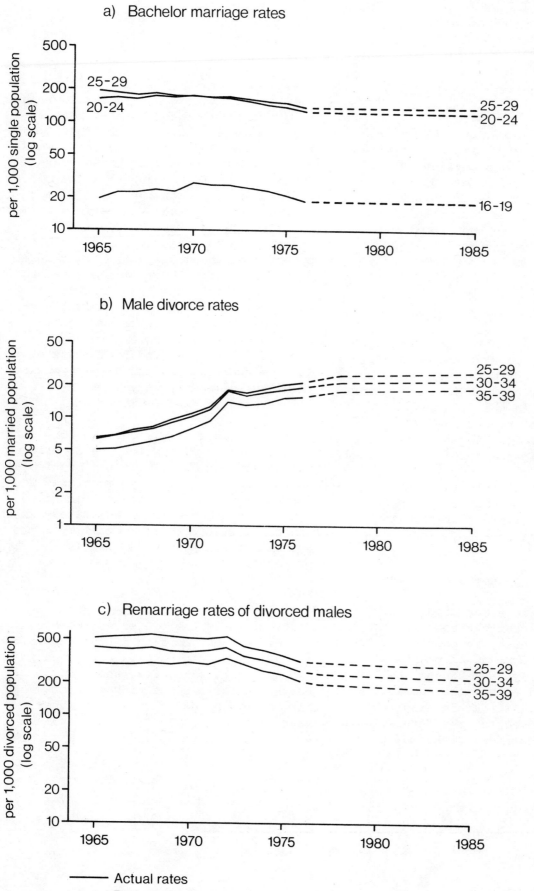

Figure 2   Rates of first marriage, remarriage and divorce, for selected age-groups, actual and projected, England and Wales, 1965-1985

a) Bachelor marriage rates

b) Male divorce rates

c) Remarriage rates of divorced males

———— Actual rates
– – – – Projected rates

Figure 2 continued

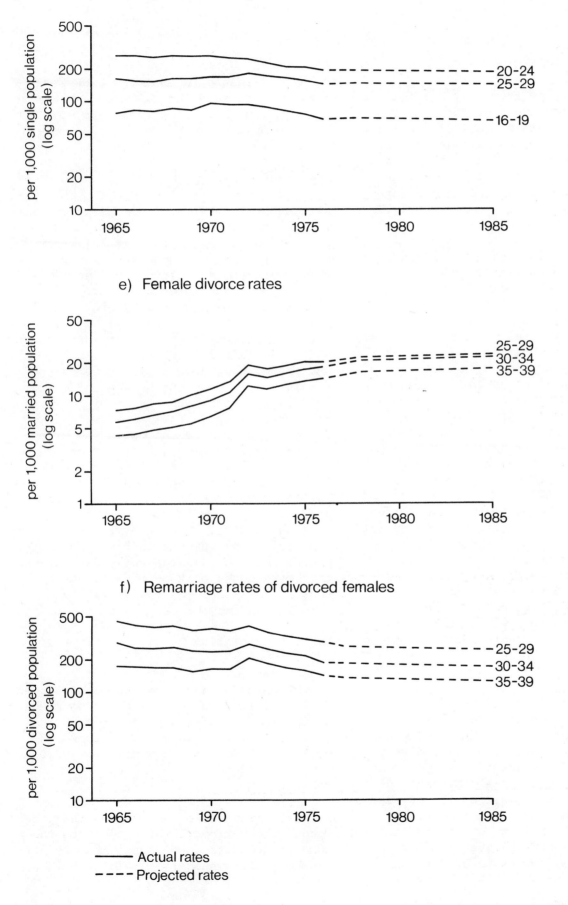

d) Spinster marriage rates

e) Female divorce rates

f) Remarriage rates of divorced females

Actual rates

Projected rates

Results of the projections

Summary

The projected populations by age for each country, and for Great Britain and the United Kingdom, are summarised in Appendix Tables 1(a) - VI(a) and are set out in detail in Appendix Tables 1(c) - VI(c). Appendix Tables 1(b) - VI(b) give the projected number of births, deaths and migrants each mid-year to mid-year. The future United Kingdom population of all ages is projected to fall slightly from 55.9 million in 1977 to 55.7 million in 1982 before rising steadily to 58.3 million in the year 2017.

The projected growth is due entirely to natural increase, ie. an excess of births over deaths; it would have been greater but for the assumption that the net balance of migration would be outwards in future. For example, over the decade ending mid-1987 the projected births average 758 thousand per annum and deaths 701 thousand, resulting in a projected natural increase of 57 thousand per annum. However this is reduced to a small net annual increase of 20 thousand in the total population over the 10 year period as a result of assumed net outward migration averaging 37 thousand per annum. The natural increase arises mainly from the relatively high propor- tion of the present population under middle age, which gives rise both to more births and to fewer deaths, as compared with those which would occur in an age-balanced population.

Sex balance

Throughout the period, the number of young males exceeds the number of young females in the population (as a direct consequence of the assumed six per cent excess of male over female births) but at the older ages the position is reversed as a result of the much higher mortality of males relative to females throughout life. The age to which an excess of males persists rises from 45 in 1977 to 53 by the year 2017. Another facet of this projected change is that the excess of females over males of all ages amounts to 1.4 million in 1977 but falls to 0.7 million by the end of the projection period.

Age structure

Although the total size of the population is expected to change relatively little over the next forty years it is likely that there will be some quite large changes in the age structure (see Table 6). The number of children under age 15 falls by 1.8 million between 1977 and 1986, rising to reach the 1977 level just before the turn of the century but falling again thereafter. At the other end of the age range, the numbers over pension age remain fairly constant between 1977 and 2011, lying within the range 9½ to 10 millions, although the last few years of the projection show the beginning of a substantial increase in the number of pensioners. Within this group, however, the numbers of the very elderly (over age 75) increase by over 25 per cent from about 2.9 million in 1977 to about 3.7 million in 2001. Figure 3 illustrates the changes in the numbers in five broad age- groups between 1955 and 2017, distinguish- ing between the part of the projection that is influenced by the fertility assumptions and the part that is not.

Married population

The projected numbers of married persons in the United Kingdom are shown in Appendix Tables I(d), IV(d) and VI(d). The number of married persons is projected to rise from 28.0 million in mid-1977 to 28.4 million in 1991 and 28.9 million in 2011.

Reliability

It must always be borne in mind that the longer the period of the projection the more the results depend upon the project- ions of future numbers of births which

Table 6 Results of the projection, United Kingdom

Age-group	1977 (base)	1981	1991	2001	2011
(a) Numbers (in thousands)					
0-14	12,557	11,378	11,477	12,530	11,237
15-29	12,271	12,785	12,820	10,765	12,512
30-44	10,225	10,829	11,841	12,889	10,891
45-59	9,825	9,497	9,267	10,530	11,500
60-74	8,127	8,041	7,695	7,141	8,063
75 & over	2,913	3,189	3,616	3,688	3,531
All ages	55,918	55,719	56,716	57,543	57,734
(b) Percentage in each age-group					
0-14	22.5	20.4	20.2	21.8	19.5
15-29	21.9	22.9	22.6	18.7	21.7
30-44	18.3	19.4	20.9	22.4	18.9
45-59	17.6	17.0	16.3	18.3	19.9
60-74	14.5	14.4	13.6	12.4	14.0
75 & over	5.2	5.7	6.4	6.4	6.1
All ages	100.0	100.0	100.0	100.0	100.0
(c) Index numbers (1977=100)					
0-14	100	91	91	100	89
15-29	100	104	104	88	102
30-44	100	106	116	126	107
45-59	100	97	94	107	117
60-74	100	99	95	88	99
75 & over	100	109	124	127	121
All ages	100	100	101	103	103
(d) Relative numbers (16-64/59* = 100)					
0-15	41	37	35	39	34
65/60† & over	29	29	29	28	28

64 for males, 59 for females   † *65 for males, 60 for females*

The figures above the broken lines include persons born after mid-1977

Figure 3 Actual and projected population by age-group, United Kingdom, 1951-2017

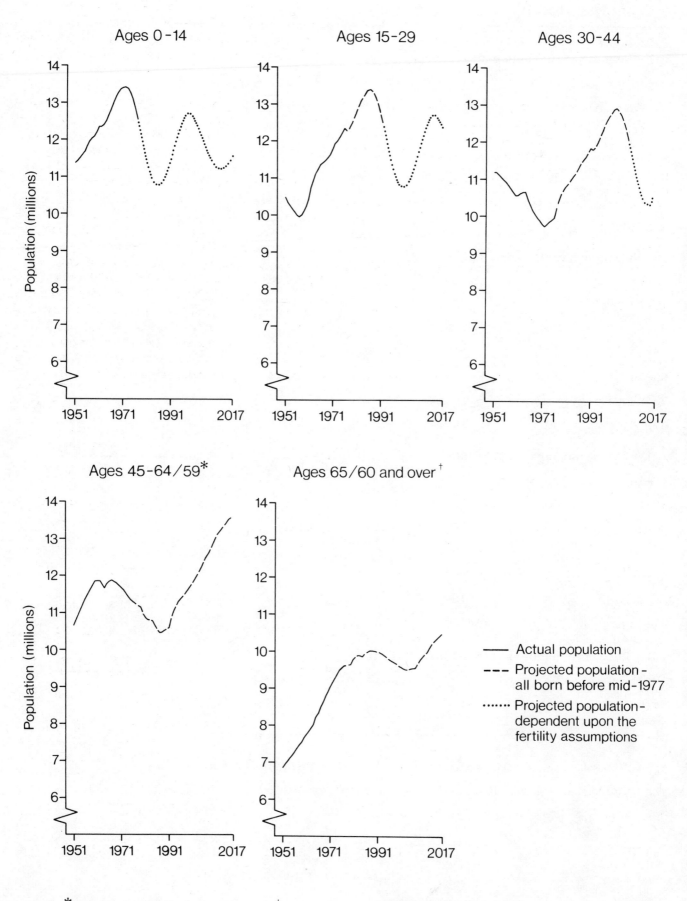

Ages 0-14

Ages 15-29

Ages 30-44

Ages 45-64/59*

Ages 65/60 and over†

——— Actual population

– – – Projected population –
all born before mid-1977

········· Projected population-
dependent upon the
fertility assumptions

*45-64 for males, 45-59 for females   † 65 and over for males, 60 and over for females

become increasingly speculative the further ahead they are carried. Estimates of the number of persons who are already alive at mid-1977 will be affected only by unforeseen changes in mortality and migration. Thus greater reliability may be attached to the projected numbers above age 20 in 1997 and above age 40 in 2017 than to the numbers below these ages.

Readers are referred to the previous booklet in this series for a discussion of possible margins of uncertainty surrounding projections of future births, and an assessment of the effects on the overall projections of possible divergences in future levels and trends of fertility from those assumed in the principal projection. An assessment was also given of the effects of uncertainties about future levels of mortality and net migration.

Previous projections

The results of the new projections differ only marginally from the principal mid-1976 based projections, since the population estimate for mid-1977 is closely in line with that previously projected for that year, and since the assumptions made for the future have not been changed to any significant extent. For the United Kingdom the number of births assumed in the first ten years of the projection is, in total, 47 thousand more than was previously assumed for these years, the net loss of migrants 7 thousand fewer and the number of deaths 6 thousand more. In the second decade, however, from 1987 to 1997, the number of births assumed is 7 thousand fewer than in the mid-1976 based projections whereas the number of deaths is 2 thousand more. The net number of outward migrants is the same as that assumed in the previous projections. By 1997 this results in 15 thousand fewer people aged under 15, and 16 thousand more aged between 15 and 60, giving an overall difference of only one thousand, the projected number aged 60 and over being unchanged. A comparison with the mid-1976 based projection is shown in Table 7. The results are so close that some users may find that they do not need to revise estimates based on the previous set of projections.

Table 7 Projected population, United Kingdom

millions

Age-group	1977		1981		1991		2001		2011	
	1976 based	1977 based	1976 based	1977 based	1976 based	1977 based	1976 based	1977 based	1976 based	1977 based
0-14	12.56	12.56	11.31	11.38	11.43	11.48	12.53	12.53	11.21	11.24
15-29	12.31	12.27	12.81	12.78	12.81	12.82	10.71	10.76	12.53	12.51
30-44	10.23	10.22	10.85	10.83	11.88	11.84	12.90	12.89	10.82	10.89
45-59	9.83	9.82	9.50	9.50	9.28	9.27	10.57	10.53	11.54	11.50
60-74	8.13	8.13	8.04	8.04	7.70	7.70	7.15	7.14	8.08	8.06
75 & over	2.91	2.91	3.19	3.19	3.61	3.62	3.68	3.69	3.53	3.53
All ages	55.96	55.92	55.70	55.72	56.71	56.72	57.54	57.54	57.71	57.73

The figures above the broken lines include persons born after mid-1977

References

(1)   OPCS (1978) *Population projections, 1976-2016*, Series PP2 No. 8, HMSO.

(2)   Martin L V and Daykin C D (1976) *The recent trend of mortality in Great Britain*, Journal of the Institute of Actuaries, Vol. 103, Part 2.

(3)   Daykin C D (1977) *The recent trend of mortality in Great Britain*, Journal of the Institute of Actuaries, Vol. 104, Part 1 and Vol 105, Part 1.

(4)   OPCS (1978) *Trends in mortality, 1951-1975*, Series DH1 no. 3, HMSO.

(5)   Scott W F (1976) *The projection of mortality rates in Great Britain*. International Congress of Actuaries, Tokyo.

(6)   OPCS (1978) *Demographic review 1977* Series DR no. 1, HMSO.

Appendix Table Ia Actual and projected Total population as at mid-year by sex and age-groups, 1951, 1961, 1971 to 2017; mid-1977 based projections

England and Wales

thousands

Year	0-14	15-44		45-64	45-59	65 and over	60 and over	All ages		
	Persons	Males	Females	Males	Females	Males	Females	Males	Females	Persons
1951	9738	9370	9464	4913	4473	1976	4073	21233	22774	44007
1961	10606	9249	9100	5655	4820	2108	4761	22449	23850	46299
1971	11604	9616	9325	5734	4612	2508	5535	23815	25119	48934
1972	11631	9665	9366	5708	4578	2559	5590	23901	25197	49098
1973	11600	9739	9431	5673	4531	2608	5646	23974	25254	49228
1974	11488	9794	9470	5636	4484	2660	5702	23988	25245	49233
1975	11343	9865	9516	5600	4440	2706	5755	23997	25228	49225
1976	11142	9956	9598	5569	4425	2745	5770	23993	25212	49205
1977	10903	10054	9698	5535	4418	2787	5780	23977	25198	49175
1978	10652	10179	9817	5486	4428	2826	5752	23965	25175	49140
1979	10386	10315	9949	5437	4429	2861	5726	23953	25150	49103
1980	10120	10447	10074	5393	4320	2894	5814	23939	25123	49062
1981	9880	10561	10186	5379	4237	2901	5876	23924	25096	49020
1982	9665	10670	10291	5382	4173	2891	5922	23918	25076	48994
1983	9517	10760	10378	5411	4132	2858	5945	23929	25072	49001
1984	9413	10851	10467	5436	4101	2828	5957	23963	25090	49053
1985	9380	10933	10546	5361	4069	2892	5963	24018	25126	49144
1986	9353	11043	10649	5285	4026	2937	5965	24085	25173	49258
1987	9387	11116	10712	5239	4006	2967	5958	24159	25226	49385
1988	9471	11139	10727	5234	4021	2985	5942	24237	25282	49519
1989	9607	11125	10705	5250	4050	2992	5926	24316	25339	49655
1990	9774	11100	10675	5264	4072	2998	5910	24397	25396	49793
1991	9967	11060	10625	5281	4101	3001	5893	24476	25452	49928
1992	10184	10919	10473	5391	4229	2999	5865	24554	25506	50060
1993	10387	10820	10366	5468	4325	2990	5828	24628	25556	50184
1994	10579	10747	10284	5519	4400	2981	5788	24696	25602	50298
1995	10753	10692	10208	5555	4467	2974	5751	24759	25641	50400
1996	10909	10651	10151	5577	4514	2969	5718	24815	25674	50489
1997	11026	10621	10115	5605	4546	2959	5691	24863	25700	50563
1998	11088	10602	10090	5649	4583	2942	5668	24903	25719	50622
1999	11085	10604	10090	5697	4615	2926	5648	24935	25730	50665
2000	11027	10633	10118	5735	4645	2912	5624	24959	25735	50694
2001	10929	10666	10149	5778	4698	2905	5586	24977	25734	50711
2002	10805	10698	10176	5826	4748	2901	5565	24990	25729	50719
2003	10667	10721	10196	5883	4784	2902	5569	25000	25722	50722
2004	10523	10740	10212	5946	4810	2901	5591	25008	25715	50723
2005	10377	10757	10223	6015	4847	2900	5607	25017	25709	50726
2006	10238	10757	10220	6115	4894	2883	5629	25029	25707	50736
2007	10111	10746	10203	6208	4870	2882	5734	25045	25709	50754
2008	10001	10724	10178	6287	4889	2903	5802	25066	25718	50784
2009	9914	10687	10139	6365	4939	2933	5850	25093	25734	50827
2010	9852	10646	10095	6444	4993	2959	5893	25126	25756	50882
2011	9817	10606	10053	6513	5053	2986	5921	25164	25785	50949
2012	9811	10559	10004	6513	5120	3081	5941	25209	25820	51029
2013	9831	10518	9964	6529	5164	3144	5968	25257	25861	51118
2014	9877	10467	9910	6567	5215	3186	5993	25309	25906	51215
2015	9944	10423	9866	6601	5256	3215	6013	25363	25955	51318
2016	10028	10363	9806	6653	5296	3235	6043	25418	26006	51424
2017	10121	10319	9764	6685	5304	3252	6083	25471	26057	51528

Appendix Table Ib **Annual changes in projected Total population**   **England and Wales**
1977 to 2017; mid-1977 based projections

thousands

Mid-year to mid-year	Population at beginning of period	Births	Deaths	Natural increase	Net migration	Total increase
1977-1978	49175	575	600	− 24	− 11	− 35
1978-1979	49140	577	604	− 26	− 11	− 37
1979-1980	49103	581	608	− 27	− 14	− 41
1980-1981	49062	588	612	− 25	− 17	− 42
1981-1982	49020	609	616	− 6	− 20	− 26
1982-1983	48994	648	620	28	− 21	7
1983-1984	49001	697	624	73	− 21	52
1984-1985	49053	738	627	112	− 21	91
1985-1986	49144	764	630	135	− 21	114
1986-1987	49258	782	632	148	− 21	127
1987-1988	49385	789	634	155	− 21	134
1988-1989	49519	793	636	157	− 21	136
1989-1990	49655	795	637	159	− 21	138
1990-1991	49793	794	637	156	− 21	135
1991-1992	49928	789	637	153	− 21	132
1992-1993	50060	782	637	145	− 21	124
1993-1994	50184	771	636	135	− 21	114
1994-1995	50298	759	635	123	− 21	102
1995-1996	50400	744	634	110	− 21	89
1996-1997	50489	727	632	95	− 21	74
1997-1998	50563	710	631	80	− 21	59
1998-1999	50622	693	629	64	− 21	43
1999-2000	50665	677	627	50	− 21	29
2000-2001	50694	664	626	38	− 21	17
2001-2002	50711	654	624	29	− 21	8
2002-2003	50719	647	623	24	− 21	3
2003-2004	50722	644	622	22	− 21	1
2004-2005	50723	645	621	24	− 21	3
2005-2006	50726	650	620	31	− 21	10
2006-2007	50736	658	619	39	− 21	18
2007-2008	50754	669	618	51	− 21	30
2008-2009	50784	681	618	64	− 21	43
2009-2010	50827	694	618	76	− 21	55
2010-2011	50882	707	618	88	− 21	67
2011-2012	50949	719	619	101	− 21	80
2012-2013	51029	730	619	110	− 21	89
2013-2014	51118	738	620	118	− 21	97
2014-2015	51215	744	620	124	− 21	103
2015-2016	51318	747	621	127	− 21	106
2016-2017	51424	748	622	125	− 21	104
2017-2018	51528					

Appendix Table Ic Projected Total population as at mid-year, by sex and single ages 1977 to 1989, 1991-2017; mid-1977 based projections.

thousands

Age-group	1977 Males	Females	Persons	1978 Males	Females	Persons	1979 Males	Females	Persons	1980 Males	Females	Persons	1981 Males	Females	Persons
0	287	272	559	290	275	565	292	276	568	293	277	570	297	281	578
1	300	283	583	286	270	556	289	273	562	290	274	564	292	276	568
2	314	296	610	299	283	582	286	269	555	288	272	560	289	273	562
3	327	309	636	314	295	609	298	282	580	285	269	554	288	271	559
4	351	331	682	326	308	634	313	295	608	298	281	579	284	268	552
0-4	1579	1491	3070	1515	1431	2946	1478	1395	2873	1454	1373	2827	1450	1369	2819
5	374	351	725	351	331	682	326	307	633	313	294	607	297	280	577
6	394	374	768	374	350	724	351	330	681	325	307	632	312	293	605
7	384	363	747	393	373	766	373	349	722	350	329	679	325	306	631
8	398	378	776	383	362	745	393	373	766	373	349	722	350	329	679
9	396	374	770	398	378	776	383	362	745	393	372	765	372	348	720
5-9	1946	1840	3786	1899	1794	3693	1826	1721	3547	1754	1651	3405	1656	1556	3212
10	410	390	800	396	374	770	397	378	775	383	362	745	392	372	764
11	412	391	803	410	390	800	396	374	770	397	377	774	383	361	744
12	421	399	820	412	390	802	410	389	799	396	373	769	397	377	774
13	421	400	821	421	399	820	412	390	802	410	389	799	395	373	768
14	412	391	803	421	400	821	421	399	820	411	390	801	410	389	799
10-14	2076	1971	4047	2060	1953	4013	2036	1930	3966	1997	1891	3888	1977	1872	3849
15	405	384	789	412	391	803	421	400	821	421	399	820	412	390	802
16	396	375	771	405	385	790	413	391	804	422	400	822	422	399	821
17	381	360	741	397	376	773	406	386	792	414	393	807	423	401	824
18	377	358	735	383	362	745	399	378	777	408	388	796	416	395	811
19	373	354	727	379	360	739	385	365	750	401	380	781	409	391	800
15-19	1932	1831	3763	1976	1874	3850	2024	1920	3944	2066	1960	4026	2082	1976	4058
20	363	344	707	375	355	730	381	362	743	386	366	752	403	382	785
21	354	334	688	364	345	709	376	356	732	383	363	746	388	367	755
22	346	324	670	355	334	689	365	345	710	377	357	734	383	363	746
23	353	331	684	346	324	670	356	334	690	366	345	711	378	357	735
24	349	333	682	354	331	685	346	325	671	356	334	690	365	346	711
20-24	1765	1666	3431	1794	1689	3483	1824	1722	3546	1868	1765	3633	1917	1815	3732
25	339	326	665	349	333	682	354	331	685	346	324	670	356	334	690
26	338	337	675	338	326	664	348	332	680	353	330	683	345	324	669
27	350	350	700	337	336	673	337	325	662	347	332	679	352	329	681
28	363	355	718	348	349	697	336	335	671	336	324	660	345	331	676
29	387	379	766	361	354	715	346	349	695	333	334	667	334	323	657
25-29	1777	1747	3524	1733	1698	3431	1721	1672	3393	1715	1644	3359	1732	1641	3373
30	425	419	844	386	378	764	360	353	713	345	348	693	332	333	665
31	334	328	662	424	418	842	384	378	762	358	352	710	343	347	690
32	331	321	652	332	328	660	421	417	838	382	377	759	356	352	708
33	335	327	662	329	320	649	331	327	658	420	416	836	381	376	757
34	319	311	630	333	326	659	328	320	648	329	326	655	418	415	833
30-34	1744	1706	3450	1804	1770	3574	1824	1795	3619	1834	1819	3653	1830	1823	3653
35	290	282	572	318	310	628	332	325	657	326	319	645	327	325	652
36	271	266	537	288	281	569	317	310	627	330	325	655	325	318	643
37	291	280	571	270	265	535	287	280	567	315	309	624	329	324	653
38	293	284	577	290	280	570	268	264	532	286	279	565	314	308	622
39	292	282	574	292	284	576	289	279	568	268	264	532	285	279	564
35-39	1437	1394	2831	1458	1420	2878	1493	1458	2951	1525	1496	3021	1580	1554	3134
40	290	278	568	292	282	574	291	283	574	289	278	567	267	263	530
41	284	275	559	289	278	567	291	281	572	290	282	572	288	277	565
42	277	269	546	284	274	558	288	277	565	290	280	570	289	281	570
43	274	264	538	276	268	544	283	274	557	288	277	565	289	280	569
44	274	268	542	273	264	537	276	267	543	282	273	555	287	276	563
40-44	1399	1354	2753	1414	1366	2780	1429	1382	2811	1439	1390	2829	1420	1377	2797

Figures above the dotted line relate to persons born after mid-1977

Age-group	1977			1978			1979			1980			1981		
	Males	Females	Persons	Males	Females	Persons	Males	Females	Persons	Males	Females	Persons	Males	Females	Persons
45	283	278	561	273	267	540	272	263	535	275	267	542	281	273	554
46	289	288	577	282	277	559	271	266	537	270	262	532	273	266	539
47	285	288	573	287	287	574	280	276	556	270	265	535	269	261	530
48	284	285	569	283	287	570	286	286	572	278	275	553	268	264	532
49	281	283	564	282	284	566	281	286	567	284	285	569	277	274	551
45-49	1422	1422	2844	1407	1402	2809	1390	1377	2767	1377	1354	2731	1368	1338	2706
50	287	292	579	279	282	561	280	283	563	279	285	564	282	283	565
51	292	296	588	284	291	575	276	280	556	277	282	559	276	283	559
52	291	298	589	290	295	585	282	289	571	274	279	553	275	281	556
53	291	302	593	288	296	584	287	293	580	279	287	566	271	277	548
54	297	308	605	288	299	587	285	295	580	284	291	575	276	286	562
50-54	1458	1496	2954	1429	1463	2892	1410	1440	2850	1393	1424	2817	1380	1410	2790
55	309	327	636	294	306	600	285	298	583	282	293	575	281	289	570
56	321	340	661	305	324	629	290	304	594	281	296	577	278	291	569
57	336	360	696	316	338	654	301	322	623	286	302	588	278	293	571
58	219	240	459	331	357	688	311	335	646	296	319	615	281	300	581
59	212	233	445	215	238	453	325	353	678	306	332	638	291	316	607
55-59	1397	1500	2897	1461	1563	3024	1512	1612	3124	1451	1542	2993	1409	1489	2898
60	235	261	496	208	231	439	211	235	446	319	350	669	300	329	629
61	246	273	519	230	258	488	204	229	433	207	233	440	313	346	659
62	265	299	564	240	270	510	225	255	480	199	226	425	202	230	432
63	260	297	557	258	295	553	234	266	500	219	252	471	194	223	417
64	252	291	543	253	292	545	251	291	542	228	262	490	213	248	461
60-64	1258	1421	2679	1189	1346	2535	1125	1276	2401	1172	1323	2495	1222	1376	2598
65	241	281	522	245	287	532	245	288	533	243	287	530	221	258	479
66	233	284	517	232	276	508	237	282	519	236	283	519	235	282	517
67	227	279	506	225	279	504	224	271	495	228	277	505	227	278	505
68	219	276	495	217	273	490	215	273	488	214	266	480	218	271	489
69	208	268	476	209	270	479	207	267	474	206	266	472	205	260	465
65-69	1128	1388	2516	1128	1385	2513	1128	1381	2509	1127	1379	2506	1106	1349	2455
70	194	257	451	197	261	458	198	263	461	197	260	457	195	260	455
71	180	249	429	183	250	433	186	254	440	187	256	443	186	253	439
72	167	240	407	169	241	410	172	242	414	175	246	421	176	248	424
73	154	228	382	156	232	388	158	233	391	161	234	395	164	238	402
74	140	216	356	143	219	362	145	223	368	147	224	371	150	225	375
70-74	835	1190	2025	848	1203	2051	859	1215	2074	867	1220	2087	871	1224	2095
75	124	201	325	129	207	336	131	210	341	134	214	348	135	214	349
76	111	194	305	114	191	305	119	197	316	121	200	321	122	204	326
77	95	179	274	101	184	285	103	181	284	108	186	294	110	189	299
78	83	163	246	86	168	254	91	173	264	93	170	263	98	176	274
79	69	146	215	74	153	227	77	157	234	81	162	243	84	159	243
75-79	482	883	1365	504	903	1407	521	918	1439	537	932	1469	549	942	1491
80	60	134	194	61	135	196	65	141	206	68	146	214	72	150	222
81	50	121	171	53	123	176	54	124	178	57	129	186	60	134	194
82	46	109	155	44	110	154	46	112	158	47	113	160	50	118	168
83	37	92	129	39	98	137	37	99	136	39	101	140	40	101	141
84	32	81	113	31	82	113	33	87	120	32	88	120	33	90	123
80-84	225	537	762	228	548	776	235	563	798	243	577	820	255	593	848
85 and over	117	361	478	118	367	485	118	373	491	120	383	503	120	392	512
All ages	23977	25198	49175	23965	25175	49140	23953	25150	49103	23939	25123	49062	23924	25096	49020

Appendix Table Ic *continued*

thousands

Age-group	1982			1983			1984			1985			1986		
	Males	Females	Persons	Males	Females	Persons	Males	Females	Persons	Males	Females	Persons	Males	Females	Persons
0	308	291	599	328	310	638	352	333	685	373	353	726	386	366	752
1	295	279	574	306	289	595	326	308	634	351	331	682	372	351	723
2	291	275	566	295	278	573	305	289	594	325	307	632	350	330	680
3	289	272	561	290	274	564	294	277	571	305	288	593	324	306	630
4	287	271	558	288	272	560	290	273	563	293	276	569	304	287	591
0–4	1470	1388	2858	1507	1423	2930	1567	1480	3047	1647	1555	3202	1736	1640	3376
5	284	267	551	287	270	557	288	271	559	289	273	562	293	276	569
6	297	280	577	283	266	549	286	269	555	287	270	557	289	272	561
7	312	292	604	296	278	574	282	265	547	285	268	553	286	269	555
8	324	305	629	311	291	602	296	278	574	282	265	547	285	267	552
9	349	328	677	324	305	629	311	291	602	296	277	573	282	264	546
5–9	1566	1472	3038	1501	1410	2911	1463	1374	2837	1439	1353	2792	1435	1348	2783
10	372	348	720	349	328	677	323	305	628	311	291	602	295	277	572
11	392	371	763	372	347	719	349	327	676	323	304	627	310	290	600
12	382	361	743	392	371	763	372	347	719	349	327	676	323	304	627
13	397	377	774	382	361	743	392	371	763	371	347	718	349	327	676
14	396	373	769	397	377	774	382	361	743	392	371	763	372	347	719
10–14	1939	1830	3769	1892	1784	3676	1818	1711	3529	1746	1640	3386	1649	1545	3194
15	410	389	799	395	373	768	397	377	774	382	360	742	392	371	763
16	412	390	802	410	389	799	396	373	769	397	377	774	383	361	744
17	423	400	823	413	391	804	411	390	801	397	374	771	398	378	776
18	425	403	828	425	402	827	415	393	808	413	392	805	398	376	774
19	417	398	815	427	406	833	426	405	831	417	396	813	415	394	809
15–19	2087	1980	4067	2070	1961	4031	2045	1938	3983	2006	1899	3905	1986	1880	3866
20	411	392	803	419	399	818	428	407	835	429	407	836	418	397	815
21	404	383	787	413	393	806	421	400	821	430	408	838	430	407	837
22	389	368	757	405	384	789	414	394	808	421	401	822	430	409	839
23	384	363	747	389	368	757	405	383	788	414	394	808	422	401	823
24	378	357	735	384	363	747	389	368	757	405	383	788	414	394	808
20–24	1966	1863	3829	2010	1907	3917	2057	1952	4009	2099	1993	4092	2114	2008	4122
25	366	345	711	378	356	734	384	362	746	389	367	756	405	383	788
26	355	333	688	365	344	709	377	356	733	383	362	745	388	367	755
27	344	323	667	354	332	686	363	343	706	376	355	731	382	361	743
28	350	328	678	342	322	664	352	332	684	362	342	704	374	354	728
29	344	330	674	348	328	676	341	321	662	350	331	681	360	341	701
25–29	1759	1659	3418	1787	1682	3469	1817	1714	3531	1860	1757	3617	1909	1806	3715
30	332	322	654	342	329	671	346	327	673	339	320	659	348	330	678
31	330	332	662	330	321	651	340	328	668	344	326	670	337	319	656
32	341	346	687	329	332	661	328	320	648	338	327	665	343	325	668
33	355	351	706	339	345	684	327	331	658	327	319	646	337	326	663
34	379	375	754	353	350	703	338	344	682	325	330	655	325	319	644
30–34	1737	1726	3463	1693	1677	3370	1679	1650	3329	1673	1622	3295	1690	1619	3309
35	417	415	832	377	374	751	352	349	701	336	344	680	323	329	652
36	326	325	651	415	414	829	375	373	748	350	348	698	334	343	677
37	323	317	640	325	324	649	413	413	826	374	373	747	348	348	696
38	328	323	651	322	316	638	323	323	646	412	412	824	373	371	744
39	313	307	620	326	322	648	321	316	637	322	322	644	411	411	822
35–39	1707	1687	3394	1765	1750	3515	1784	1774	3558	1794	1799	3593	1789	1802	3591
40	284	278	562	312	306	618	326	321	647	320	315	635	321	321	642
41	266	262	528	284	277	561	311	306	617	325	320	645	319	314	633
42	287	276	563	265	262	527	283	276	559	310	305	615	324	320	644
43	289	281	570	286	276	562	264	261	525	282	276	558	310	304	614
44	288	279	567	288	280	568	285	275	560	264	260	524	281	275	556
40–44	1414	1376	2790	1435	1401	2836	1469	1439	2908	1501	1476	2977	1555	1534	3089

Figures above the dotted line relate to persons born after mid-1977.

Age-group	1982 Males	1982 Females	1982 Persons	1983 Males	1983 Females	1983 Persons	1984 Males	1984 Females	1984 Persons	1985 Males	1985 Females	1985 Persons	1986 Males	1986 Females	1986 Persons
45	286	275	561	287	278	565	286	279	565	284	275	559	262	259	521
46	279	272	551	285	274	559	286	277	563	285	278	563	283	274	557
47	272	265	537	278	271	549	283	273	556	284	276	560	284	277	561
48	267	260	527	270	264	534	276	270	546	281	272	553	282	275	557
49	266	263	529	265	259	524	268	263	531	274	268	542	279	271	550
45-49	1370	1335	2705	1385	1346	2731	1399	1362	2761	1408	1369	2777	1390	1356	2746
50	274	273	547	264	262	526	263	258	521	266	262	528	272	267	539
51	279	282	561	272	272	544	262	261	523	261	257	518	264	260	524
52	274	282	556	277	280	557	270	270	540	259	259	518	258	255	513
53	273	279	552	271	280	551	274	279	553	267	268	535	257	258	515
54	268	275	543	269	277	546	268	278	546	271	277	548	264	267	531
50-54	1368	1391	2759	1353	1371	2724	1337	1346	2683	1324	1323	2647	1315	1307	2622
55	273	284	557	265	274	539	266	275	541	265	277	542	268	275	543
56	277	287	564	269	282	551	262	272	534	263	273	536	262	275	537
57	274	288	562	273	285	558	265	280	545	258	270	528	259	271	530
58	273	291	564	270	286	556	269	283	552	262	277	539	254	267	521
59	276	297	573	269	288	557	266	283	549	264	280	544	257	275	532
55-59	1373	1447	2820	1346	1415	2761	1328	1393	2721	1312	1377	2689	1300	1363	2663
60	286	313	599	271	294	565	263	285	548	260	281	541	260	277	537
61	294	325	619	280	310	590	266	291	557	258	282	540	255	278	533
62	305	342	647	287	321	608	273	306	579	260	287	547	252	279	531
63	197	227	424	298	338	636	280	317	597	267	302	569	253	284	537
64	189	220	409	191	224	415	290	333	623	272	313	585	260	298	558
60-64	1271	1427	2698	1327	1487	2814	1372	1532	2904	1317	1465	2782	1280	1416	2696
65	207	244	451	183	217	400	185	220	405	281	328	609	264	308	572
66	213	254	467	200	240	440	177	213	390	179	217	396	272	322	594
67	226	277	503	205	249	454	192	236	428	170	209	379	173	213	386
68	218	272	490	217	271	488	197	244	441	185	231	416	163	205	368
69	208	265	473	208	266	474	207	265	472	188	238	426	176	226	402
65-69	1072	1312	2384	1013	1243	2256	958	1178	2136	1003	1223	2226	1048	1274	2322
70	194	253	447	198	259	457	198	259	457	197	259	456	179	233	412
71	185	253	438	184	246	430	187	252	439	188	252	440	186	252	438
72	175	245	420	174	245	419	173	239	412	176	244	420	177	245	422
73	165	240	405	164	237	401	163	237	400	162	231	393	165	236	401
74	152	229	381	153	231	384	153	228	381	151	228	379	151	222	373
70-74	871	1220	2091	873	1218	2091	874	1215	2089	874	1214	2088	858	1188	2046
75	138	216	354	141	219	360	142	221	363	141	219	360	140	219	359
76	124	204	328	127	206	333	129	209	338	130	211	341	129	209	338
77	112	193	305	113	193	306	116	195	311	118	198	316	119	200	319
78	99	178	277	100	182	282	102	183	285	104	184	288	106	187	293
79	87	165	252	89	167	256	90	170	260	92	171	263	94	172	266
75-79	560	956	1516	570	967	1537	579	978	1557	585	983	1568	588	987	1575
80	74	148	222	77	152	229	79	155	234	80	158	238	82	159	241
81	63	138	201	65	136	201	68	141	209	70	143	213	71	146	217
82	52	122	174	55	126	181	57	124	181	59	128	187	60	130	190
83	43	106	149	45	110	155	47	113	160	49	112	161	51	115	166
84	34	91	125	36	95	131	38	98	136	40	101	141	41	100	141
80-84	266	605	871	278	619	897	289	631	920	298	642	940	305	650	955
85 and over	122	402	524	124	411	535	128	423	551	132	436	568	138	450	588
All ages	23918	25076	48994	23929	25072	49001	23963	25090	49053	24018	25126	49144	24085	25173	49258

thousands

Age-group	1987			1988			1989			1991			1996		
	Males	Females	Persons	Males	Females	Persons	Males	Females	Persons	Males	Females	Persons	Males	Females	Persons
0	395	374	769	399	377	776	401	379	780	402	380	782	376	356	732
1	385	364	749	394	372	766	397	375	772	400	379	779	382	361	743
2	371	350	721	384	363	747	393	371	764	399	376	775	388	366	754
3	349	329	678	370	349	719	383	362	745	395	373	768	392	371	763
4	324	305	629	348	329	677	369	349	718	391	369	760	396	373	769
0-4	1824	1722	3546	1895	1790	3685	1943	1836	3779	1987	1877	3864	1934	1827	3761
5	304	286	590	323	305	628	348	328	676	382	360	742	397	375	772
6	292	275	567	303	285	588	323	304	627	368	347	715	397	374	771
7	288	271	559	291	274	565	302	284	586	346	326	672	395	372	767
8	286	268	554	288	270	558	291	273	564	322	302	624	393	369	762
9	285	267	552	286	268	554	287	270	557	302	283	585	389	366	755
5-9	1455	1367	2822	1491	1402	2893	1551	1459	3010	1720	1618	3338	1971	1856	3827
10	282	264	546	284	267	551	285	268	553	290	273	563	380	357	737
11	295	277	572	281	263	544	284	266	550	287	269	556	366	344	710
12	310	290	600	295	276	571	281	263	544	285	267	552	345	324	669
13	323	303	626	310	290	600	295	276	571	384	266	550	321	301	622
14	348	327	675	323	304	627	310	290	600	281	263	544	301	282	583
10-14	1558	1461	3019	1493	1400	2893	1455	1363	2818	1427	1338	2765	1713	1608	3321
15	372	347	719	349	327	676	323	303	626	295	276	571	290	272	562
16	392	371	763	372	347	719	349	327	676	311	290	601	287	268	555
17	384	362	746	393	372	765	373	348	721	325	304	629	287	268	555
18	400	380	780	385	364	749	395	374	769	352	330	682	287	269	556
19	400	378	778	402	382	784	388	366	754	376	353	729	287	269	556
15-19	1948	1838	3786	1901	1792	3693	1828	1718	3546	1659	1553	3212	1438	1346	2784
20	416	397	813	402	380	782	404	384	788	399	378	777	302	284	586
21	420	398	818	418	397	815	404	381	785	390	369	759	319	298	617
22	430	408	838	420	399	819	418	398	816	406	385	791	333	312	645
23	431	409	840	431	408	839	421	399	820	405	382	787	358	336	694
24	422	400	822	431	409	840	431	408	839	419	398	817	381	356	737
20-24	2119	2012	4131	2102	1993	4095	2078	1970	4048	2019	1912	3931	1693	1586	3279
25	414	393	807	422	400	822	431	408	839	421	398	819	402	379	781
26	404	382	786	413	392	805	421	399	820	430	407	837	391	368	759
27	387	366	753	403	381	784	412	392	804	428	406	834	404	383	787
28	380	360	740	385	365	750	401	380	781	418	397	815	401	379	780
29	372	353	725	378	359	737	383	364	747	408	390	798	413	394	807
25-29	1957	1854	3811	2001	1897	3898	2048	1943	3991	2105	1998	4103	2011	1903	3914
30	358	341	699	370	352	722	376	358	734	398	379	777	413	394	807
31	346	329	675	356	340	696	368	351	719	379	362	741	421	402	823
32	335	318	653	345	328	673	355	339	694	372	356	728	419	402	821
33	341	324	665	334	317	651	343	327	670	365	349	714	408	393	801
34	335	325	660	339	323	662	332	317	649	351	337	688	399	385	784
30-34	1715	1637	3352	1744	1660	3404	1774	1692	3466	1865	1783	3648	2060	1976	4036
35	323	318	641	333	325	658	338	323	661	340	326	666	389	374	763
36	322	328	650	322	317	639	331	324	655	329	315	644	371	358	729
37	333	342	675	320	327	647	321	316	637	334	321	655	364	352	716
38	347	347	694	332	341	673	319	327	646	329	322	651	357	345	702
39	372	371	743	346	346	692	331	340	671	318	315	633	344	333	677
35-39	1697	1706	3403	1653	1656	3309	1640	1630	3270	1650	1599	3249	1825	1762	3587
40	410	410	820	371	370	741	345	345	690	318	325	643	334	321	655
41	321	320	641	408	409	817	370	369	739	329	339	668	323	311	634
42	318	313	631	320	320	640	407	408	815	343	343	686	329	317	646
43	323	319	642	317	312	629	319	319	638	367	367	734	324	318	642
44	308	303	611	322	318	640	316	311	627	405	406	811	314	311	625
40-44	1680	1665	3345	1738	1729	3467	1757	1752	3509	1762	1780	3542	1624	1578	3202

Figures above the dotted line relate to persons born after mid-1977

Age-group	1987 Males	1987 Females	1987 Persons	1988 Males	1988 Females	1988 Persons	1989 Males	1989 Females	1989 Persons	1991 Males	1991 Females	1991 Persons	1996 Males	1996 Females	1996 Persons
45	280	274	554	307	302	609	320	317	637	316	317	633	312	321	633
46	261	259	520	278	273	551	306	302	608	314	310	624	323	334	657
47	281	273	554	260	258	518	277	272	549	317	315	632	336	338	674
48	282	276	558	279	272	551	258	257	515	302	299	601	359	362	721
49	280	274	554	280	275	555	277	270	547	273	270	543	394	399	793
45-49	1384	1356	2740	1404	1380	2784	1438	1418	2856	1522	1511	3033	1724	1754	3478
50	277	270	547	278	273	551	277	274	551	254	255	509	306	311	617
51	270	266	536	274	269	543	276	271	547	273	268	541	303	304	607
52	261	259	520	267	264	531	272	267	539	273	271	544	305	308	613
53	256	254	510	259	257	516	265	263	528	271	268	539	290	292	582
54	254	256	510	254	252	506	256	256	512	266	264	530	261	263	524
50-54	1318	1305	2623	1332	1315	2647	1346	1331	2677	1337	1326	2663	1465	1478	2943
55	261	265	526	251	255	506	250	250	500	259	259	518	242	247	489
56	265	273	538	258	263	521	248	253	501	250	252	502	258	260	518
57	258	273	531	261	271	532	254	261	515	243	247	490	257	262	519
58	255	269	524	254	270	524	257	269	526	241	249	490	254	259	513
59	250	265	515	251	267	518	250	268	518	246	257	503	248	254	502
55-59	1289	1345	2634	1275	1326	2601	1259	1301	2560	1239	1264	2503	1259	1282	2541
60	252	272	524	245	262	507	246	264	510	248	264	512	240	249	489
61	254	275	529	247	269	516	240	259	499	240	262	502	230	241	471
62	250	274	524	248	271	519	242	266	508	236	258	494	222	235	457
63	246	275	521	244	271	515	242	268	510	229	253	482	217	235	452
64	246	280	526	239	272	511	237	267	504	230	259	489	220	242	462
60-64	1248	1376	2624	1223	1345	2568	1207	1324	2531	1183	1296	2479	1129	1202	2331
65	252	293	545	239	275	514	232	267	499	229	260	489	219	248	467
66	255	303	558	244	289	533	231	271	502	222	259	481	210	245	455
67	262	317	579	246	298	544	235	283	518	217	258	475	204	239	443
68	166	209	375	252	310	562	237	292	529	214	261	475	195	233	428
69	156	200	356	158	204	362	241	304	545	216	272	488	191	236	427
65-69	1091	1322	2413	1139	1376	2515	1176	1417	2593	1098	1310	2408	1019	1201	2220
70	168	220	388	149	195	344	151	199	350	216	279	495	188	236	424
71	169	227	396	159	215	374	141	190	331	217	289	506	179	232	411
72	176	244	420	160	220	380	150	208	358	135	188	323	170	229	399
73	165	237	402	164	236	400	149	213	362	124	178	302	165	228	393
74	154	227	381	154	228	382	153	228	381	131	194	325	161	234	395
70-74	832	1155	1987	786	1094	1880	744	1038	1782	823	1128	1951	863	1159	2022
75	140	213	353	143	218	361	143	219	362	129	197	326	157	236	393
76	128	209	337	128	204	332	131	208	339	131	209	340	154	240	394
77	118	198	316	117	198	315	117	194	311	120	198	318	92	153	245
78	107	189	296	107	187	294	106	187	293	108	187	295	82	142	224
79	96	175	271	97	177	274	96	175	271	96	171	267	84	151	235
75-79	589	984	1573	592	984	1576	593	983	1576	584	962	1546	569	922	1491
80	84	160	244	85	163	248	86	165	251	85	163	248	79	148	227
81	72	146	218	73	148	221	75	150	225	76	151	227	77	152	229
82	61	133	194	63	133	196	64	135	199	66	139	205	68	139	207
83	52	118	170	53	120	173	54	121	175	56	124	180	58	125	183
84	43	103	146	44	105	149	45	107	152	47	109	156	49	110	159
80-84	312	660	972	318	669	987	324	678	1002	330	686	1016	331	674	1005
85 and over	143	461	604	150	474	624	155	486	641	166	511	677	187	560	747
All ages	24159	25226	49385	24237	25282	49519	24316	25339	49655	24476	25452	49928	24815	25674	50489

29

thousands

Age-group	2001			2006			2011			2016			2017		
	Males	Females	Persons	Males	Females	Persons	Males	Females	Persons	Males	Females	Persons	Males	Females	Persons
0	336	318	654	329	311	640	358	339	697	379	358	737	380	359	739
1	342	323	665	326	308	634	351	331	682	376	355	731	378	357	735
2	349	329	678	324	306	630	343	323	666	372	351	723	375	354	729
3	356	336	692	325	306	631	336	317	653	367	346	713	371	350	721
4	364	344	708	327	309	636	330	311	641	361	341	702	366	345	711
0–4	1747	1650	3397	1631	1540	3171	1718	1621	3339	1855	1751	3606	1870	1765	3635
5	372	351	723	332	313	645	326	306	632	355	334	689	360	340	700
6	379	357	736	338	318	656	322	303	625	347	327	674	354	333	687
7	385	362	747	346	325	671	321	302	623	340	320	660	347	326	673
8	389	366	755	354	333	687	322	303	625	333	313	646	340	319	659
9	393	370	763	362	340	702	325	305	630	328	307	635	333	312	645
5–9	1918	1806	3724	1732	1629	3361	1616	1519	3135	1703	1601	3304	1734	1630	3364
10	395	371	766	370	348	718	330	309	639	323	303	626	327	307	634
11	395	371	766	377	354	731	337	316	653	321	301	622	323	303	626
12	394	370	764	383	360	743	344	323	667	320	300	620	320	300	620
13	391	368	759	389	365	754	353	331	684	321	301	622	320	300	620
14	388	365	753	392	368	760	361	339	700	324	304	628	321	301	622
10–14	1963	1845	3808	1911	1795	3706	1725	1618	3343	1609	1509	3118	1611	1511	3122
15	379	356	735	395	370	765	370	346	716	330	309	639	324	304	628
16	367	344	711	395	371	766	377	354	731	337	315	652	330	309	639
17	347	324	671	395	371	766	385	361	746	346	324	670	338	316	654
18	324	304	628	395	371	766	392	368	760	356	334	690	348	326	674
19	306	288	594	393	370	763	397	374	771	366	345	711	358	337	695
15–19	1723	1616	3339	1973	1853	3826	1921	1803	3724	1735	1627	3362	1698	1592	3290
20	298	279	577	386	363	749	401	378	779	377	354	731	369	346	715
21	296	277	573	375	352	727	403	379	782	385	362	747	378	355	733
22	295	276	571	354	332	686	403	379	782	392	369	761	386	363	749
23	294	275	569	331	310	641	401	376	777	398	373	771	393	369	762
24	291	272	563	311	291	602	398	373	771	402	377	779	398	373	771
20–24	1474	1379	2853	1757	1648	3405	2006	1885	3891	1954	1835	3789	1924	1806	3730
25	305	285	590	301	280	581	389	364	753	404	379	783	402	377	779
26	320	298	618	296	277	573	375	351	726	404	378	782	403	378	781
27	331	310	641	294	274	568	353	331	684	401	377	778	402	377	779
28	355	333	688	291	272	563	327	307	634	397	373	770	400	376	776
29	375	352	727	286	268	554	306	287	593	392	369	761	395	372	767
25–29	1686	1578	3264	1468	1371	2839	1750	1640	3390	1998	1876	3874	2002	1880	3882
30	394	375	769	298	281	579	294	276	570	381	360	741	390	369	759
31	382	363	745	311	293	604	288	272	560	367	347	714	380	359	739
32	395	379	774	322	306	628	285	270	555	344	326	670	365	346	711
33	392	374	766	346	328	674	282	268	550	319	303	622	342	325	667
34	404	389	793	367	348	715	278	264	542	297	283	580	317	302	619
30–34	1967	1880	3847	1644	1556	3200	1427	1350	2777	1708	1619	3327	1794	1701	3495
35	404	390	794	385	370	755	290	277	567	285	272	557	296	282	578
36	412	398	810	374	360	734	303	290	593	280	269	549	284	272	556
37	411	398	809	386	375	761	314	302	616	277	266	543	279	268	547
38	400	388	788	384	370	754	338	324	662	275	264	539	276	265	541
39	392	381	773	397	385	782	360	344	704	272	261	533	274	264	538
35–39	2019	1955	3974	1926	1860	3786	1605	1537	3142	1389	1332	2721	1409	1351	2760
40	382	370	752	397	385	782	378	366	744	284	273	557	271	260	531
41	365	353	718	406	393	799	368	355	723	298	286	584	283	272	555
42	359	348	707	405	393	798	381	370	751	310	298	608	297	285	582
43	352	341	693	395	384	779	379	366	745	333	321	654	309	298	607
44	339	329	668	386	377	763	391	381	772	354	339	693	332	319	651
40–44	1797	1741	3538	1989	1932	3921	1897	1838	3735	1579	1517	3096	1492	1434	2926

Figures above the dotted line relate to persons born after mid-1977.

Age-group	2001 Males	2001 Females	2001 Persons	2006 Males	2006 Females	2006 Persons	2011 Males	2011 Females	2011 Persons	2016 Males	2016 Females	2016 Persons	2017 Males	2017 Females	2017 Persons
45	328	317	645	376	365	741	391	380	771	372	362	734	353	338	691
46	318	307	625	359	349	708	399	388	787	362	350	712	371	361	732
47	323	312	635	352	343	695	397	388	785	373	365	738	360	349	709
48	316	313	629	343	336	679	386	378	764	370	360	730	371	364	735
49	305	306	611	330	323	653	375	370	745	381	374	755	367	358	725
45-49	1590	1555	3145	1760	1716	3476	1948	1904	3852	1858	1811	3669	1822	1770	3592
50	303	314	617	318	311	629	365	359	724	379	374	753	378	372	750
51	312	327	639	307	301	608	346	342	688	386	380	766	376	372	748
52	323	331	654	311	305	616	338	335	673	382	379	761	382	378	760
53	344	353	697	303	306	609	330	327	657	370	369	739	378	377	755
54	377	389	766	291	297	588	315	315	630	359	360	719	366	367	733
50-54	1659	1714	3373	1530	1520	3050	1694	1678	3372	1876	1862	3738	1880	1866	3746
55	292	302	594	288	306	594	303	303	606	347	349	696	355	358	713
56	287	294	581	296	317	613	290	292	582	329	331	660	343	346	689
57	288	298	586	305	320	625	293	295	588	319	324	643	324	329	653
58	271	282	553	323	341	664	285	295	580	309	316	625	314	322	636
59	243	253	496	351	374	725	272	286	558	294	303	597	304	313	617
55-59	1381	1429	2810	1563	1658	3221	1443	1471	2914	1598	1623	3221	1640	1668	3308
60	224	237	461	271	290	561	267	294	561	281	290	571	289	300	589
61	238	248	486	264	281	545	273	303	576	268	279	547	276	287	563
62	235	250	485	263	284	547	279	305	584	268	281	549	263	276	539
63	229	246	475	246	267	513	293	323	616	259	280	539	262	278	540
64	222	239	461	218	239	457	316	354	670	245	271	516	253	277	530
60-64	1148	1220	2368	1262	1361	2623	1428	1579	3007	1321	1401	2722	1343	1418	2761
65	213	234	447	199	223	422	241	273	514	239	276	515	239	267	506
66	201	225	426	209	232	441	233	263	496	241	284	525	232	272	504
67	192	218	410	204	232	436	229	264	493	244	284	528	233	280	513
68	185	217	402	196	227	423	211	247	458	253	299	552	236	279	515
69	185	221	406	187	219	406	185	219	404	269	326	595	243	293	536
65-69	976	1115	2091	995	1133	2128	1099	1266	2365	1246	1469	2715	1183	1391	2574
70	181	225	406	176	212	388	166	203	369	202	249	451	258	319	577
71	170	220	390	163	203	366	170	209	379	191	238	429	192	243	435
72	161	212	373	153	194	347	163	207	370	184	236	420	182	232	414
73	150	204	354	144	191	335	154	200	354	167	219	386	174	229	403
74	144	205	349	140	192	332	143	191	334	142	191	333	157	211	368
70-74	806	1066	1872	776	992	1768	796	1010	1806	886	1133	2019	963	1234	2197
75	138	201	339	133	192	325	131	182	313	124	175	299	132	185	317
76	127	194	321	122	185	307	118	171	289	125	177	302	115	168	283
77	118	187	305	112	175	287	108	161	269	115	172	287	115	169	284
78	110	182	292	102	164	266	98	154	252	106	162	268	106	163	269
79	104	183	287	94	160	254	92	151	243	95	151	246	96	153	249
75-79	597	947	1544	563	876	1439	547	819	1366	565	837	1402	564	838	1402
80	98	179	277	87	153	240	85	147	232	84	141	225	86	142	228
81	91	176	267	77	143	220	74	137	211	73	128	201	75	131	206
82	53	108	161	68	133	201	65	126	191	63	116	179	64	118	182
83	45	96	141	60	125	185	56	114	170	55	108	163	55	107	162
84	43	98	141	54	120	174	50	106	156	49	101	150	48	98	146
80-84	330	657	987	346	674	1020	330	630	960	324	594	918	328	596	924
85 and over	196	581	777	203	593	796	214	617	831	214	609	823	214	606	820
All ages	24977	25734	50711	25029	25707	50736	25164	25785	50949	25418	26006	51424	25471	26057	51528

Appendix Table Id Projected Total population as at mid-year, by sex, age and marital condition, 1977-2017; mid-1977 based projections

Age	1977	1978	1979	1980	1981	1982	1986	1991	1996	2001	2006	2011	2016	2017
Married males *(thousands)*														
0-14	-	-	-	-	-	-	-	-	-	-	-	-	-	-
15-19	26	27	29	31	31	31	31	27	20	21	28	28	26	25
20-24	541	525	515	522	531	543	588	558	469	386	453	541	528	520
25-29	1228	1166	1131	1103	1096	1098	1166	1276	1199	995	863	1033	1185	1186
30-34	1422	1459	1459	1453	1436	1350	1264	1367	1495	1410	1175	1023	1226	1287
35-39	1225	1233	1255	1274	1312	1411	1448	1293	1406	1541	1462	1216	1054	1069
40-44	1206	1214	1221	1223	1202	1192	1298	1444	1294	1410	1553	1475	1225	1157
45-49	1220	1205	1186	1173	1163	1163	1172	1275	1421	1279	1399	1542	1462	1433
50-54	1250	1219	1199	1180	1166	1154	1108	1124	1226	1368	1235	1354	1493	1494
55-59	1201	1253	1292	1233	1192	1157	1085	1037	1054	1153	1289	1167	1280	1312
60-64	1065	1004	948	988	1030	1069	1064	976	936	954	1047	1172	1065	1079
65-69	924	924	924	923	906	878	859	889	821	791	811	894	1004	950
70-74	638	651	661	670	673	674	665	639	662	618	601	620	691	751
75-79	324	340	353	366	377	385	410	409	402	416	394	388	403	404
80-84	120	124	132	135	142	149	174	192	195	198	204	196	196	199
85 and over	45	43	41	43	43	45	52	65	72	77	82	87	86	86
All ages	12435	12387	12346	12317	12300	12299	12384	12571	12672	12617	12596	12736	12924	12952
Other males *(thousands)*														
0-14	5600	5474	5337	5203	5082	4972	4818	5134	5616	5627	5273	5057	5164	5213
15-19	1906	1949	1995	2036	2051	2056	1956	1632	1418	1702	1945	1893	1710	1674
20-24	1224	1269	1309	1346	1386	1423	1526	1461	1225	1088	1304	1465	1426	1404
25-29	549	567	590	613	637	661	743	829	812	691	605	717	813	816
30-34	322	345	365	381	394	387	426	498	566	557	469	404	482	507
35-39	212	225	238	251	268	296	341	357	419	478	464	389	335	340
40-44	193	200	208	216	218	222	257	318	330	387	436	422	355	335
45-49	202	202	204	204	205	208	218	247	303	311	361	407	396	389
50-54	208	210	211	213	214	214	207	213	239	291	295	340	383	386
55-59	196	208	220	218	217	216	215	202	205	228	274	276	318	328
60-64	193	185	177	184	192	202	216	207	193	195	215	256	257	264
65-69	204	204	204	204	200	195	190	209	198	185	185	205	242	233
70-74	197	197	198	197	198	198	193	184	201	188	175	176	195	212
75-79	158	164	169	171	172	175	178	175	167	181	169	159	162	161
80-84	105	104	104	108	113	117	131	138	136	132	142	134	128	129
85 and over	73	75	78	77	77	77	86	101	115	119	121	128	128	128
All ages	11542	11578	11607	11622	11624	11619	11701	11905	12143	12360	12433	12428	12494	12519
Males - *proportions married*														
0-14	-	-	-	-	-	-	-	-	-	-	-	-	-	-
15-19	0.013	0.014	0.014	0.015	0.015	0.015	0.016	0.016	0.014	0.012	0.014	0.015	0.015	0.015
20-24	0.307	0.293	0.282	0.279	0.277	0.276	0.278	0.276	0.277	0.262	0.258	0.270	0.270	0.270
25-29	0.691	0.673	0.657	0.643	0.632	0.624	0.611	0.606	0.596	0.590	0.588	0.590	0.593	0.592
30-34	0.815	0.809	0.800	0.792	0.785	0.777	0.748	0.733	0.725	0.717	0.715	0.717	0.718	0.717
35-39	0.852	0.846	0.841	0.835	0.830	0.827	0.809	0.784	0.770	0.763	0.759	0.758	0.759	0.759
40-44	0.862	0.859	0.854	0.850	0.846	0.843	0.835	0.820	0.797	0.785	0.781	0.778	0.775	0.775
45-49	0.858	0.856	0.853	0.852	0.850	0.848	0.843	0.838	0.824	0.804	0.795	0.791	0.787	0.786
50-54	0.857	0.853	0.850	0.847	0.845	0.844	0.843	0.841	0.837	0.825	0.807	0.799	0.796	0.795
55-59	0.860	0.858	0.854	0.850	0.846	0.843	0.835	0.837	0.837	0.835	0.825	0.809	0.801	0.800
60-64	0.847	0.844	0.843	0.843	0.843	0.841	0.831	0.825	0.829	0.830	0.830	0.821	0.806	0.803
65-69	0.819	0.819	0.819	0.819	0.819	0.818	0.819	0.810	0.806	0.810	0.814	0.813	0.806	0.803
70-74	0.764	0.768	0.769	0.773	0.773	0.773	0.775	0.776	0.767	0.767	0.774	0.779	0.780	0.780
75-79	0.672	0.675	0.676	0.682	0.687	0.688	0.697	0.700	0.707	0.697	0.700	0.709	0.713	0.715
80-84	0.533	0.544	0.559	0.556	0.557	0.560	0.570	0.582	0.589	0.600	0.590	0.594	0.605	0.607
85 and over	0.381	0.364	0.345	0.358	0.358	0.369	0.377	0.392	0.385	0.393	0.404	0.405	0.402	0.402
15 and over	0.677	0.670	0.663	0.657	0.653	0.649	0.643	0.650	0.660	0.652	0.638	0.C33	0.638	0.639

Age	1977	1978	1979	1980	1981	1982	1986	1991	1996	2001	2006	2011	2016	2017
Married females *(thousands)*														
0-14	-	-	-	-	-	-	-	-	-	-	-	-	-	-
15-19	119	121	125	128	131	133	130	116	96	107	130	129	120	118
20-24	913	892	879	882	894	911	993	964	832	718	833	961	948	937
25-29	1417	1352	1313	1282	1268	1268	1341	1493	1442	1215	1050	1243	1426	1431
30-34	1487	1534	1544	1546	1537	1445	1325	1435	1602	1539	1278	1106	1322	1389
35-39	1225	1239	1266	1291	1335	1443	1513	1319	1441	1608	1537	1273	1102	1118
40-44	1180	1185	1193	1194	1178	1173	1295	1483	1300	1424	1584	1511	1251	1183
45-49	1215	1195	1168	1144	1127	1121	1129	1253	1442	1268	1388	1540	1471	1439
50-54	1224	1198	1179	1164	1150	1133	1059	1070	1196	1377	1211	1325	1472	1476
55-59	1141	1190	1225	1174	1133	1102	1037	961	977	1096	1260	1110	1216	1250
60-64	943	894	849	891	934	971	965	889	829	845	950	1095	967	977
65-69	756	757	759	760	744	724	725	749	696	653	670	761	877	830
70-74	481	485	490	493	496	495	491	487	503	473	449	463	533	584
75-79	229	233	236	241	244	248	258	259	264	273	261	250	262	264
80-84	81	80	80	80	82	83	90	96	100	105	108	105	104	105
85 and over	27	24	22	22	20	21	19	24	24	28	31	33	33	33
All ages	12438	12379	12328	12292	12273	12271	12370	12598	12744	12729	12740	12905	13104	13134
Other females *(thousands)*														
0-14	5300	5176	5044	4914	4795	4688	4531	4832	5289	5298	4961	4757	4858	4904
15-19	1712	1753	1795	1832	1845	1847	1750	1437	1250	1509	1723	1674	1507	1474
20-24	754	797	843	883	921	952	1015	948	754	661	816	924	887	869
25-29	330	346	359	362	373	391	465	505	461	363	321	397	450	449
30-34	219	237	251	273	286	282	294	348	374	342	278	244	297	312
35-39	170	181	193	205	219	244	289	280	322	347	323	264	230	233
40-44	174	181	189	196	199	203	239	297	278	317	348	327	266	251
45-49	207	208	209	210	211	214	228	258	312	287	328	364	340	332
50-54	272	265	261	260	260	258	249	256	282	338	310	353	390	390
55-59	359	373	387	368	356	345	326	303	305	334	398	361	408	418
60-64	478	452	428	432	442	456	451	408	374	375	411	484	434	441
65-69	632	628	622	619	605	588	549	561	505	462	463	506	593	561
70-74	709	718	725	727	728	725	697	641	656	593	544	547	601	651
75-79	654	670	682	692	699	708	729	703	658	674	615	569	575	574
80-84	456	468	483	497	512	522	560	590	574	552	566	525	490	491
85 and over	334	343	351	361	372	382	431	487	536	553	562	584	576	573
All ages	12760	12796	12811	12831	12823	12805	12803	12854	12930	13005	12967	12880	12902	12923
Females - *proportions married*														
0-14	-	-	-	-	-	-	-	-	-	-	-	-	-	-
15-19	0.065	0.065	0.065	0.065	0.066	0.067	0.069	0.075	0.071	0.066	0.070	0.072	0.074	0.074
20-24	0.548	0.528	0.510	0.500	0.493	0.489	0.495	0.504	0.525	0.521	0.505	0.510	0.517	0.519
25-29	0.811	0.796	0.785	0.780	0.773	0.764	0.743	0.747	0.758	0.770	0.766	0.758	0.760	0.761
30-34	0.872	0.866	0.860	0.850	0.843	0.837	0.818	0.805	0.811	0.818	0.821	0.819	0.817	0.817
35-39	0.878	0.873	0.868	0.863	0.859	0.855	0.840	0.825	0.817	0.823	0.826	0.828	0.827	0.828
40-44	0.871	0.867	0.863	0.859	0.855	0.852	0.844	0.833	0.824	0.818	0.820	0.822	0.825	0.825
45-49	0.854	0.852	0.848	0.845	0.842	0.840	0.832	0.829	0.822	0.815	0.809	0.809	0.812	0.813
50-54	0.818	0.819	0.819	0.817	0.816	0.815	0.810	0.807	0.809	0.803	0.796	0.790	0.791	0.791
55-59	0.761	0.761	0.760	0.761	0.761	0.762	0.761	0.760	0.762	0.766	0.760	0.755	0.749	0.749
60-64	0.664	0.664	0.665	0.673	0.679	0.680	0.681	0.685	0.689	0.693	0.698	0.693	0.690	0.689
65-69	0.545	0.547	0.550	0.551	0.552	0.552	0.569	0.572	0.580	0.586	0.591	0.601	0.597	0.597
70-74	0.404	0.403	0.403	0.404	0.405	0.406	0.413	0.432	0.434	0.444	0.452	0.458	0.470	0.473
75-79	0.259	0.258	0.257	0.258	0.259	0.259	0.261	0.269	0.286	0.288	0.298	0.305	0.313	0.315
80-84	0.151	0.146	0.142	0.139	0.138	0.137	0.138	0.140	0.148	0.160	0.160	0.167	0.175	0.176
85 and over	0.075	0.065	0.059	0.057	0.051	0.052	0.042	0.047	0.043	0.048	0.052	0.053	0.054	0.054
15 and over	0.625	0.619	0.613	0.608	0.605	0.602	0.599	0.611	0.625	0.623	0.614	0.614	0.620	0.621

Appendix Table 1e Mortality rates by sex and single ages,
mid-1977-78 to mid-2011-12

Age last birthday	1977–78		1991–92		2011–12	
	Males	Females	Males	Females	Males	Females
0*	0.01815	0.01488	0.01640	0.01345	0.01419	0.01164
0	0.00257	0.00212	0.00233	0.00191	0.00201	0.00165
1	0.00091	0.00068	0.00082	0.00062	0.00071	0.00053
2	0.00064	0.00049	0.00058	0.00044	0.00050	0.00038
3	0.00054	0.00040	0.00048	0.00036	0.00042	0.00031
4	0.00047	0.00033	0.00042	0.00030	0.00037	0.00026
5	0.00041	0.00029	0.00037	0.00026	0.00032	0.00023
6	0.00037	0.00026	0.00033	0.00024	0.00029	0.00021
7	0.00033	0.00023	0.00030	0.00021	0.00026	0.00018
8	0.00030	0.00021	0.00027	0.00019	0.00024	0.00017
9	0.00029	0.00020	0.00026	0.00018	0.00023	0.00015
10	0.00029	0.00020	0.00026	0.00018	0.00023	0.00015
11	0.00030	0.00020	0.00027	0.00018	0.00024	0.00015
12	0.00033	0.00020	0.00030	0.00018	0.00026	0.00015
13	0.00037	0.00021	0.00033	0.00019	0.00029	0.00017
14	0.00042	0.00026	0.00038	0.00024	0.00033	0.00021
15	0.00054	0.00033	0.00050	0.00031	0.00045	0.00028
16	0.00083	0.00038	0.00080	0.00036	0.00076	0.00034
17	0.00112	0.00040	0.00112	0.00040	0.00112	0.00040
18	0.00114	0.00042	0.00114	0.00042	0.00114	0.00042
19	0.00112	0.00043	0.00110	0.00043	0.00109	0.00042
20	0.00106	0.00043	0.00104	0.00042	0.00101	0.00041
21	0.00102	0.00042	0.00099	0.00040	0.00094	0.00038
22	0.00097	0.00041	0.00093	0.00039	0.00087	0.00036
23	0.00093	0.00041	0.00088	0.00039	0.00082	0.00035
24	0.00089	0.00042	0.00084	0.00039	0.00078	0.00035
25	0.00086	0.00043	0.00081	0.00040	0.00075	0.00035
26	0.00085	0.00045	0.00080	0.00041	0.00073	0.00036
27	0.00086	0.00048	0.00080	0.00043	0.00073	0.00037
28	0.00089	0.00051	0.00083	0.00046	0.00077	0.00040
29	0.00092	0.00054	0.00087	0.00048	0.00080	0.00042
30	0.00096	0.00058	0.00091	0.00052	0.00085	0.00045
31	0.00101	0.00061	0.00097	0.00056	0.00091	0.00048
32	0.00106	0.00067	0.00102	0.00061	0.00097	0.00053
33	0.00113	0.00074	0.00109	0.00067	0.00103	0.00059
34	0.00122	0.00082	0.00118	0.00075	0.00112	0.00067
35	0.00132	0.00091	0.00127	0.00085	0.00121	0.00077
36	0.00144	0.00102	0.00139	0.00096	0.00132	0.00089
37	0.00159	0.00114	0.00153	0.00110	0.00145	0.00104
38	0.00179	0.00127	0.00173	0.00123	0.00166	0.00118
39	0.00204	0.00142	0.00200	0.00139	0.00194	0.00135
40	0.00232	0.00160	0.00229	0.00158	0.00224	0.00155
41	0.00262	0.00182	0.00260	0.00180	0.00257	0.00179
42	0.00294	0.00204	0.00294	0.00203	0.00294	0.00202
43	0.00331	0.00229	0.00331	0.00229	0.00331	0.00229
44	0.00375	0.00255	0.00375	0.00255	0.00375	0.00255

Probability that a baby born in the year will not survive until the end of the year

Age last birthday	1977-78		1991-92		2011-12	
	Males	Females	Males	Females	Males	Females
45	0.00425	0.00284	0.00425	0.00284	0.00425	0.00284
46	0.00482	0.00316	0.00482	0.00316	0.00482	0.00316
47	0.00546	0.00350	0.00546	0.00350	0.00546	0.00350
48	0.00616	0.00384	0.00616	0.00384	0.00616	0.00384
49	0.00692	0.00418	0.00692	0.00418	0.00692	0.00418
50	0.00774	0.00455	0.00774	0.00455	0.00774	0.00455
51	0.00862	0.00495	0.00862	0.00495	0.00862	0.00495
52	0.00957	0.00540	0.00957	0.00540	0.00957	0.00540
53	0.01059	0.00588	0.01054	0.00588	0.01048	0.00588
54	0.01170	0.00639	0.01162	0.00639	0.01150	0.00639
55	0.01290	0.00694	0.01276	0.00691	0.01256	0.00687
56	0.01422	0.00756	0.01402	0.00750	0.01374	0.00743
57	0.01564	0.00824	0.01531	0.00815	0.01486	0.00802
58	0.01718	0.00897	0.01668	0.00884	0.01600	0.00867
59	0.01889	0.00977	0.01821	0.00959	0.01729	0.00934
60	0.02076	0.01063	0.01985	0.01041	0.01861	0.01010
61	0.02281	0.01157	0.02163	0.01124	0.02004	0.01078
62	0.02503	0.01261	0.02363	0.01216	0.02176	0.01155
63	0.02754	0.01381	0.02593	0.01326	0.02379	0.01251
64	0.03039	0.01516	0.02849	0.01449	0.02598	0.01359
65	0.03362	0.01668	0.03138	0.01588	0.02845	0.01481
66	0.03722	0.01838	0.03455	0.01743	0.03107	0.01615
67	0.04117	0.02030	0.03806	0.01924	0.03402	0.01783
68	0.04551	0.02243	0.04207	0.02117	0.03760	0.01950
69	0.05019	0.02487	0.04659	0.02348	0.04189	0.02163
70	0.05519	0.02766	0.05152	0.02611	0.04670	0.02405
71	0.06042	0.03080	0.05641	0.02900	0.05113	0.02660
72	0.06597	0.03436	0.06184	0.03235	0.05640	0.02968
73	0.07169	0.03833	0.06721	0.03608	0.06129	0.03310
74	0.07780	0.04270	0.07324	0.04003	0.06719	0.03650
75	0.08422	0.04760	0.07929	0.04462	0.07274	0.04069
76	0.09112	0.05304	0.08603	0.04972	0.07924	0.04534
77	0.09840	0.05915	0.09290	0.05545	0.08558	0.05057
78	0.10628	0.06596	0.10077	0.06157	0.09338	0.05581
79	0.11463	0.07366	0.10868	0.06877	0.10071	0.06233
80	0.12375	0.08220	0.11782	0.07674	0.10985	0.06956
81	0.13344	0.09143	0.12705	0.08536	0.11845	0.07737
82	0.14382	0.10125	0.13693	0.09453	0.12766	0.08568
83	0.15490	0.11147	0.14748	0.10406	0.13749	0.09432
84	0.16666	0.12200	0.15868	0.11325	0.14793	0.10183
85	0.17912	0.13328	0.17054	0.12372	0.15899	0.11125
86	0.19236	0.14534	0.18315	0.13492	0.17075	0.12132
87	0.20660	0.15844	0.19670	0.14708	0.18338	0.13225
88	0.22202	0.17290	0.21138	0.16051	0.19707	0.14432
89	0.23872	0.18904	0.22729	0.17549	0.21190	0.15779
90 and over	0.27905	0.24274	0.26569	0.22534	0.24770	0.20262

Appendix Table IIa Actual and projected Total population as at mid-year by sex and age-groups, 1951, 1961, 1971 to 2017; mid-1977 based projections.

Wales

thousands

Year	Age in years 0-14	15-44		45-64	45-59	65 and over	60 and over	All ages		
	Persons	Males	Females	Males	Females	Males	Females	Males	Females	Persons
1951	591	535	546	307	259	125	224	1269	1318	2587
1961	619	514	508	325	272	128	269	1283	1352	2635
1971	644	522	505	328	265	149	318	1329	1402	2731
1972	646	526	508	326	263	151	321	1335	1408	2743
1973	647	532	514	325	261	154	325	1341	1416	2757
1974	642	536	518	324	261	156	328	1345	1420	2765
1975	636	542	523	322	258	157	331	1348	1422	2770
1976	626	549	530	320	256	159	333	1350	1423	2773
1977	614	550	540	319	256	160	334	1346	1427	2773
1978	602	558	545	316	256	163	335	1347	1428	2775
1979	590	566	553	313	253	165	337	1348	1429	2777
1980	575	573	561	312	249	168	341	1350	1429	2779
1981	566	579	566	310	245	170	345	1351	1430	2781
1982	555	588	573	310	240	169	350	1353	1432	2785
1983	550	592	577	312	237	169	353	1356	1434	2790
1984	546	599	584	311	235	169	355	1361	1438	2799
1985	546	602	589	309	233	173	356	1366	1442	2808
1986	545	610	597	305	230	175	357	1372	1447	2819
1987	547	614	600	302	227	179	360	1378	1451	2829
1988	553	616	602	302	228	180	359	1384	1456	2840
1989	561	617	601	303	228	180	361	1390	1461	2851
1990	569	616	601	304	231	182	359	1396	1466	2862
1991	579	615	597	305	234	183	360	1402	1471	2873
1992	590	608	589	310	242	184	359	1407	1475	2882
1993	602	604	583	314	249	184	356	1413	1479	2892
1994	614	600	577	317	253	184	356	1418	1483	2901
1995	623	597	574	320	260	184	352	1423	1487	2910
1996	629	595	570	322	263	185	353	1427	1490	2917
1997	636	596	568	323	266	184	350	1431	1492	2923
1998	637	596	568	326	270	183	349	1434	1495	2929
1999	637	596	567	330	273	182	349	1437	1497	2934
2000	633	600	568	332	277	181	347	1440	1498	2938
2001	627	602	569	335	282	181	345	1442	1499	2941
2002	622	605	571	337	285	181	343	1444	1500	2944
2003	613	608	572	341	288	180	345	1446	1501	2947
2004	606	611	573	345	291	179	345	1448	1502	2950
2005	600	613	573	347	293	180	347	1450	1503	2953
2006	591	614	574	353	295	180	349	1452	1504	2956
2007	588	614	573	357	293	180	356	1455	1506	2961
2008	582	614	573	362	293	181	361	1458	1508	2966
2009	578	613	572	366	295	183	364	1461	1510	2971
2010	578	611	570	370	296	184	368	1464	1513	2977
2011	575	609	569	375	298	187	371	1468	1516	2984
2012	577	607	567	375	301	192	372	1472	1519	2991
2013	578	607	565	376	302	194	376	1476	1522	2998
2014	582	604	562	378	305	198	378	1481	1526	3007
2015	588	601	559	380	306	200	381	1485	1530	3015
2016	592	599	557	383	308	202	383	1490	1534	3024
2017	597	598	556	386	307	202	386	1494	1538	3032

Figures for the years 1971-1976 relate to the old series estimates of Total population and are not directly comparable with the data for subsequent years. (See Population Trends *10, 11 and 12 for further details of the new series estimates.)*

Appendix Table IIb Annual changes in projected Total population
1977 to 2017; mid-1977 based projections

Wales

thousands

Mid-year to mid-year	Population at beginning of period	Births	Deaths	Natural increase	Net migration	Total increase
1977-1978	2773	32	34	- 2	4	2
1978-1979	2775	32	35	- 2	4	2
1979-1980	2777	33	35	- 2	4	2
1980-1981	2779	34	35	- 2	4	2
1981-1982	2781	35	36	0	4	4
1982-1983	2785	37	36	1	4	5
1983-1984	2790	40	36	5	4	9
1984-1985	2799	42	37	5	4	9
1985-1986	2808	43	37	7	4	11
1986-1987	2819	44	37	6	4	10
1987-1988	2829	44	37	7	4	11
1988-1989	2840	44	37	7	4	11
1989-1990	2851	44	38	7	4	11
1990-1991	2862	44	38	7	4	11
1991-1992	2873	44	38	5	4	9
1992-1993	2882	44	38	6	4	10
1993-1994	2892	43	38	5	4	9
1994-1995	2901	42	38	5	4	9
1995-1996	2910	42	38	3	4	7
1996-1997	2917	41	38	2	4	6
1997-1998	2923	40	38	2	4	6
1998-1999	2929	39	38	1	4	5
1999-2000	2934	38	38	0	4	4
2000-2001	2938	38	38	- 1	4	3
2001-2002	2941	37	38	- 1	4	3
2002-2003	2944	37	38	- 1	4	3
2003-2004	2947	37	38	- 1	4	3
2004-2005	2950	37	38	- 1	4	3
2005-2006	2953	37	38	- 1	4	3
2006-2007	2956	38	38	1	4	5
2007-2008	2961	39	38	1	4	5
2008-2009	2966	39	38	1	4	5
2009-2010	2971	40	38	2	4	6
2010-2011	2977	41	38	3	4	7
2011-2012	2984	41	38	3	4	7
2012-2013	2991	42	38	3	4	7
2013-2014	2998	42	38	5	4	9
2014-2015	3007	43	38	4	4	8
2015-2016	3015	43	38	5	4	9
2016-2017	3024	43	38	4	4	8
2017-2018	3032					

Appendix Table IIc **Projected Total population as at mid-year, by sex and single ages 1977 to 1989, 1991-2017; mid-1977 based projections.**

thousands

Age-group	1977			1978			1979			1980			1981		
	Males	Females	Persons	Males	Females	Persons	Males	Females	Persons	Males	Females	Persons	Males	Females	Persons
0	16	15	31	16	15	31	17	16	33	17	16	33	17	16	33
1	17	16	33	16	15	31	16	15	31	16	15	31	17	16	33
2	18	17	35	17	16	33	16	15	31	16	15	31	17	16	33
3	19	18	37	19	17	36	17	16	33	17	15	32	16	15	31
4	20	18	38	19	18	37	19	17	36	17	16	33	16	15	31
0-4	90	84	174	87	81	168	85	79	164	83	77	160	83	78	161
5	21	20	41	20	19	39	19	18	37	19	17	36	17	16	33
6	22	21	43	21	20	41	20	18	38	19	17	36	19	17	36
7	22	21	43	22	21	43	21	20	41	20	19	39	19	18	37
8	23	21	44	22	21	43	22	21	43	21	20	41	20	18	38
9	22	20	42	22	21	43	22	21	43	22	21	43	21	20	41
5-9	110	103	213	107	102	209	104	98	202	101	94	195	96	89	185
10	23	22	45	22	21	43	23	22	45	22	21	43	22	21	43
11	23	22	45	23	22	45	22	21	43	23	21	44	22	21	43
12	24	22	46	23	22	45	23	22	45	22	21	43	23	22	45
13	24	22	46	24	22	46	23	22	45	23	22	45	22	21	43
14	23	22	45	24	22	46	24	22	46	23	22	45	24	22	46
10-14	117	110	227	116	109	225	115	109	224	113	107	220	113	107	220
15	22	22	44	23	22	45	24	22	46	24	22	46	24	22	46
16	22	21	43	23	21	44	23	22	45	24	22	46	24	22	46
17	21	20	41	21	21	42	22	21	43	24	22	46	24	22	46
18	21	21	42	21	20	41	22	21	43	22	21	43	23	21	44
19	20	20	40	21	21	42	21	20	41	21	21	42	22	21	43
15-19	106	104	210	109	105	214	112	106	218	115	108	223	117	108	225
20	20	19	39	20	20	40	21	20	41	21	20	41	21	21	42
21	19	19	38	20	19	39	20	20	40	21	20	41	21	20	41
22	19	18	37	19	19	38	20	19	39	20	20	40	21	20	41
23	19	19	38	19	18	37	19	19	38	19	19	38	20	19	39
24	19	19	38	19	19	38	19	18	37	19	19	38	19	19	38
20-24	96	94	190	97	95	192	99	96	195	100	98	198	102	99	201
25	18	18	36	19	18	37	19	19	38	18	18	36	19	19	38
26	19	18	37	18	18	36	19	18	37	19	19	38	18	18	36
27	19	20	39	19	18	37	18	18	36	19	18	37	19	19	38
28	20	20	40	19	20	39	19	19	38	18	18	36	19	18	37
29	21	22	43	19	20	39	19	20	39	19	19	38	18	18	36
25-29	97	98	195	94	94	188	94	94	188	93	92	185	93	92	185
30	23	23	46	21	22	43	20	20	40	19	20	39	19	19	38
31	18	18	36	23	23	46	21	22	43	20	20	40	19	20	39
32	18	18	36	18	18	36	23	23	46	21	22	43	19	20	39
33	18	18	36	19	18	37	18	18	36	23	23	46	21	22	43
34	18	17	35	18	18	36	18	18	36	18	18	36	23	23	46
30-34	95	94	189	99	99	198	100	101	201	101	103	204	101	104	205
35	16	15	31	18	17	35	18	18	36	18	18	36	18	19	37
36	15	15	30	16	15	31	18	17	35	18	18	36	18	18	36
37	16	15	31	15	15	30	16	15	31	18	17	35	18	18	36
38	16	15	31	16	15	31	15	15	30	16	15	31	18	17	35
39	16	16	32	16	15	31	16	15	31	15	15	30	16	15	31
35-39	79	76	155	81	77	158	83	80	163	85	83	168	88	87	175
40	16	15	31	16	16	32	16	15	31	16	16	32	15	15	30
41	16	15	31	16	15	31	16	16	32	16	15	31	16	15	31
42	15	15	30	16	15	31	16	15	31	16	16	32	16	15	31
43	15	14	29	15	15	30	15	15	30	16	15	31	16	16	32
44	15	15	30	15	14	29	15	15	30	15	15	30	15	15	30
40-44	77	74	151	78	75	153	78	76	154	79	77	156	78	76	154

Figures above the dotted line relate to persons born after mid-1977.

Age-group	1977			1978			1979			1980			1981		
	Males	Females	Persons	Males	Females	Persons	Males	Females	Persons	Males	Females	Persons	Males	Females	Persons
45	16	15	31	15	15	30	15	14	29	15	15	30	16	15	31
46	17	16	33	16	15	31	15	15	30	15	14	29	15	15	30
47	16	17	33	16	16	32	16	15	31	15	14	29	15	14	29
48	16	16	32	16	17	33	16	16	32	16	15	31	15	15	30
49	16	16	32	16	16	32	16	16	32	16	16	32	15	15	30
45-49	81	80	161	79	79	158	78	76	154	77	74	151	76	74	150
50	17	17	34	16	16	32	16	16	32	16	17	33	16	16	32
51	17	18	35	17	17	34	16	16	32	16	16	32	16	17	33
52	17	17	34	17	18	35	16	17	33	16	16	32	16	16	32
53	17	18	35	17	17	34	17	18	35	16	17	33	16	16	32
54	16	17	33	16	18	34	17	17	34	17	18	35	16	17	33
50-54	84	87	171	83	86	169	82	84	166	81	84	165	80	82	162
55	18	20	38	17	17	34	16	18	34	17	17	34	17	18	35
56	18	20	38	18	20	38	16	17	33	16	18	34	16	17	33
57	18	19	37	18	20	38	18	20	38	16	17	33	16	18	34
58	14	16	30	17	19	36	18	19	37	17	20	37	16	17	33
59	13	14	27	14	15	29	17	19	36	18	19	37	17	19	36
55-59	81	89	170	84	91	175	85	93	178	84	91	175	82	89	171
60	14	15	29	13	14	27	14	16	30	17	19	36	17	20	37
61	14	16	30	14	16	30	12	14	26	14	15	29	17	19	36
62	15	18	33	14	16	30	13	15	28	12	14	26	13	15	28
63	15	17	32	15	17	32	14	16	30	13	15	28	12	14	26
64	15	17	32	14	17	31	15	17	32	14	16	30	13	15	28
60-64	73	83	156	70	80	150	68	78	146	70	79	149	72	83	155
65	14	17	31	14	17	31	14	17	31	14	17	31	14	15	29
66	14	17	31	14	17	31	14	17	31	14	16	30	14	17	31
67	13	16	29	13	17	30	13	16	29	13	17	30	13	16	29
68	12	16	28	13	16	29	13	16	29	13	16	29	13	16	29
69	12	15	27	12	15	27	12	15	27	12	16	28	12	16	28
65-69	65	81	146	66	82	148	66	81	147	66	82	148	66	80	146
70	11	15	26	11	15	26	11	15	26	11	15	26	12	16	28
71	10	15	25	10	14	24	11	15	26	11	15	26	11	15	26
72	10	14	24	10	14	24	10	14	24	10	14	24	10	14	24
73	9	13	22	9	14	23	9	14	23	9	14	23	10	13	23
74	8	12	20	9	13	22	8	13	21	9	13	22	8	13	21
70-74	48	69	117	49	70	119	49	71	120	50	71	121	51	71	122
75	7	12	19	8	12	20	8	12	20	8	13	21	8	13	21
76	6	12	18	6	11	17	7	11	18	7	11	18	7	12	19
77	6	10	16	6	11	17	6	11	17	6	11	17	6	11	17
78	5	9	14	5	10	15	5	11	16	5	10	15	4	10	16
79	4	8	12	4	8	12	4	9	13	5	10	15	4	10	14
75-79	28	51	79	29	52	81	30	54	84	31	55	86	31	56	87
80	3	8	11	4	8	12	4	8	12	4	9	13	4	9	13
81	3	7	10	3	7	10	3	7	10	3	7	10	4	8	12
82	3	6	9	2	6	8	3	7	10	3	6	9	3	6	9
83	2	5	7	2	5	7	2	6	8	2	6	8	2	6	8
84	2	4	6	2	5	7	2	4	6	2	5	7	2	5	7
80-84	13	30	43	13	31	44	14	32	46	14	33	47	15	34	49
85 & over	6	20	26	6	20	26	6	21	27	7	21	28	7	21	28
All ages	1346	1427	2773	1347	1428	2775	1348	1429	2777	1350	1429	2779	1351	1430	2781

thousands

Age-group	1982			1983			1984			1985			1986		
	Males	Females	Persons	Males	Females	Persons	Males	Females	Persons	Males	Females	Persons	Males	Females	Persons
0	18	17	35	19	18	37	20	19	39	21	20	41	22	20	42
1	17	16	33	18	17	35	19	18	37	20	19	39	22	20	42
2	17	16	33	17	16	33	18	17	35	19	18	37	20	19	39
3	17	15	32	17	16	33	17	16	33	18	17	35	19	18	37
4	16	15	31	16	15	31	17	15	32	18	16	34	18	17	35
0-4	85	79	164	87	82	169	91	85	176	96	90	186	101	94	195
5	16	15	31	16	15	31	17	16	33	17	16	33	17	16	33
6	17	16	33	17	15	32	16	15	31	17	16	33	17	16	33
7	19	17	36	17	16	33	17	15	32	16	15	31	17	15	32
8	19	17	36	19	17	36	17	16	33	17	15	32	16	15	31
9	20	19	39	19	18	37	19	17	36	17	16	33	17	16	33
5-9	91	84	175	88	81	169	86	79	165	84	78	162	84	78	162
10	21	20	41	20	19	39	19	18	37	19	17	36	18	16	34
11	22	22	44	21	20	41	20	19	39	19	18	37	19	18	37
12	22	21	43	22	22	44	21	20	41	20	19	39	19	18	37
13	23	22	45	22	21	43	23	22	45	21	20	41	20	19	39
14	22	21	43	23	22	45	22	21	43	23	22	45	21	20	41
10-14	110	106	216	108	104	212	105	100	205	102	96	198	97	91	188
15	23	22	45	22	21	43	23	22	45	22	21	43	23	22	45
16	24	22	46	23	21	44	22	21	43	23	22	45	22	21	43
17	24	22	46	24	21	45	23	21	44	22	21	43	23	22	45
18	24	22	46	24	22	46	24	21	45	24	21	45	22	20	42
19	23	21	44	24	22	46	24	22	46	23	21	44	23	21	44
15-19	118	109	227	117	107	224	116	107	223	114	106	220	113	106	219
20	22	21	43	23	21	44	24	22	46	23	22	45	24	21	45
21	21	21	42	22	21	43	23	21	44	24	21	45	23	22	45
22	21	20	41	21	20	41	22	21	43	23	21	44	24	21	45
23	21	20	41	21	20	41	21	20	41	22	21	43	23	21	44
24	20	19	39	21	20	41	21	20	41	21	20	41	22	21	43
20-24	105	101	206	108	102	210	111	104	215	113	105	218	116	106	222
25	20	19	39	20	19	39	21	20	41	20	20	40	21	20	41
26	19	19	38	20	19	39	20	19	39	20	20	40	20	20	40
27	18	18	36	19	19	38	19	19	38	20	19	39	20	20	40
28	19	19	38	18	18	36	19	19	38	19	19	38	20	20	40
29	19	18	37	19	19	38	18	18	36	19	19	38	19	19	38
25-29	95	93	188	96	94	190	97	95	192	98	97	195	100	99	199
30	18	18	36	18	19	37	19	19	38	18	18	36	19	19	38
31	19	19	38	18	18	36	18	19	37	19	19	38	18	19	37
32	19	20	39	19	19	38	18	18	36	18	19	37	19	19	38
33	19	20	39	19	20	39	19	19	38	18	18	36	18	19	37
34	21	22	43	19	20	39	19	20	39	19	19	38	18	18	36
30-34	96	99	195	93	96	189	93	95	188	92	93	185	92	94	186
35	23	23	46	21	22	43	19	20	39	19	20	39	19	19	38
36	18	19	37	23	23	46	21	22	43	19	21	40	19	20	39
37	18	18	36	18	19	37	23	24	47	21	22	43	19	21	40
38	18	18	36	18	18	36	18	19	37	23	23	46	21	22	43
39	18	17	35	18	18	36	18	18	36	18	19	37	23	23	46
35-39	95	95	190	98	100	198	99	103	202	100	105	205	101	105	206
40	16	15	31	18	17	35	18	18	36	18	18	36	18	19	37
41	15	15	30	16	15	31	18	17	35	18	18	36	18	18	36
42	16	15	31	15	15	30	16	15	31	18	17	35	18	18	36
43	16	15	31	16	16	32	15	15	30	16	15	31	18	17	35
44	16	16	32	15	15	30	16	15	31	15	15	30	16	15	31
40-44	79	76	155	80	78	158	83	80	163	85	83	168	88	87	175

Figures above the dotted line relate to persons born after mid-1977.

Age-group	1982			1983			1984			1985			1986		
	Males	Females	Persons	Males	Females	Persons	Males	Females	Persons	Males	Females	Persons	Males	Females	Persons
45	16	15	31	16	16	32	16	15	31	16	15	31	15	15	30
46	16	15	31	16	15	31	16	16	32	16	15	31	16	15	31
47	15	15	30	15	15	30	15	15	30	16	16	32	15	15	30
48	14	14	28	15	14	29	15	15	30	15	15	30	16	15	31
49	15	14	29	15	14	29	15	14	29	15	15	30	15	15	30
45-49	76	73	149	77	74	151	77	75	152	78	76	154	77	75	152
50	15	15	30	15	15	30	14	14	28	15	15	30	15	15	30
51	16	16	32	15	15	30	15	15	30	14	14	28	15	15	30
52	16	17	33	16	16	32	15	15	30	15	14	29	14	14	28
53	16	16	32	16	16	32	16	16	32	15	15	30	15	14	29
54	16	16	32	15	16	31	16	16	32	16	16	32	15	15	30
50-54	79	80	159	77	78	155	76	76	152	75	74	149	74	73	147
55	16	17	33	16	16	32	16	16	32	16	17	33	16	16	32
56	16	18	34	16	17	33	15	16	31	15	16	31	15	17	32
57	16	17	33	16	18	34	16	17	33	15	16	31	15	16	31
58	16	18	34	16	17	33	16	18	34	16	17	33	15	16	31
59	16	17	33	16	17	33	16	17	33	16	17	33	16	17	33
55-59	80	87	167	80	85	165	79	84	163	78	83	161	77	82	159
60	17	19	36	15	17	32	16	17	33	16	17	33	16	17	33
61	17	19	36	17	19	36	15	17	32	15	17	32	15	17	32
62	16	19	35	17	19	36	16	19	35	15	17	32	15	17	32
63	13	15	28	16	19	35	16	19	35	16	19	35	15	17	32
64	12	14	26	13	15	28	16	19	35	16	19	35	16	19	35
60-64	75	86	161	78	89	167	79	91	170	78	89	167	77	87	164
65	13	15	28	12	14	26	13	15	28	15	18	33	15	19	34
66	13	15	28	12	15	27	11	14	25	12	15	27	15	18	33
67	13	16	29	13	15	28	12	14	26	11	14	25	12	14	26
68	13	16	29	13	16	29	12	15	27	12	14	26	11	13	24
69	12	16	28	12	16	28	12	16	28	12	14	26	11	14	25
65-69	64	78	142	62	76	138	60	74	134	62	75	137	64	78	142
70	12	16	28	12	15	27	12	15	27	12	16	28	11	14	25
71	11	15	26	11	15	26	11	15	26	11	15	26	11	15	26
72	10	14	24	10	15	25	10	15	25	11	14	25	11	14	25
73	9	14	23	10	14	24	10	14	24	10	14	24	10	14	24
74	9	13	22	9	13	22	9	13	22	9	14	23	9	14	23
70-74	51	72	123	52	72	124	52	72	124	53	73	126	52	71	123
75	8	13	21	8	12	20	8	13	21	8	13	21	8	13	21
76	7	13	20	7	12	19	8	12	20	7	12	19	8	12	20
77	6	11	17	6	12	18	6	11	17	7	11	18	7	12	19
78	6	10	16	6	11	17	6	11	17	6	11	17	6	11	17
79	5	9	14	5	10	15	5	10	15	5	10	15	5	10	15
75-79	32	56	88	32	57	89	33	57	90	33	57	90	34	58	92
80	4	9	13	5	9	14	4	9	13	5	9	14	5	10	15
81	4	8	12	3	8	11	4	8	12	4	8	12	4	8	12
82	3	7	10	3	8	11	3	7	10	3	7	10	3	7	10
83	2	6	8	3	6	9	3	7	10	3	7	10	3	7	10
84	2	5	7	2	5	7	2	6	8	2	6	8	2	6	8
80-84	15	35	50	16	36	52	16	37	53	17	37	54	17	38	55
85 & over	7	23	30	7	23	30	8	24	32	8	25	33	8	25	33
All ages	1353	1432	2785	1356	1434	2790	1361	1438	2799	1366	1442	2808	1372	1447	2819

Appendix Table IIc *continued*

thousands

Age-group	1987 Males	1987 Females	1987 Persons	1988 Males	1988 Females	1988 Persons	1989 Males	1989 Females	1989 Persons	1991 Males	1991 Females	1991 Persons	1996 Males	1996 Females	1996 Persons
0	23	21	44	23	21	44	23	21	44	22	22	44	21	20	41
1	22	20	42	23	21	44	23	21	44	23	21	44	22	20	42
2	21	20	41	22	21	43	22	21	43	23	21	44	22	20	42
3	20	19	39	21	20	41	22	21	43	23	21	44	22	21	43
4	19	18	37	20	19	39	21	20	41	22	21	43	22	21	43
0 - 4	105	98	203	109	102	211	111	104	215	113	106	219	109	102	211
5	18	17	35	19	18	37	20	19	39	22	20	42	23	21	44
6	17	16	33	18	17	35	19	18	37	22	20	42	23	22	45
7	17	16	33	17	16	33	18	17	35	20	19	39	23	21	44
8	17	15	32	17	16	33	18	16	34	19	18	37	22	21	43
9	17	15	32	17	15	32	17	16	33	18	17	35	22	21	43
5 - 9	86	79	165	88	82	170	92	86	178	101	94	195	113	106	219
10	17	16	33	16	16	32	17	16	33	17	16	33	22	21	43
11	17	17	34	17	16	33	16	16	32	17	16	33	22	21	43
12	19	17	36	18	16	34	17	16	33	17	16	33	21	19	40
13	19	18	37	19	17	36	18	16	34	17	16	33	19	18	37
14	20	19	39	19	18	37	19	17	36	17	16	33	19	17	36
10-14	92	87	179	89	83	172	87	81	168	85	80	165	103	96	199
15	21	20	41	20	19	39	19	18	37	18	16	34	18	17	35
16	23	22	45	21	20	41	20	19	39	19	17	36	17	16	33
17	22	21	43	23	21	44	22	20	42	19	18	37	17	15	32
18	23	21	44	22	21	43	23	21	44	20	19	39	17	15	32
19	22	20	42	23	21	44	22	20	42	22	19	41	17	15	32
15-19	111	104	215	109	102	211	106	98	204	98	89	187	86	78	164
20	23	21	44	22	20	42	23	21	44	23	21	44	18	16	34
21	23	21	44	23	21	44	22	20	42	22	20	42	19	17	36
22	23	22	45	23	21	44	23	21	44	22	21	43	19	17	36
23	24	21	45	23	21	44	23	21	44	22	20	42	19	18	37
24	23	21	44	24	22	46	23	21	44	23	21	44	21	19	40
20-24	116	106	222	115	105	220	114	104	218	112	103	215	96	87	183
25	22	21	43	23	21	44	23	21	44	23	21	44	22	20	42
26	21	20	41	22	21	43	23	21	44	23	21	44	21	20	41
27	20	20	40	21	20	41	22	21	43	23	21	44	22	21	43
28	20	20	40	20	20	40	21	20	41	23	21	44	22	20	42
29	20	19	39	20	20	40	20	20	40	22	21	43	23	21	44
25-29	103	100	203	106	102	208	109	103	212	114	105	219	110	102	212
30	19	19	38	20	20	40	20	20	40	21	21	42	23	21	44
31	19	19	38	19	19	38	20	20	40	20	20	40	23	21	44
32	18	19	37	19	19	38	19	19	38	20	20	40	23	22	45
33	19	19	38	18	19	37	19	19	38	19	20	39	23	21	44
34	19	19	38	19	19	38	18	19	37	19	19	38	21	21	42
30-34	94	95	189	95	96	191	96	97	193	99	100	199	113	106	219
35	18	18	36	18	19	37	19	19	38	19	19	38	21	21	42
36	19	19	38	18	19	37	18	19	37	18	19	37	20	20	40
37	19	20	39	19	19	38	18	19	37	19	20	39	20	21	41
38	19	21	40	19	20	39	19	19	38	18	19	37	19	20	39
39	21	22	43	19	20	39	19	20	39	18	18	36	19	20	39
35-39	96	100	196	93	97	190	93	96	189	92	95	187	99	102	201
40	22	23	45	21	22	43	19	21	40	19	19	38	19	20	39
41	18	19	37	23	23	46	21	22	43	19	21	40	18	19	37
42	18	18	36	18	19	37	23	23	46	19	20	39	19	19	38
43	18	18	36	18	18	36	18	19	37	21	22	43	18	19	37
44	18	17	35	18	18	36	18	18	36	22	23	45	17	18	35
40-44	94	95	189	98	100	198	99	103	202	100	105	205	91	95	186

Figures above the dotted line relate to persons born after mid-1977.

Age-group	1987			1988			1989			1991			1996		
	Males	Females	Persons	Males	Females	Persons	Males	Females	Persons	Males	Females	Persons	Males	Females	Persons
45	16	15	31	17	17	34	18	18	36	18	19	37	18	19	37
46	15	15	30	16	15	31	17	17	34	18	18	36	19	20	39
47	16	15	31	15	15	30	16	15	31	18	17	35	19	20	39
48	15	15	30	16	15	31	15	14	29	17	17	34	21	22	43
49	16	15	31	15	15	30	16	15	31	16	15	31	22	23	45
45-49	78	75	153	79	77	156	82	79	161	87	86	173	99	104	203
50	15	15	30	16	15	31	15	15	30	15	14	29	17	18	35
51	15	15	30	15	15	30	16	15	31	15	15	30	18	18	36
52	15	15	30	15	15	30	15	15	30	15	15	30	17	17	34
53	14	14	28	15	15	30	15	15	30	15	16	31	17	17	34
54	15	14	29	14	14	28	14	14	28	15	15	30	15	15	30
50-54	74	73	147	75	74	149	75	74	149	75	75	150	84	85	169
55	15	15	30	14	14	28	14	14	28	15	15	30	14	14	28
56	15	16	31	15	15	30	14	14	28	14	15	29	15	15	30
57	15	16	31	15	16	31	15	15	30	14	14	28	15	15	30
58	15	16	31	15	16	31	15	16	31	14	14	28	15	15	30
59	15	16	31	15	16	31	15	16	31	14	15	29	14	15	29
55-59	75	79	154	74	77	151	73	75	148	71	73	144	73	74	147
60	15	17	32	15	16	31	15	16	31	15	16	31	14	15	29
61	16	17	33	15	17	32	14	16	30	15	16	31	13	14	27
62	15	17	32	15	17	32	15	17	32	14	16	30	13	14	27
63	15	17	32	15	16	31	15	17	32	14	16	30	13	14	27
64	14	16	30	14	17	31	14	16	30	14	16	30	13	15	28
60-64	75	84	159	74	83	157	73	82	155	72	80	152	66	72	138
65	15	19	34	14	17	31	14	17	31	15	17	32	14	15	29
66	15	18	33	15	18	33	14	16	30	14	16	30	13	16	29
67	15	18	33	15	18	33	15	18	33	13	16	29	13	15	28
68	12	14	26	14	17	31	14	18	32	13	16	29	12	15	27
69	10	13	23	11	14	25	13	17	30	13	17	30	12	15	27
65-69	67	82	149	69	84	153	70	86	156	68	82	150	64	76	140
70	11	14	25	10	13	23	11	14	25	13	17	30	12	15	27
71	10	14	24	10	13	23	9	12	21	12	16	28	12	15	27
72	11	15	26	10	14	24	10	13	23	10	13	23	11	14	25
73	10	14	24	10	14	24	9	13	22	9	12	21	10	14	24
74	9	13	22	9	13	22	9	14	23	8	12	20	10	15	25
70-74	51	70	121	49	67	116	48	66	114	52	70	122	55	73	128
75	9	13	22	9	13	22	9	13	22	8	12	20	10	15	25
76	8	13	21	8	13	21	8	13	21	8	13	21	9	14	23
77	7	11	18	7	12	19	7	12	19	7	12	19	6	11	17
78	6	11	17	6	11	17	6	11	17	6	11	17	5	9	14
79	5	10	15	5	10	15	5	10	15	6	10	16	5	9	14
75-79	35	58	93	35	59	94	35	59	94	35	58	93	35	58	93
80	5	9	14	5	9	14	5	10	15	5	10	15	5	9	14
81	4	9	13	4	9	13	4	9	13	4	9	13	5	9	14
82	4	8	12	4	8	12	3	8	11	4	8	12	4	8	12
83	3	7	10	3	7	10	3	7	10	3	7	10	3	8	11
84	2	6	8	2	6	8	3	6	9	3	6	9	3	7	10
80-84	18	39	57	18	39	57	18	40	58	19	40	59	20	41	61
85 & over	8	27	35	9	27	36	9	28	37	9	30	39	11	33	44
All ages	1378	1451	2829	1384	1456	2840	1390	1461	2851	1402	1471	2873	1427	1490	2917

thousands

Age-group	2001			2006			2011			2016			2017		
	Males	Females	Persons	Males	Females	Persons	Males	Females	Persons	Males	Females	Persons	Males	Females	Persons
0	19	18	37	19	18	37	21	20	41	22	21	43	22	21	43
1	20	18	38	19	18	37	21	19	40	22	20	42	22	21	43
2	20	19	39	18	18	36	20	19	39	22	20	42	22	20	42
3	20	19	39	19	17	36	20	18	38	21	20	41	21	20	41
4	21	19	40	19	18	37	19	18	37	21	20	41	21	20	41
0-4	100	93	193	94	89	183	101	94	195	108	101	209	108	102	210
5	21	20	41	19	18	37	19	18	37	21	19	40	21	20	41
6	22	20	42	20	18	38	19	18	37	21	19	40	21	19	40
7	22	20	42	20	19	39	19	17	36	20	19	39	21	19	40
8	22	21	43	20	19	39	19	18	37	20	19	39	20	19	39
9	23	21	44	21	19	40	19	18	37	19	18	37	20	19	39
5-9	110	102	212	100	93	193	95	89	184	101	94	195	103	96	199
10	22	21	43	21	20	41	19	18	37	20	19	39	20	19	39
11	23	22	45	22	21	43	20	19	39	19	18	37	20	18	38
12	23	22	45	22	21	43	20	19	39	19	18	37	19	18	37
13	23	22	45	23	21	44	21	19	40	19	18	37	19	18	37
14	23	21	44	23	21	44	21	20	41	20	18	38	19	18	37
10-14	114	108	222	111	104	215	101	95	196	97	91	188	97	91	188
15	23	21	44	23	22	45	22	20	42	20	18	38	20	18	38
16	22	20	42	23	21	44	22	20	42	20	19	39	20	18	38
17	21	19	40	23	21	44	22	21	43	20	19	39	20	18	38
18	19	18	37	23	21	44	23	21	44	21	19	40	20	19	39
19	18	16	34	23	21	44	23	21	44	21	19	40	21	19	40
15-19	103	94	197	115	106	221	112	103	215	102	94	196	101	92	193
20	18	16	34	22	20	42	23	21	44	22	20	42	21	19	40
21	17	15	32	22	20	42	23	21	44	22	20	42	22	20	42
22	17	15	32	21	19	40	23	21	44	22	20	42	22	20	42
23	17	15	32	19	17	36	23	20	43	22	20	42	22	20	42
24	16	14	30	18	16	34	22	20	42	23	20	43	22	20	42
20-24	85	75	160	102	92	194	114	103	217	111	100	211	109	99	208
25	17	15	32	17	15	32	22	20	42	23	20	43	23	20	43
26	19	17	36	17	15	32	21	20	41	23	21	44	23	21	44
27	19	17	36	17	15	32	20	19	39	22	21	43	22	20	42
28	19	18	37	16	15	31	19	17	36	22	21	43	22	21	43
29	21	19	40	16	15	31	18	16	34	22	20	42	22	21	43
25-29	95	86	181	83	75	158	100	92	192	112	103	215	112	103	215
30	22	21	43	17	16	33	17	16	33	22	20	42	22	20	42
31	21	21	42	18	17	35	17	16	33	21	20	41	22	20	42
32	22	21	43	19	17	36	16	15	31	20	19	39	21	20	41
33	21	20	41	19	18	37	16	15	31	19	17	36	20	19	39
34	23	21	44	21	20	41	16	15	31	17	17	34	19	18	37
30-34	109	104	213	94	88	182	82	77	159	99	93	192	104	97	201
35	23	21	44	22	21	43	17	16	33	17	16	33	18	17	35
36	23	22	45	21	21	42	18	17	35	17	16	33	17	16	33
37	23	22	45	22	21	43	18	18	36	16	16	32	17	16	33
38	22	22	44	22	20	42	19	18	37	16	15	31	16	16	32
39	21	21	42	22	22	44	21	20	41	16	15	31	16	15	31
35-39	112	108	220	109	105	214	93	89	182	82	78	160	84	80	164
40	20	21	41	22	22	44	22	21	43	17	16	33	16	15	31
41	20	20	40	23	22	45	21	21	42	18	17	35	17	16	33
42	20	21	41	23	22	45	22	21	43	18	18	36	18	17	35
43	19	20	39	22	21	43	21	21	42	19	18	37	18	18	36
44	19	20	39	21	21	42	22	21	43	21	20	41	19	19	38
40-44	98	102	200	111	108	219	108	105	213	93	89	182	88	85	173

Figures above the dotted line relate to persons born after mid-1977.

Age-group	2001			2006			2011			2016			2017		
	Males	Females	Persons	Males	Females	Persons	Males	Females	Persons	Males	Females	Persons	Males	Females	Persons
45	18	19	37	20	21	41	22	21	43	21	21	42	20	20	40
46	18	19	37	20	20	40	22	22	44	21	21	42	22	21	43
47	19	19	38	20	20	40	23	22	45	21	21	42	21	20	41
48	18	19	37	19	20	39	22	21	43	21	20	41	21	21	42
49	17	18	35	18	19	37	21	21	42	22	21	43	21	20	41
45-49	90	94	184	97	100	197	110	107	217	106	104	210	105	102	207
50	18	19	37	18	19	37	20	20	40	22	21	43	22	21	43
51	18	20	38	18	18	36	19	20	39	22	21	43	22	21	43
52	19	20	39	18	19	37	19	20	39	22	21	43	22	21	43
53	20	22	42	17	19	36	19	20	39	21	21	42	21	21	42
54	21	22	43	17	18	35	18	19	37	20	21	41	21	21	42
50-54	96	103	199	88	93	181	95	99	194	107	105	212	108	105	213
55	17	18	35	17	19	36	17	19	36	19	21	40	20	21	41
56	17	18	35	18	20	38	17	18	35	19	20	39	19	20	39
57	17	17	34	18	20	38	17	19	36	18	20	38	18	20	38
58	16	17	33	19	21	40	17	18	35	18	19	37	18	20	38
59	14	15	29	20	22	42	16	18	34	17	19	36	18	19	37
55-59	81	85	166	92	102	194	84	92	176	91	99	190	93	100	193
60	13	14	27	16	18	34	16	18	34	17	19	36	17	19	36
61	14	15	29	16	17	33	17	19	36	16	18	34	16	18	34
62	14	15	29	16	17	33	17	19	36	16	18	34	16	18	34
63	14	15	29	15	16	31	18	21	39	15	18	33	16	18	34
64	13	14	27	13	15	28	18	22	40	15	17	32	15	18	33
60-64	68	73	141	76	83	159	86	99	185	79	90	169	80	91	171
65	13	14	27	12	14	26	15	17	32	15	18	33	14	17	31
66	12	14	26	13	14	27	14	17	31	15	19	34	15	18	33
67	12	13	25	12	14	26	14	16	30	15	18	33	15	18	33
68	11	13	24	12	14	26	13	15	28	16	19	35	14	18	32
69	11	14	25	12	14	26	12	14	26	16	20	36	15	19	34
65-69	59	68	127	61	70	131	68	79	147	77	94	171	73	90	163
70	12	14	26	11	13	24	10	13	23	13	16	29	15	20	35
71	11	14	25	10	12	22	11	13	24	12	15	27	12	16	28
72	10	14	24	10	12	22	10	13	23	11	14	25	12	15	27
73	10	13	23	9	12	21	10	12	22	11	14	25	11	14	25
74	9	13	22	9	12	21	9	12	21	9	12	21	10	13	23
70-74	52	68	120	49	61	110	50	63	113	56	71	127	60	78	138
75	9	13	22	9	12	21	8	11	19	8	11	19	9	11	20
76	8	12	20	8	12	20	7	11	18	8	11	19	8	11	19
77	7	12	19	7	11	18	7	10	17	7	11	18	7	11	18
78	7	11	18	6	11	17	6	10	16	6	10	16	6	10	16
79	7	12	19	6	10	16	6	9	15	6	9	15	6	9	15
75-79	38	60	98	36	56	92	34	51	85	35	52	87	36	52	88
80	6	11	17	6	10	16	5	9	14	5	9	14	5	9	14
81	5	10	15	5	9	14	5	9	14	5	8	13	5	8	13
82	4	8	12	4	8	12	4	8	12	4	7	11	4	7	11
83	3	6	9	4	8	12	4	7	11	3	7	10	3	7	10
84	2	6	8	3	8	11	3	7	10	3	6	9	3	6	9
80-84	20	41	61	22	43	65	21	40	61	20	37	57	20	37	57
85 and over	12	35	47	12	36	48	14	39	53	14	39	53	13	38	51
All ages	1442	1499	2941	1452	1504	2956	1468	1516	2984	1490	1534	3024	1494	1538	3032

Appendix Table IIIa Actual and projected Total population as at mid-year by sex and age-groups, 1951, 1961, 1971 to 2017; mid-1977 based projections.

Scotland

thousands

Year	0-14	15-44		45-64	45-59	65 and over	60 and over	All ages		
	Persons	Males	Females	Males	Females	Males	Females	Males	Females	Persons
1951	1258	1120	1134	527	493	215	421	2503	2666	5169
1961	1340	1033	1041	593	521	215	482	2526	2700	5226
1971	1351	1018	1009	575	484	246	561	2532	2712	5244
1972	1340	1020	1009	570	480	249	567	2527	2708	5235
1973	1325	1029	1015	566	475	254	573	2528	2709	5237
1974	1305	1042	1025	562	470	258	580	2532	2710	5242
1975	1280	1047	1029	558	467	262	585	2524	2704	5227
1976	1256	1058	1040	554	466	265	586	2522	2703	5225
1977	1221	1073	1051	551	466	267	585	2518	2696	5214
1978	1189	1084	1062	547	468	270	582	2512	2690	5202
1979	1154	1098	1073	543	468	272	581	2506	2683	5189
1980	1120	1111	1086	539	458	276	588	2501	2677	5178
1981	1094	1121	1094	537	453	276	593	2496	2672	5168
1982	1069	1132	1103	538	448	274	596	2493	2667	5160
1983	1052	1142	1111	540	445	270	597	2492	2665	5157
1984	1040	1151	1120	542	442	267	597	2494	2665	5159
1985	1037	1158	1126	536	440	271	597	2497	2668	5165
1986	1037	1166	1134	531	434	274	598	2503	2671	5174
1987	1041	1171	1139	527	432	276	597	2508	2675	5183
1988	1054	1170	1139	528	432	275	595	2514	2679	5193
1989	1070	1168	1136	527	431	277	595	2521	2683	5204
1990	1088	1165	1134	527	429	277	594	2527	2687	5214
1991	1107	1160	1131	527	428	277	592	2532	2690	5222
1992	1130	1144	1114	536	439	278	590	2538	2693	5231
1993	1154	1130	1101	542	446	278	587	2542	2696	5238
1994	1172	1120	1092	548	452	277	583	2546	2698	5244
1995	1191	1110	1082	551	456	277	581	2549	2699	5248
1996	1204	1102	1073	555	461	277	579	2552	2699	5251
1997	1212	1097	1068	558	464	276	576	2553	2698	5251
1998	1213	1093	1064	562	468	275	574	2553	2696	5249
1999	1209	1090	1062	568	473	274	570	2552	2694	5246
2000	1196	1090	1061	573	477	273	570	2550	2690	5240
2001	1181	1090	1061	580	484	272	566	2548	2686	5234
2002	1162	1090	1062	586	491	272	564	2545	2682	5227
2003	1143	1090	1062	593	497	271	562	2541	2677	5218
2004	1123	1088	1058	602	504	272	564	2538	2673	5211
2005	1103	1087	1057	610	512	271	562	2534	2668	5202
2006	1083	1084	1054	621	520	270	563	2531	2664	5195
2007	1068	1078	1049	631	520	271	572	2528	2661	5189
2008	1055	1075	1045	639	524	271	575	2526	2658	5184
2009	1044	1066	1036	648	530	274	581	2524	2655	5179
2010	1036	1059	1030	658	537	274	583	2523	2654	5177
2011	1031	1054	1024	664	541	276	586	2523	2653	5176
2012	1030	1044	1016	666	547	284	589	2523	2653	5176
2013	1032	1037	1009	667	550	290	592	2524	2653	5177
2014	1037	1028	1000	670	552	295	597	2525	2654	5179
2015	1043	1020	993	672	555	298	600	2526	2654	5181
2016	1052	1014	986	673	554	300	604	2527	2656	5183
2017	1061	1006	979	673	552	303	610	2527	2657	5184

Appendix Table IIIb Annual changes in projected Total population
1977 to 2017; mid-1977 based projections

Scotland

thousands

Mid-year to mid-year	Population at beginning or period	Births	Deaths	Natural increase	Net migration	Total increase
1977-1978	5214	63	65	- 2	- 10	- 12
1978-1979	5202	63	66	- 3	- 10	- 13
1979-1980	5189	64	66	- 1	- 10	- 11
1980-1981	5178	66	66	0	- 10	- 10
1981-1982	5168	69	67	2	- 10	- 8
1982-1983	5160	74	67	7	- 10	- 3
1983-1984	5157	79	67	12	- 10	2
1984-1985	5159	84	68	16	- 10	6
1985-1986	5165	86	68	19	- 10	9
1986-1987	5174	88	68	19	- 10	9
1987-1988	5183	88	68	20	- 10	10
1988-1989	5193	88	68	21	- 10	11
1989-1990	5204	88	68	20	- 10	10
1990-1991	5214	87	68	18	- 10	8
1991-1992	5222	87	68	19	- 10	9
1992-1993	5231	85	68	17	- 10	7
1993-1994	5238	84	68	16	- 10	6
1994-1995	5244	82	68	14	- 10	4
1995-1996	5248	80	67	13	- 10	3
1996-1997	5251	78	67	10	- 10	0
1997-1998	5251	75	67	8	- 10	- 2
1998-1999	5249	73	67	7	- 10	- 3
1999-2000	5246	72	67	4	- 10	- 6
2000-2001	5240	70	66	4	- 10	- 6
2001-2002	5234	69	66	3	- 10	- 7
2002-2003	5227	68	66	1	- 10	- 9
2003-2004	5218	68	66	3	- 10	- 7
2004-2005	5211	68	66	1	- 10	- 9
2005-2006	5202	69	66	3	- 10	- 7
2006-2007	5195	70	66	4	- 10	- 6
2007-2008	5189	71	66	5	- 10	- 5
2008-2009	5184	72	66	5	- 10	- 5
2009-2010	5179	74	66	8	- 10	- 2
2010-2011	5177	75	66	9	- 10	- 1
2011-2012	5176	76	66	10	- 10	0
2012-2013	5176	77	66	11	- 10	1
2013-2014	5177	78	66	12	- 10	2
2014-2015	5179	78	66	12	- 10	2
2015-2016	5181	78	66	12	- 10	2
2016-2017	5183	78	67	11	- 10	1
2017-2018	5184					

Appendix Table IIIc   Projected Total population as at mid-year, by sex and single ages 1977 to 1989, 1991-2017; mid-1977 based projections.

thousands

Age-group	1977 Males	Females	Persons	1978 Males	Females	Persons	1979 Males	Females	Persons	1980 Males	Females	Persons	1981 Males	Females	Persons
0	32	30	62	32	30	62	32	30	62	32	31	63	33	32	65
1	34	32	66	32	29	61	32	30	62	32	30	62	32	30	62
2	35	33	68	34	32	66	31	29	60	31	29	60	32	30	62
3	35	33	68	34	33	67	34	32	66	31	29	60	31	29	60
4	38	36	74	35	34	69	34	33	67	34	32	66	31	29	60
0-4	174	164	338	167	158	325	163	154	317	160	151	311	159	150	309
5	41	39	80	38	36	74	35	33	68	34	33	67	34	32	66
6	43	41	84	41	39	80	38	36	74	35	33	68	34	33	67
7	43	41	84	43	41	84	41	39	80	37	36	73	35	33	68
8	45	42	87	43	40	83	43	41	84	41	39	80	37	35	72
9	45	43	88	45	42	87	43	40	83	43	40	83	41	39	80
5-9	217	206	423	210	198	408	200	189	389	190	181	371	181	172	353
10	47	44	91	45	43	88	45	42	87	43	41	84	43	41	84
11	46	44	90	47	44	91	45	43	88	45	42	87	43	41	84
12	48	45	93	46	44	90	47	44	91	45	43	88	45	42	87
13	48	46	94	48	45	93	46	44	90	46	44	90	45	42	87
14	47	45	92	48	46	94	47	45	92	46	43	89	46	44	90
10-14	236	224	460	234	222	456	230	218	448	225	213	438	222	210	432
15	47	45	92	47	45	92	47	46	93	48	45	93	46	43	89
16	46	44	90	47	44	91	47	45	92	47	46	93	48	45	93
17	45	43	88	46	44	90	47	44	91	47	45	92	47	46	93
18	45	42	87	45	43	88	46	44	90	47	44	91	47	45	92
19	44	41	85	44	42	86	45	42	87	46	44	90	46	44	90
15-19	227	215	442	229	218	447	232	221	453	235	224	459	234	223	457
20	42	40	82	44	41	85	44	42	86	44	42	86	46	44	90
21	42	39	81	42	40	82	43	41	84	44	42	86	44	42	86
22	39	38	77	41	39	80	42	39	81	43	41	84	43	42	85
23	39	37	76	38	37	75	40	38	78	41	39	80	42	40	82
24	37	36	73	38	37	75	38	37	75	39	38	77	40	38	78
20-24	199	190	389	203	194	397	207	197	404	211	202	413	215	206	421
25	36	35	71	37	36	73	38	37	75	37	37	74	39	37	76
26	36	36	72	36	35	71	37	36	73	38	36	74	38	36	74
27	37	36	73	36	36	72	35	34	69	36	35	71	37	36	73
28	37	36	73	37	35	72	36	35	71	35	34	69	36	35	71
29	39	38	77	37	36	73	36	35	71	36	35	71	35	34	69
25-29	185	181	366	183	178	361	182	177	359	182	177	359	185	178	363
30	43	41	84	39	38	77	37	36	73	36	35	71	35	35	70
31	32	31	63	43	41	84	39	38	77	37	36	73	36	35	71
32	32	31	63	32	31	63	42	41	83	38	38	76	37	36	73
33	32	32	64	31	31	62	32	32	64	42	41	83	38	38	76
34	32	32	64	32	32	64	31	31	62	32	32	64	41	42	83
30-34	171	167	338	177	173	350	181	178	359	185	182	367	187	186	373
35	30	30	60	32	32	64	32	32	64	31	31	62	32	31	63
36	29	29	58	30	30	60	32	32	64	32	32	64	31	31	62
37	29	30	59	28	29	57	30	29	59	32	31	63	32	32	64
38	29	30	59	29	29	58	28	29	57	30	29	59	31	31	62
39	30	30	60	29	30	59	29	29	58	28	29	57	30	29	59
35-39	147	149	296	148	150	298	151	151	302	153	152	305	156	154	310
40	29	30	59	30	30	60	29	30	59	29	29	58	28	28	56
41	29	30	59	29	30	59	30	30	60	29	30	59	29	29	58
42	29	30	59	29	30	59	29	30	59	29	30	59	29	30	59
43	28	29	57	28	30	58	29	30	59	29	30	59	29	30	59
44	29	30	59	28	29	57	28	29	57	29	30	59	29	30	59
40-44	144	149	293	144	149	293	145	149	294	145	149	294	144	147	291

Figures above the dotted line relate to persons born after mid-1977.

Age-group	1977			1978			1979			1980			1981		
	Males	Females	Persons	Males	Females	Persons	Males	Females	Persons	Males	Females	Persons	Males	Females	Persons
45	29	30	59	28	30	58	28	29	57	28	29	57	28	30	58
46	30	31	61	29	30	59	28	30	58	28	29	57	28	29	57
47	29	31	60	30	31	61	29	30	59	28	29	57	28	29	57
48	29	31	60	29	31	60	29	31	60	29	30	59	28	29	57
49	29	31	60	29	31	60	29	31	60	29	31	60	28	30	58
45-49	146	154	300	145	153	298	143	151	294	142	148	290	140	147	287
50	29	31	60	29	31	60	29	31	60	29	31	60	29	31	60
51	30	32	62	29	31	60	29	30	59	29	30	59	28	31	59
52	29	31	60	29	32	61	29	31	60	28	30	58	28	30	58
53	30	32	62	29	31	60	29	31	60	28	31	59	28	30	58
54	29	31	60	29	31	60	28	31	59	29	31	60	28	30	58
50-54	147	157	304	145	156	301	144	154	298	143	153	296	141	152	293
55	30	33	63	29	31	60	29	31	60	28	31	59	28	31	59
56	30	34	64	30	33	63	28	31	59	28	31	59	28	30	58
57	32	37	69	30	34	64	29	32	61	27	30	57	28	31	59
58	22	26	48	31	36	67	29	33	62	29	32	61	27	30	57
59	22	25	47	21	25	46	31	36	67	29	33	62	28	32	60
55-59	136	155	291	141	159	300	146	163	309	141	157	298	139	154	293
60	23	27	50	21	25	46	21	26	47	30	35	65	28	33	61
61	23	29	52	23	26	49	20	25	45	20	25	45	29	35	64
62	26	31	57	23	28	51	22	26	48	20	24	44	20	25	45
63	25	31	56	25	31	56	23	27	50	21	26	47	19	23	42
64	25	30	55	24	30	54	24	30	54	22	27	49	21	25	46
60-64	122	148	270	116	140	256	110	134	244	113	137	250	117	141	258
65	24	29	53	24	30	54	23	30	53	23	30	53	21	26	47
66	23	29	52	23	29	52	23	29	52	23	29	52	22	29	51
67	22	29	51	22	29	51	22	28	50	22	29	51	22	29	51
68	22	29	51	21	28	49	21	28	49	21	27	48	21	28	49
69	20	28	48	20	28	48	20	28	48	20	28	48	20	27	47
65-69	111	144	255	110	144	254	109	143	252	109	143	252	106	139	245
70	19	26	45	19	27	46	20	27	47	19	27	46	19	27	46
71	17	26	43	18	25	43	18	26	44	19	27	46	18	26	44
72	16	25	41	16	25	41	16	24	40	17	25	42	17	26	43
73	15	23	38	15	24	39	15	24	39	15	23	38	16	24	40
74	13	22	35	14	22	36	14	23	37	14	23	37	14	22	36
70-74	80	122	202	82	123	205	83	124	207	84	125	209	84	125	209
75	12	21	33	12	21	33	13	21	34	13	22	35	13	22	35
76	10	20	30	11	19	30	11	20	31	11	20	31	12	20	32
77	9	18	27	9	19	28	10	18	28	10	19	29	10	19	29
78	8	16	24	8	17	25	8	18	26	9	17	26	9	18	27
79	6	14	20	7	15	22	7	16	23	7	16	23	8	16	24
75-79	45	89	134	47	91	138	49	93	142	50	94	144	52	95	147
80	6	13	19	6	13	19	6	14	20	6	15	21	7	15	22
81	4	12	16	5	12	17	5	12	17	5	12	17	6	13	19
82	4	10	14	4	10	14	4	11	15	4	11	15	4	11	15
83	3	9	12	3	9	12	3	9	12	4	10	14	3	10	13
84	3	7	10	3	8	11	3	8	11	3	8	11	3	9	12
80-84	20	51	71	21	52	73	21	54	75	22	56	78	23	58	81
85 and over	11	31	42	10	32	42	10	33	43	11	33	44	11	35	46
All ages	2518	2696	5214	2512	2690	5202	2506	2683	5189	2501	2677	5178	2496	2672	5168

thousands

Age-group	1982 Males	1982 Females	1982 Persons	1983 Males	1983 Females	1983 Persons	1984 Males	1984 Females	1984 Persons	1985 Males	1985 Females	1985 Persons	1986 Males	1986 Females	1986 Persons
0	35	33	68	37	35	72	40	38	78	42	40	82	44	41	85
1	33	31	64	35	33	68	37	35	72	40	38	78	42	40	82
2	32	30	62	33	31	64	35	32	67	37	35	72	40	37	77
3	31	30	61	32	30	62	33	31	64	34	32	66	36	35	71
4	31	29	60	31	30	61	31	30	61	33	31	64	34	33	67
0–4	162	153	315	168	159	327	176	166	342	186	176	362	196	186	382
5	31	29	60	31	29	60	31	29	60	31	30	61	33	31	64
6	34	32	66	31	29	60	31	29	60	31	29	60	31	30	61
7	34	33	67	33	32	65	31	29	60	31	29	60	31	29	60
8	35	33	68	34	33	67	33	32	65	31	29	60	31	29	60
9	37	36	73	35	33	68	34	33	67	33	32	65	30	29	59
5–9	171	163	334	164	156	320	160	152	312	157	149	306	156	148	304
10	41	39	80	37	36	73	35	33	68	34	33	67	33	32	65
11	42	41	83	41	39	80	37	36	73	35	33	68	34	33	67
12	43	40	83	42	40	82	41	39	80	37	35	72	35	33	68
13	45	42	87	43	40	83	42	40	82	41	39	80	37	35	72
14	45	42	87	45	42	87	43	40	83	42	40	82	41	38	79
10–14	216	204	420	208	197	405	198	188	386	189	180	369	180	171	351
15	47	44	91	45	42	87	45	42	87	43	40	83	42	40	82
16	46	43	89	47	44	91	45	42	87	45	42	87	43	40	83
17	48	45	93	46	43	89	46	43	89	44	42	86	45	42	87
18	47	45	92	47	45	92	45	43	88	46	43	89	44	42	86
19	46	45	91	47	45	92	47	45	92	45	43	88	46	43	89
15–19	234	222	456	232	219	451	228	215	443	223	210	433	220	207	427
20	47	44	91	46	44	90	47	45	92	47	45	92	45	43	88
21	45	43	88	46	44	90	46	44	90	47	45	92	47	45	92
22	44	42	86	45	43	88	46	44	90	46	44	90	46	44	90
23	42	41	83	43	41	84	44	42	86	45	43	88	45	43	88
24	41	40	81	42	41	83	42	41	83	43	42	85	44	43	87
20–24	219	210	429	222	213	435	225	216	441	228	219	447	227	218	445
25	40	38	78	41	40	81	42	40	82	42	41	83	43	42	85
26	39	37	76	39	38	77	41	39	80	41	40	81	42	40	82
27	37	36	73	39	37	76	39	37	76	41	39	80	41	40	81
28	37	35	72	37	35	72	38	37	75	39	37	76	40	38	78
29	36	35	71	37	35	72	37	35	72	38	36	74	39	37	76
25–29	189	181	370	193	185	378	197	188	385	201	193	394	205	197	402
30	35	34	69	36	35	71	37	36	73	36	35	71	38	37	75
31	35	35	70	34	34	68	35	35	70	37	35	72	36	35	71
32	36	35	71	35	35	70	34	34	68	35	35	70	36	35	71
33	36	36	72	35	35	70	34	35	69	34	34	68	35	35	70
34	37	38	75	36	36	72	35	35	70	34	35	69	33	34	67
30–34	179	178	357	176	175	351	175	175	350	176	174	350	178	176	354
35	41	41	82	37	38	75	36	36	72	35	35	70	34	35	69
36	32	31	63	41	41	82	37	38	75	36	36	72	35	35	70
37	31	31	62	32	31	63	41	41	82	37	38	75	36	36	72
38	32	32	64	31	31	62	32	32	64	41	41	82	37	37	74
39	31	31	62	32	31	63	31	30	61	31	31	62	41	41	82
35–39	167	166	333	173	172	345	177	177	354	180	181	361	183	184	367
40	29	29	58	31	31	62	32	32	64	31	30	61	31	31	62
41	28	28	56	29	29	58	31	31	62	32	31	63	30	30	60
42	29	29	58	28	28	56	29	29	58	31	31	62	32	31	63
43	29	30	59	29	29	58	28	28	56	29	29	58	31	31	62
44	29	30	59	29	30	59	29	29	58	27	28	55	29	29	58
40–44	144	146	290	146	147	293	149	149	298	150	149	299	153	152	305

Figures above the dotted line relate to persons born after mid-1977

Age-group	1982			1983			1984			1985			1986		
	Males	Females	Persons	Males	Females	Persons	Males	Females	Persons	Males	Females	Persons	Males	Females	Persons
45	28	30	58	29	30	59	29	29	58	28	29	57	28	28	56
46	28	30	58	28	30	58	29	30	59	28	29	57	28	29	57
47	28	29	57	28	29	57	28	30	58	29	30	59	28	29	57
48	28	28	56	28	29	57	28	29	57	28	30	58	28	30	58
49	28	29	57	27	28	55	27	29	56	28	29	57	28	29	57
45–49	140	146	286	140	146	286	141	147	288	141	147	288	140	145	285
50	28	30	58	27	29	56	27	28	55	27	29	56	27	29	56
51	28	30	58	28	30	58	27	29	56	27	28	55	27	29	56
52	28	31	59	28	30	58	28	30	58	27	29	56	27	28	55
53	28	30	58	28	30	58	28	30	58	27	29	56	27	28	55
54	28	30	58	28	30	58	27	30	57	28	30	58	27	29	56
50–54	140	151	291	139	149	288	137	147	284	136	145	281	135	143	278
55	28	30	58	27	30	57	27	30	57	27	30	57	27	29	56
56	28	31	59	27	30	57	27	29	56	27	29	56	27	30	57
57	27	30	57	28	30	58	27	30	57	26	29	55	26	29	55
58	27	30	57	27	30	57	27	30	57	26	30	56	26	29	55
59	27	30	57	27	30	57	26	29	55	27	30	57	26	29	55
55–59	137	151	288	136	150	286	134	148	282	133	148	281	132	146	278
60	27	32	59	26	29	55	26	30	56	26	29	55	26	30	56
61	27	32	59	27	31	58	25	29	54	26	29	55	25	29	54
62	29	34	63	26	32	58	26	31	57	24	29	53	25	29	54
63	19	25	44	28	34	62	26	31	57	25	30	55	24	28	52
64	19	23	42	18	24	42	27	33	60	25	31	56	24	29	53
60–64	121	146	267	125	150	275	130	154	284	126	148	274	124	145	269
65	20	25	45	18	23	41	18	24	42	26	33	59	24	30	54
66	20	26	46	19	25	44	17	22	39	17	23	40	25	32	57
67	21	29	50	19	25	44	18	24	42	17	22	39	17	23	40
68	21	28	49	20	28	48	18	25	43	17	23	40	16	22	38
69	20	27	47	20	27	47	20	27	47	18	24	42	16	23	39
65–69	102	135	237	96	128	224	91	122	213	95	125	220	98	130	228
70	19	26	45	19	27	46	19	27	46	19	27	46	17	24	41
71	18	26	44	18	25	43	18	26	44	18	26	44	18	26	44
72	17	25	42	17	25	42	16	24	40	17	25	42	16	25	41
73	16	25	41	15	24	39	16	24	40	15	23	38	16	24	40
74	14	23	37	15	24	39	14	23	37	14	23	37	14	22	36
70–74	84	125	209	84	125	209	83	124	207	83	124	207	81	121	202
75	13	21	34	14	22	36	14	22	36	13	22	35	13	22	35
76	12	21	33	12	20	32	12	21	33	12	21	33	12	21	33
77	11	19	30	11	19	30	11	19	30	11	20	31	11	20	31
78	9	18	27	9	18	27	10	18	28	10	18	28	10	18	28
79	8	16	24	8	17	25	8	17	25	9	17	26	9	17	26
75–79	53	95	148	54	96	150	55	97	152	55	98	153	55	98	153
80	7	15	22	7	15	22	7	15	22	7	15	22	8	16	24
81	5	14	19	6	14	20	6	14	20	6	14	20	6	14	20
82	5	12	17	5	12	17	5	12	17	5	13	18	5	13	18
83	4	10	14	4	11	15	4	11	15	4	11	15	4	11	15
84	3	8	11	3	9	12	4	10	14	4	10	14	4	9	13
80–84	24	59	83	25	61	86	26	62	88	26	63	89	27	63	90
85 and over	11	36	47	11	37	48	12	38	50	12	39	51	13	41	54
All ages	2493	2667	5160	2492	2665	5157	2494	2665	5159	2497	2668	5165	2503	2671	5174

thousands

Age-group	1987			1988			1989			1991			1996		
	Males	Females	Persons	Males	Females	Persons	Males	Females	Persons	Males	Females	Persons	Males	Females	Persons
0	44	42	86	45	42	87	45	42	87	44	42	86	40	38	78
1	43	41	84	44	42	86	44	42	86	44	42	86	41	39	80
2	42	40	82	43	41	84	44	41	85	44	42	86	42	39	81
3	40	37	77	42	39	81	43	41	84	44	41	85	43	40	83
4	36	34	70	39	37	76	41	39	80	44	41	85	43	41	84
0-4	205	194	399	213	201	414	217	205	422	220	208	428	209	197	406
5	34	33	67	36	35	71	39	37	76	43	41	84	43	41	84
6	33	31	64	34	32	66	36	35	71	41	39	80	44	42	86
7	31	30	61	33	31	64	34	32	66	39	37	76	44	41	85
8	31	29	60	31	30	61	33	31	64	36	35	71	43	41	84
9	30	29	59	31	29	60	31	30	61	34	32	66	43	41	84
5-9	159	152	311	165	157	322	173	165	338	193	184	377	217	206	423
10	31	29	60	30	29	59	31	29	60	32	31	63	42	41	83
11	33	32	65	31	29	60	30	29	59	31	30	61	41	39	80
12	34	32	66	33	32	65	31	29	60	31	29	60	39	37	76
13	35	33	68	34	32	66	33	32	65	30	29	59	36	34	70
14	37	35	72	35	33	68	34	32	66	31	28	59	34	32	66
10-14	170	161	331	163	155	318	159	151	310	155	147	302	192	183	375
15	41	38	79	37	35	72	35	33	68	33	31	64	32	31	63
16	42	40	82	40	38	78	37	35	72	33	32	65	31	29	60
17	43	40	83	42	40	82	40	38	78	35	33	68	30	29	59
18	44	42	86	43	40	83	42	40	82	37	35	72	30	28	58
19	44	42	86	44	42	86	43	40	83	40	38	78	30	28	58
15-19	214	202	416	206	195	401	197	186	383	178	169	347	153	145	298
20	46	43	89	44	42	86	44	41	85	42	40	82	32	31	63
21	45	43	88	46	43	89	44	42	86	42	39	81	33	31	64
22	46	44	90	44	42	86	45	42	87	43	40	83	33	32	65
23	46	44	90	45	44	89	43	42	85	42	41	83	35	34	69
24	44	43	87	45	43	88	45	43	88	44	42	86	38	36	74
20-24	227	217	444	224	214	438	221	210	431	213	202	415	171	164	335
25	44	42	86	44	43	87	45	43	88	43	41	84	39	38	77
26	43	41	84	44	42	86	44	42	86	44	43	87	40	37	77
27	41	40	81	43	41	84	43	41	84	44	42	86	41	39	80
28	41	39	80	41	39	80	42	41	83	43	42	85	41	39	80
29	40	39	79	40	39	79	41	40	81	43	41	84	42	40	82
25-29	209	201	410	212	204	416	215	207	422	217	209	426	203	193	396
30	38	37	75	40	38	78	40	39	79	42	41	83	41	40	81
31	38	37	75	38	37	75	40	38	78	40	39	79	43	42	85
32	36	35	71	37	37	74	38	37	75	40	39	79	43	42	85
33	36	35	71	35	35	70	37	37	74	39	38	77	42	41	83
34	34	35	69	36	35	71	35	35	70	37	37	74	41	41	82
30-34	182	179	361	186	182	368	190	186	376	198	194	392	210	206	416
35	33	34	67	34	35	69	35	35	70	37	37	74	41	41	82
36	34	35	69	33	34	67	34	35	69	35	35	70	39	39	78
37	34	35	69	34	35	69	33	34	67	35	35	70	39	39	78
38	36	36	72	35	35	70	34	35	69	34	35	69	38	38	76
39	37	37	74	36	35	71	35	34	69	33	33	66	37	36	73
35-39	174	177	351	172	174	346	171	173	344	174	175	349	194	193	387
40	41	41	82	37	37	74	35	36	71	34	35	69	36	36	72
41	31	31	62	41	41	82	37	37	74	34	35	69	34	34	68
42	31	30	61	31	31	62	41	40	81	35	35	70	35	35	70
43	31	31	62	30	30	60	31	31	62	37	37	74	34	34	68
44	31	30	61	31	31	62	30	30	60	40	40	80	32	33	65
40-44	165	163	328	170	170	340	174	174	348	180	182	362	171	172	343

Figures above the dotted line relate to persons born after mid-1977

Age-group	1987			1988			1989			1991			1996		
	Males	Females	Persons	Males	Females	Persons	Males	Females	Persons	Males	Females	Persons	Males	Females	Persons
45	29	29	58	30	31	61	31	31	62	30	30	60	33	34	67
46	27	28	55	29	29	58	30	30	60	30	30	60	34	34	68
47	28	29	57	27	28	55	29	29	58	31	31	62	34	35	69
48	28	29	57	28	28	56	27	28	55	30	30	60	35	36	71
49	28	29	57	28	29	57	28	28	56	28	28	56	39	40	79
45-49	140	144	284	142	145	287	145	146	291	149	149	298	175	179	354
50	28	29	57	28	29	57	27	29	56	27	28	55	29	30	59
51	27	29	56	27	29	56	28	29	57	27	28	55	29	29	58
52	27	29	56	27	29	56	27	29	56	27	29	56	29	30	59
53	26	28	54	27	28	55	27	28	55	27	28	55	29	30	59
54	26	28	54	26	28	54	26	28	54	26	28	54	27	27	54
50-54	134	143	277	135	143	278	135	143	278	134	141	275	143	146	289
55	27	29	56	26	28	54	26	28	54	26	28	54	25	27	52
56	27	29	56	27	29	56	25	28	53	25	28	53	26	27	53
57	26	29	55	26	29	55	26	28	54	25	27	52	25	28	53
58	26	29	55	26	29	55	26	29	55	25	27	52	25	27	52
59	25	29	54	25	29	54	25	29	54	25	28	53	24	27	51
55-59	131	145	276	130	144	274	128	142	270	126	138	264	125	136	261
60	25	29	54	25	28	53	25	28	53	25	28	53	23	27	50
61	26	29	55	24	28	52	24	28	52	24	28	52	23	26	49
62	24	29	53	25	29	54	23	28	51	24	28	52	22	25	47
63	24	28	52	24	28	52	24	28	52	23	27	50	22	26	48
64	23	28	51	23	28	51	23	28	51	22	27	49	22	26	48
60-64	122	143	265	121	141	262	119	140	259	118	138	256	112	130	242
65	24	29	53	22	27	49	23	27	50	22	27	49	21	26	47
66	23	30	53	23	28	51	21	27	48	21	27	48	21	26	47
67	24	31	55	22	29	51	22	28	50	21	26	47	20	25	45
68	16	22	38	23	31	54	21	29	50	20	26	46	19	25	44
69	15	21	36	15	22	37	22	30	52	20	27	47	18	25	43
65-69	102	133	235	105	137	242	109	141	250	104	133	237	99	127	226
70	16	22	38	14	20	34	14	21	35	19	27	46	18	25	43
71	16	23	39	15	22	37	14	20	34	20	28	48	17	24	41
72	16	25	41	15	22	37	14	21	35	13	20	33	16	23	39
73	15	24	39	16	24	40	14	21	35	12	19	31	15	22	37
74	15	23	38	14	23	37	14	23	37	12	19	31	15	22	37
70-74	78	117	195	74	111	185	70	106	176	76	113	189	81	116	197
75	13	21	34	13	22	35	13	22	35	12	19	31	14	22	36
76	12	21	33	12	20	32	12	21	33	12	21	33	14	23	37
77	11	20	31	11	20	31	11	19	30	11	20	31	8	16	24
78	10	19	29	10	19	29	10	19	29	10	18	28	8	14	22
79	9	17	26	9	17	26	9	17	26	9	17	26	7	15	22
75-79	55	98	153	55	98	153	55	98	153	54	95	149	51	90	141
80	8	16	24	8	16	24	8	16	24	8	16	24	7	14	21
81	6	14	20	6	14	20	7	15	22	6	15	21	7	15	22
82	5	13	18	5	13	18	5	13	18	6	13	19	6	14	20
83	5	11	16	5	12	17	5	12	17	5	12	17	5	12	17
84	4	10	14	4	10	14	4	10	14	4	10	14	4	10	14
80-84	28	64	92	28	65	93	29	66	95	29	66	95	29	65	94
85 and over	13	42	55	13	43	56	14	44	58	14	47	61	17	51	68
All ages	2508	2675	5183	2514	2679	5193	2521	2683	5204	2532	2690	5222	2552	2699	5251

Appendix Table IIIc *continued*

thousands

Age-group	2001 Males	Females	Persons	2006 Males	Females	Persons	2011 Males	Females	Persons	2016 Males	Females	Persons	2017 Males	Females	Persons
0	35	33	68	35	33	68	38	36	74	40	38	78	40	38	78
1	36	34	70	34	32	66	37	35	72	39	37	76	40	37	77
2	37	35	72	34	32	66	36	34	70	39	37	76	39	37	76
3	38	36	74	34	32	66	35	33	68	39	36	75	39	37	76
4	38	36	74	34	32	66	35	33	68	38	36	74	38	36	74
0-4	184	174	358	171	161	332	181	171	352	195	184	379	196	185	381
5	40	38	78	35	33	68	34	32	66	37	35	72	38	36	74
6	40	38	78	35	34	69	34	32	66	36	35	71	37	35	72
7	41	39	80	36	34	70	33	32	65	36	34	70	36	34	70
8	42	40	82	37	35	72	33	32	65	35	33	68	36	34	70
9	43	41	84	38	36	74	34	32	66	34	32	66	35	33	68
5-9	206	196	402	181	172	353	168	160	328	178	169	347	182	172	354
10	43	41	84	39	37	76	34	33	67	34	32	66	34	33	67
11	44	41	85	40	38	78	35	33	68	33	32	65	34	32	66
12	43	41	84	41	39	80	36	34	70	33	32	65	33	32	65
13	43	41	84	42	40	82	37	35	72	33	31	64	33	31	64
14	43	41	84	42	40	82	38	36	74	34	32	66	33	31	64
10-14	216	205	421	204	194	398	180	171	351	167	159	326	167	159	326
15	42	40	82	43	40	83	39	37	76	34	32	66	34	32	66
16	41	39	80	43	41	84	40	38	78	35	33	68	34	32	66
17	38	36	74	43	41	84	41	38	79	36	34	70	35	33	68
18	36	34	70	43	41	84	41	39	80	36	35	71	35	34	69
19	33	31	64	42	40	82	42	40	82	37	35	72	36	34	70
15-19	190	180	370	214	203	417	203	192	395	178	169	347	174	165	339
20	31	30	61	41	40	81	42	40	82	38	36	74	37	35	72
21	30	29	59	40	38	78	42	40	82	39	37	76	38	36	74
22	29	28	57	37	35	72	42	40	82	39	38	77	38	37	75
23	28	27	55	34	32	66	41	39	80	40	38	78	39	37	76
24	28	26	54	31	30	61	40	39	79	40	38	78	39	38	77
20-24	146	140	286	183	175	358	207	198	405	196	187	383	191	183	374
25	30	29	59	29	28	57	39	38	77	40	38	78	39	38	77
26	30	29	59	28	27	55	37	36	73	40	38	78	40	38	78
27	31	30	61	27	26	53	35	33	68	39	38	77	39	38	77
28	34	32	66	27	25	52	32	31	63	39	38	77	39	37	76
29	36	35	71	26	25	51	30	28	58	39	37	76	39	37	76
25-29	161	155	316	137	131	268	173	166	339	197	189	386	196	188	384
30	38	37	75	29	28	57	28	27	55	38	37	75	39	37	76
31	38	37	75	29	29	58	27	26	53	36	35	71	38	37	75
32	40	38	78	30	29	59	26	26	52	34	33	67	36	35	71
33	39	39	78	32	32	64	25	25	50	31	31	62	33	33	66
34	41	40	81	35	35	70	25	25	50	28	28	56	30	31	61
30-34	196	191	387	155	153	308	131	129	260	167	164	331	176	173	349
35	40	40	80	37	37	74	28	28	56	27	27	54	28	28	56
36	42	42	84	37	37	74	28	29	57	25	26	51	27	27	54
37	42	42	84	39	38	77	29	29	58	25	25	50	25	26	51
38	41	41	82	39	38	77	32	32	64	25	25	50	25	25	50
39	41	40	81	40	40	80	34	34	68	25	25	50	25	25	50
35-39	206	205	411	192	190	382	151	152	303	127	128	255	130	131	261
40	40	40	80	40	39	79	36	36	72	27	27	54	25	24	49
41	39	39	78	42	41	83	37	36	73	28	28	56	27	27	54
42	38	38	76	41	41	82	38	38	76	29	29	58	28	28	56
43	38	37	75	40	41	81	38	38	76	31	31	62	28	29	57
44	36	36	72	40	40	80	40	39	79	34	34	68	31	31	62
40-44	191	190	381	203	202	405	189	187	376	149	149	298	139	139	278

Figures above the dotted line relate to persons born after mid-1977.

Age-group	2001			2006			2011			2016			2017		
	Males	Females	Persons	Males	Females	Persons	Males	Females	Persons	Males	Females	Persons	Males	Females	Persons
45	35	36	71	39	39	78	39	39	78	36	36	72	34	34	68
46	34	34	68	38	38	76	40	40	80	36	36	72	35	36	71
47	34	34	68	37	38	75	40	41	81	37	37	74	35	35	70
48	33	33	66	37	37	74	39	40	79	37	37	74	37	37	74
49	31	32	63	35	35	70	39	39	78	38	38	76	37	37	74
45-49	167	169	336	186	187	373	197	199	396	184	184	368	178	179	357
50	32	34	66	34	35	69	38	39	77	37	38	75	38	38	76
51	32	33	65	33	33	66	36	37	73	39	39	78	37	38	75
52	33	34	67	32	33	65	36	37	73	38	40	78	38	39	77
53	34	35	69	31	33	64	35	36	71	38	39	77	38	39	77
54	37	38	75	30	31	61	33	34	67	37	38	75	37	39	76
50-54	168	174	342	160	165	325	178	183	361	189	194	383	188	193	381
55	28	29	57	30	32	62	32	34	66	36	37	73	36	38	74
56	27	28	55	30	32	62	31	32	63	34	36	70	35	37	72
57	28	29	57	31	33	64	30	32	62	33	36	69	34	36	70
58	26	29	55	31	34	65	29	31	60	32	34	66	33	35	68
59	24	26	50	34	37	71	27	30	57	31	33	64	32	34	66
55-59	133	141	274	156	168	324	149	159	308	166	176	342	170	180	350
60	23	25	48	25	28	53	27	31	58	30	32	62	30	32	62
61	23	26	49	24	27	51	27	30	57	27	31	58	29	32	61
62	23	26	49	25	27	52	28	31	59	27	30	57	27	30	57
63	22	26	48	24	27	51	28	32	60	26	29	55	26	30	56
64	21	25	46	21	24	45	30	34	64	24	28	52	25	29	54
60-64	112	128	240	119	133	252	140	158	298	134	150	284	137	153	290
65	20	25	45	20	24	44	22	26	48	24	29	53	23	28	51
66	20	24	44	20	24	44	21	25	46	24	28	52	23	28	51
67	19	24	43	19	24	43	21	25	46	24	29	53	23	28	51
68	18	23	41	19	23	42	20	24	44	23	29	52	23	28	51
69	18	24	42	17	23	40	18	22	40	25	31	56	23	28	51
65-69	95	120	215	95	118	213	102	122	224	120	146	266	115	140	255
70	17	24	41	17	23	40	16	22	38	18	24	42	24	31	55
71	16	23	39	16	22	38	16	21	37	17	22	39	18	23	41
72	15	22	37	15	21	36	15	21	36	17	22	39	16	22	38
73	15	21	36	14	20	34	15	20	35	15	21	36	16	21	37
74	14	21	35	13	20	33	13	20	33	14	19	33	14	20	34
70-74	77	111	188	75	106	181	75	104	179	81	108	189	88	117	205
75	13	21	34	13	20	33	13	19	32	12	18	30	13	19	32
76	12	19	31	12	19	31	11	18	29	11	18	29	11	17	28
77	11	18	29	11	17	28	10	17	27	11	17	28	11	17	28
78	10	17	27	9	17	26	9	16	25	10	16	26	9	16	25
79	9	17	26	8	16	24	9	15	24	8	15	23	9	15	24
75-79	55	92	147	53	89	142	52	85	137	52	84	136	53	84	137
80	8	17	25	8	15	23	7	15	22	8	14	22	7	14	21
81	8	16	24	7	14	21	7	14	21	6	13	19	7	13	20
82	5	11	16	6	13	19	6	12	18	6	12	18	6	12	18
83	4	9	13	5	11	16	5	11	16	5	11	16	5	11	16
84	3	9	12	4	11	15	4	10	14	4	10	14	4	10	14
80-84	28	62	90	30	64	94	29	62	91	29	60	89	29	60	89
85 and over	17	53	70	17	53	70	18	55	73	18	56	74	18	56	74
All ages	2548	2686	5234	2531	2664	5195	2523	2653	5176	2527	2656	5183	2527	2657	5184

**Appendix Table IIIe Mortality rates by sex and single ages,
mid-1977-78 to mid-2011-12**

Age last birthday	1977-78		1991-92		2011-12	
	Males	Females	Males	Females	Males	Females
0*	0.01969	0.01544	0.01779	0.01396	0.01540	0.01208
0	0.00278	0.00266	0.00251	0.00241	0.00217	0.00208
1	0.00098	0.00087	0.00088	0.00078	0.00076	0.00068
2	0.00081	0.00053	0.00073	0.00048	0.00063	0.00041
3	0.00070	0.00043	0.00063	0.00039	0.00055	0.00034
4	0.00060	0.00035	0.00055	0.00032	0.00047	0.00027
5	0.00054	0.00031	0.00048	0.00028	0.00042	0.00024
6	0.00048	0.00028	0.00043	0.00026	0.00037	0.00022
7	0.00043	0.00026	0.00039	0.00024	0.00034	0.00021
8	0.00039	0.00024	0.00035	0.00022	0.00031	0.00019
9	0.00036	0.00022	0.00033	0.00020	0.00028	0.00018
10	0.00034	0.00020	0.00031	0.00019	0.00027	0.00016
11	0.00034	0.00020	0.00031	0.00018	0.00027	0.00015
12	0.00036	0.00020	0.00033	0.00018	0.00028	0.00015
13	0.00040	0.00020	0.00036	0.00018	0.00031	0.00015
14	0.00047	0.00022	0.00042	0.00020	0.00037	0.00018
15	0.00058	0.00028	0.00053	0.00026	0.00048	0.00023
16	0.00076	0.00040	0.00074	0.00038	0.00070	0.00036
17	0.00110	0.00046	0.00110	0.00046	0.00110	0.00046
18	0.00132	0.00046	0.00132	0.00046	0.00132	0.00045
19	0.00135	0.00045	0.00133	0.00045	0.00131	0.00044
20	0.00129	0.00043	0.00127	0.00042	0.00123	0.00041
21	0.00121	0.00042	0.00117	0.00040	0.00111	0.00038
22	0.00113	0.00040	0.00108	0.00038	0.00101	0.00036
23	0.00107	0.00041	0.00102	0.00039	0.00095	0.00035
24	0.00105	0.00043	0.00099	0.00040	0.00092	0.00036
25	0.00104	0.00047	0.00098	0.00043	0.00090	0.00038
26	0.00104	0.00050	0.00098	0.00045	0.00090	0.00040
27	0.00107	0.00054	0.00101	0.00048	0.00092	0.00042
28	0.00111	0.00059	0.00105	0.00053	0.00096	0.00046
29	0.00116	0.00064	0.00110	0.00058	0.00101	0.00050
30	0.00122	0.00070	0.00117	0.00063	0.00109	0.00055
31	0.00131	0.00078	0.00125	0.00070	0.00118	0.00061
32	0.00142	0.00087	0.00137	0.00078	0.00130	0.00068
33	0.00155	0.00096	0.00149	0.00087	0.00141	0.00076
34	0.00171	0.00107	0.00165	0.00098	0.00157	0.00086
35	0.00190	0.00119	0.00183	0.00111	0.00174	0.00101
36	0.00212	0.00133	0.00204	0.00126	0.00194	0.00117
37	0.00237	0.00151	0.00228	0.00145	0.00217	0.00138
38	0.00265	0.00169	0.00257	0.00164	0.00247	0.00157
39	0.00296	0.00189	0.00290	0.00185	0.00282	0.00180
40	0.00329	0.00209	0.00324	0.00206	0.00318	0.00202
41	0.00363	0.00231	0.00361	0.00229	0.00357	0.00227
42	0.00404	0.00255	0.00404	0.00254	0.00404	0.00252
43	0.00450	0.00280	0.00450	0.00280	0.00450	0.00280
44	0.00500	0.00308	0.00500	0.00308	0.00500	0.00308

* *Probability that a baby born in the year will not survive until the end of the year*

Age last birthday	1977–78		1991–92		2011–12	
	Males	Females	Males	Females	Males	Females
45	0.00553	0.00340	0.00553	0.00340	0.00553	0.00340
46	0.00616	0.00376	0.00616	0.00376	0.00616	0.00376
47	0.00686	0.00415	0.00686	0.00415	0.00686	0.00415
48	0.00764	0.00456	0.00764	0.00456	0.00764	0.00456
49	0.00850	0.00502	0.00850	0.00502	0.00850	0.00502
50	0.00945	0.00554	0.00945	0.00554	0.00945	0.00554
51	0.01047	0.00610	0.01047	0.00610	0.01047	0.00610
52	0.01158	0.00669	0.01158	0.00669	0.01158	0.00669
53	0.01279	0.00731	0.01273	0.00731	0.01266	0.00731
54	0.01411	0.00797	0.01401	0.00797	0.01387	0.00797
55	0.01554	0.00869	0.01536	0.00865	0.01512	0.00860
56	0.01710	0.00948	0.01686	0.00942	0.01653	0.00932
57	0.01878	0.01033	0.01839	0.01022	0.01785	0.01005
58	0.02061	0.01124	0.02001	0.01108	0.01919	0.01086
59	0.02261	0.01220	0.02180	0.01198	0.02070	0.01168
60	0.02478	0.01323	0.02369	0.01296	0.02222	0.01257
61	0.02713	0.01431	0.02572	0.01390	0.02383	0.01333
62	0.02969	0.01551	0.02803	0.01495	0.02582	0.01419
63	0.03246	0.01687	0.03056	0.01620	0.02803	0.01528
64	0.03540	0.01839	0.03319	0.01759	0.03027	0.01649
65	0.03859	0.02008	0.03603	0.01912	0.03266	0.01783
66	0.04205	0.02195	0.03904	0.02081	0.03510	0.01928
67	0.04581	0.02402	0.04235	0.02277	0.03785	0.02110
68	0.04991	0.02629	0.04614	0.02482	0.04123	0.02286
69	0.05441	0.02886	0.05051	0.02725	0.04541	0.02510
70	0.05928	0.03178	0.05534	0.03000	0.05016	0.02764
71	0.06445	0.03509	0.06017	0.03303	0.05454	0.03030
72	0.07009	0.03886	0.06571	0.03658	0.05992	0.03356
73	0.07610	0.04312	0.07134	0.04060	0.06506	0.03725
74	0.08264	0.04783	0.07781	0.04484	0.07138	0.04089
75	0.08958	0.05309	0.08433	0.04977	0.07737	0.04538
76	0.09707	0.05885	0.09165	0.05517	0.08442	0.05031
77	0.10500	0.06516	0.09913	0.06109	0.09131	0.05571
78	0.11354	0.07198	0.10764	0.06720	0.09975	0.06091
79	0.12251	0.07956	0.11615	0.07427	0.10763	0.06732
80	0.13216	0.08788	0.12583	0.08204	0.11731	0.07436
81	0.14227	0.09698	0.13546	0.09053	0.12629	0.08206
82	0.15303	0.10692	0.14570	0.09981	0.13583	0.09047
83	0.16448	0.11774	0.15660	0.10991	0.14600	0.09963
84	0.17667	0.12931	0.16821	0.12004	0.15682	0.10794
85	0.18965	0.14208	0.18056	0.13190	0.16834	0.11860
86	0.20347	0.15607	0.19372	0.14488	0.18060	0.13027
87	0.21823	0.17163	0.20777	0.15932	0.19370	0.14326
88	0.23407	0.18925	0.22286	0.17568	0.20777	0.15797
89	0.25120	0.20961	0.23917	0.19459	0.22297	0.17497
90 and over	0.28231	0.23793	0.26879	0.22087	0.25059	0.19860

Appendix Table IVa Actual and projected Total population as at mid-year by sex and age-groups, 1951, 1961, 1971 to 2017; mid-1977 based projections.

Great Britain

thousands

Year	0–14 Persons	15–44 Males	15–44 Females	45–64 Males	45–59 Females	65 and over Males	60 and over Females	All ages Males	All ages Females	All ages Persons
1951	10996	10490	10598	5440	4966	2191	4494	23736	25440	49176
1961	11946	10282	10141	6248	5341	2323	5244	24975	26550	51525
1971	12954	10635	10333	6309	5096	2754	6096	26348	27830	54178
1972	12971	10685	10375	6278	5058	2809	6158	26428	27905	54333
1973	12925	10768	10447	6239	5006	2862	6220	26502	27963	54465
1974	12792	10836	10494	6198	4954	2919	6281	26520	27955	54475
1975	12623	10912	10545	6158	4907	2968	6340	26521	27931	54452
1976	12397	11015	10639	6124	4891	3010	6356	26515	27915	54430
1977	12123	11127	10750	6087	4885	3054	6364	26496	27894	54390
1978	11840	11264	10879	6033	4896	3095	6334	26477	27864	54341
1979	11538	11413	11022	5980	4897	3135	6307	26459	27833	54292
1980	11240	11558	11161	5932	4778	3169	6401	26439	27800	54239
1981	10974	11684	11279	5916	4690	3175	6470	26420	27768	54188
1982	10734	11801	11395	5920	4620	3165	6518	26410	27743	54153
1983	10569	11902	11490	5951	4576	3128	6543	26421	27738	54159
1984	10453	12002	11586	5978	4543	3095	6555	26457	27755	54212
1985	10418	12090	11671	5897	4508	3163	6562	26515	27794	54309
1986	10388	12209	11782	5816	4461	3211	6564	26587	27844	54431
1987	10429	12287	11852	5766	4436	3244	6555	26668	27901	54569
1988	10525	12311	11866	5760	4452	3260	6538	26751	27961	54712
1989	10678	12291	11840	5778	4482	3268	6522	26837	28022	54859
1990	10863	12264	11807	5790	4502	3275	6505	26923	28083	55006
1991	11074	12220	11755	5807	4530	3279	6485	27008	28142	55150
1992	11315	12062	11588	5927	4666	3276	6456	27091	28199	55290
1993	11540	11950	11468	6011	4771	3267	6415	27170	28252	55422
1994	11752	11867	11374	6067	4853	3259	6370	27243	28299	55542
1995	11944	11802	11289	6107	4924	3251	6332	27309	28340	55649
1996	12112	11754	11225	6132	4974	3245	6298	27367	28373	55740
1997	12236	11719	11182	6162	5010	3236	6269	27416	28398	55814
1998	12301	11697	11154	6211	5051	3215	6242	27456	28415	55871
1999	12293	11695	11152	6265	5088	3199	6219	27487	28424	55911
2000	12221	11723	11179	6309	5123	3185	6194	27509	28425	55934
2001	12109	11757	11210	6357	5183	3177	6152	27525	28420	55945
2002	11965	11789	11237	6411	5240	3174	6130	27535	28411	55946
2003	11809	11811	11255	6477	5281	3173	6135	27541	28400	55941
2004	11644	11830	11271	6547	5314	3173	6155	27546	28388	55934
2005	11479	11844	11281	6626	5360	3171	6168	27552	28377	55929
2006	11321	11840	11274	6735	5414	3155	6192	27560	28371	55931
2007	11179	11824	11252	6840	5390	3152	6306	27573	28370	55943
2008	11055	11797	11221	6927	5413	3174	6381	27592	28376	55968
2009	10956	11754	11176	7013	5469	3207	6431	27617	28389	56006
2010	10888	11705	11124	7102	5530	3234	6476	27649	28410	56059
2011	10848	11658	11076	7178	5594	3264	6508	27688	28438	56126
2012	10839	11604	11019	7178	5667	3367	6531	27732	28473	56205
2013	10862	11556	10972	7196	5715	3434	6560	27781	28514	56295
2014	10912	11497	10910	7236	5768	3480	6591	27834	28560	56394
2015	10986	11444	10859	7272	5809	3514	6615	27889	28610	56499
2016	11078	11376	10791	7327	5851	3535	6648	27944	28662	56606
2017	11181	11325	10742	7359	5856	3556	6694	27999	28714	56713

**Appendix Table IVb Annual changes in projected Total population
1977 to 2017; mid-1977 based projections**

Great Britain

thousands

Mid-year to mid-year	Population at beginning of period	Births	Deaths	Natural increase	Net migration	Total increase
1977-1978	54390	638	665	- 28	-21	- 49
1978-1979	54341	641	669	- 28	-21	- 49
1979-1980	54292	645	674	- 29	-24	- 53
1980-1981	54239	654	678	- 24	-27	- 51
1981-1982	54188	678	682	- 5	-30	- 35
1982-1983	54153	722	687	37	-31	6
1983-1984	54159	776	691	84	-31	53
1984-1985	54212	822	695	128	-31	97
1985-1986	54309	851	698	153	-31	122
1986-1987	54431	870	701	169	-31	138
1987-1988	54569	877	702	174	-31	143
1988-1989	54712	881	704	178	-31	147
1989-1990	54859	883	705	178	-31	147
1990-1991	55006	881	705	175	-31	144
1991-1992	55150	876	705	171	-31	140
1992-1993	55290	867	705	163	-31	132
1993-1994	55422	855	704	151	-31	120
1994-1995	55542	840	703	138	-31	107
1995-1996	55649	824	701	122	-31	91
1996-1997	55740	805	700	105	-31	74
1997-1998	55814	786	698	88	-31	57
1998-1999	55871	767	696	71	-31	40
1999-2000	55911	749	694	54	-31	23
2000-2001	55934	734	692	42	-31	11
2001-2002	55945	722	691	32	-31	1
2002-2003	55946	715	689	26	-31	- 5
2003-2004	55941	712	688	24	-31	- 7
2004-2005	55934	713	687	26	-31	- 5
2005-2006	55929	719	686	33	-31	2
2006-2007	55931	728	685	43	-31	12
2007-2008	55943	740	684	56	-31	25
2008 2009	55968	753	684	69	-31	38
2009-2010	56006	768	684	84	-31	53
2010-2011	56059	782	685	98	-31	67
2011-2012	56126	795	685	110	-31	79
2012-2013	56205	807	685	121	-31	90
2013-2014	56295	816	686	130	-31	99
2014-2015	56394	822	686	136	-31	105
2015-2016	56499	826	687	138	-31	107
2016-2017	56606	827	689	138	-31	107
2017-2018	56713					

Appendix Table IVc Projected Total population as at mid-year, by sex and single ages 1977 to 1989, 1991-2017; mid-1977 based projections.

thousands

Age-group	1977			1978			1979			1980			1981		
	Males	Females	Persons	Males	Females	Persons	Males	Females	Persons	Males	Females	Persons	Males	Females	Persons
0	319	301	620	322	304	626	323	306	629	325	308	633	330	312	642
1	334	316	650	318	300	618	320	303	623	322	304	626	324	306	630
2	349	329	678	333	315	648	317	298	615	319	302	621	321	303	624
3	362	342	704	348	328	676	332	314	646	316	297	613	319	301	620
4	389	367	756	361	341	702	348	327	675	332	313	645	315	297	612
0- 4	1753	1655	3408	1682	1588	3270	1640	1548	3188	1614	1524	3138	1609	1519	3128
5	415	390	805	389	367	756	361	341	702	347	326	673	331	312	643
6	437	415	852	414	389	803	388	366	754	360	340	700	346	326	672
7	427	403	830	436	414	850	414	388	802	388	365	753	360	339	699
8	443	420	863	427	403	830	436	413	849	414	388	802	387	364	751
9	441	417	858	443	420	863	426	403	829	435	413	848	413	387	800
5- 9	2163	2045	4208	2109	1993	4102	2025	1911	3936	1944	1832	3776	1837	1728	3565
10	457	434	891	441	416	857	442	420	862	426	402	828	435	412	847
11	458	434	892	457	434	891	441	416	857	442	419	861	426	402	828
12	469	445	914	458	434	892	457	433	890	441	416	857	442	419	861
13	469	446	915	469	445	914	457	434	891	456	433	889	440	416	856
14	459	436	895	469	445	914	469	445	914	457	434	891	456	433	889
10-14	2312	2195	4507	2294	2174	4468	2266	2148	4414	2222	2104	4326	2199	2082	4281
15	451	429	880	459	437	896	469	445	914	469	445	914	458	433	891
16	443	419	862	452	429	881	460	437	897	470	446	916	470	445	915
17	426	403	829	444	419	863	453	430	883	461	437	898	471	446	917
18	422	400	822	428	405	833	445	422	867	454	432	886	462	440	902
19	417	395	812	423	402	825	429	407	836	447	424	871	456	435	891
15-19	2159	2046	4205	2206	2092	4298	2256	2141	4397	2301	2184	4485	2317	2199	4516
20	405	384	789	419	397	816	425	404	829	431	409	840	448	426	874
21	396	373	769	406	384	790	420	397	817	426	404	830	432	409	841
22	385	362	747	396	373	769	406	384	790	420	397	817	427	404	831
23	392	368	760	384	361	745	396	373	769	406	384	790	420	397	817
24	386	370	756	392	368	760	384	361	745	396	373	769	406	384	790
20-24	1964	1857	3821	1997	1883	3880	2031	1919	3950	2079	1967	4046	2133	2020	4153
25	375	361	736	386	369	755	391	367	758	384	361	745	395	372	767
26	374	372	746	374	360	734	385	368	753	391	366	757	383	359	742
27	386	386	772	373	371	744	373	359	732	383	367	750	389	365	754
28	401	392	793	384	385	769	371	370	741	371	358	729	381	366	747
29	426	417	843	399	391	790	383	384	767	369	369	738	369	357	726
25-29	1962	1928	3890	1916	1876	3792	1903	1848	3751	1898	1821	3719	1917	1819	3736
30	468	460	928	424	417	841	397	390	787	381	383	764	367	368	735
31	367	360	727	466	459	925	422	416	838	395	389	784	379	382	761
32	363	352	715	365	359	724	464	458	922	420	415	835	393	388	781
33	367	359	726	361	351	712	363	358	721	462	458	920	418	414	832
34	351	342	693	365	358	723	359	350	709	361	357	718	460	457	917
30-34	1916	1873	3789	1981	1944	3925	2005	1972	3977	2019	2002	4021	2017	2009	4026
35	319	311	630	350	342	692	364	358	722	357	350	707	359	357	716
36	299	295	594	318	310	628	348	341	689	362	357	719	355	349	704
37	321	310	631	298	294	592	317	310	627	347	340	687	361	355	716
38	322	313	636	319	309	628	297	293	590	316	309	625	346	339	685
39	322	313	635	321	314	635	318	308	626	296	292	588	315	308	623
35-39	1583	1543	3126	1606	1569	3175	1644	1610	3254	1678	1648	3326	1736	1708	3444
40	319	309	628	321	312	633	321	313	634	318	308	626	295	291	586
41	314	305	619	318	308	626	320	311	631	319	312	631	317	307	624
42	306	298	604	313	305	618	317	307	624	319	310	629	319	311	630
43	302	294	596	305	297	602	312	304	616	316	306	622	318	309	627
44	302	297	599	301	293	594	304	297	601	311	303	614	315	306	621
40-44	1543	1503	3046	1558	1515	3073	1574	1532	3106	1583	1539	3122	1564	1524	3088

Figures above the dotted line relate to persons born after mid-1977.

Age-group	1977			1978			1979			1980			1981		
	Males	Females	Persons	Males	Females	Persons	Males	Females	Persons	Males	Females	Persons	Males	Females	Persons
45	312	308	620	301	297	598	300	292	592	303	296	599	309	302	611
46	319	319	638	311	307	618	299	296	595	298	291	589	301	295	596
47	314	320	634	317	318	635	309	306	615	298	295	593	297	290	587
48	313	316	629	312	318	630	315	316	631	307	305	612	296	294	590
49	310	314	624	311	315	626	310	317	627	313	315	628	305	304	609
45-49	1568	1577	3145	1552	1555	3107	1533	1527	3060	1519	1502	3021	1508	1485	2993
50	316	323	639	307	312	619	309	314	623	308	316	624	310	314	624
51	322	328	650	313	322	635	305	311	616	306	312	618	305	314	619
52	320	329	649	319	326	645	310	320	630	302	309	611	303	311	614
53	321	333	654	317	327	644	316	324	640	307	318	625	299	307	606
54	326	340	666	318	331	649	314	325	639	313	322	635	204	316	620
50-54	1605	1653	3258	1574	1618	3192	1554	1594	3148	1536	1577	3113	1521	1562	3083
55	339	359	698	322	337	659	314	329	643	310	323	633	309	320	629
56	351	375	726	335	357	692	318	335	653	310	327	637	306	321	627
57	368	396	764	346	372	718	330	354	684	313	333	646	305	324	629
58	241	266	507	363	393	756	340	369	709	325	351	676	308	330	638
59	234	259	493	236	264	500	356	389	745	334	365	699	320	348	668
55-59	1533	1655	3188	1602	1723	3325	1658	1776	3434	1592	1699	3291	1548	1643	3191
60	258	288	546	229	256	485	232	261	493	349	385	734	328	362	690
61	270	301	571	253	285	538	224	253	477	227	258	485	342	381	723
62	291	331	622	263	297	560	247	281	528	219	250	469	222	255	477
63	285	327	612	283	326	609	257	294	551	241	278	519	213	247	460
64	277	322	599	277	323	600	275	321	596	249	289	538	234	273	507
60-64	1381	1569	2950	1305	1487	2792	1235	1410	2645	1285	1460	2745	1339	1518	2857
65	264	310	574	269	316	585	268	318	586	266	317	583	242	285	527
66	257	314	571	255	305	560	260	311	571	259	312	571	257	311	568
67	249	308	557	247	307	554	246	299	545	250	305	555	249	306	555
68	241	305	546	239	302	541	236	301	537	235	293	528	239	299	538
69	228	295	523	229	298	527	227	295	522	226	294	520	224	286	510
65-69	1239	1532	2771	1239	1528	2767	1237	1524	2761	1236	1521	2757	1211	1487	2698
70	213	283	496	216	288	504	218	290	508	216	287	503	214	287	501
71	197	274	471	201	275	476	205	280	485	206	283	489	204	279	483
72	183	265	448	185	266	451	189	267	456	192	271	463	193	274	467
73	168	251	419	171	256	427	173	256	429	176	257	433	180	262	442
74	154	239	393	156	241	397	158	246	404	161	247	408	164	248	412
70-74	915	1312	2227	929	1326	2255	943	1339	2282	951	1345	2296	955	1350	2305
75	136	221	357	142	228	370	144	231	375	146	235	381	148	236	384
76	121	214	335	125	211	336	130	217	347	132	220	352	134	224	358
77	105	197	302	110	203	313	113	199	312	118	206	324	120	208	328
78	90	179	269	94	185	279	99	191	290	102	187	289	107	194	301
79	75	160	235	80	167	247	84	173	257	89	178	267	91	175	266
75-79	527	971	1498	551	994	1545	570	1011	1581	587	1026	1613	600	1037	1637
80	66	148	214	66	148	214	71	155	226	74	160	234	79	165	244
81	55	133	188	58	136	194	58	136	194	62	142	204	65	147	212
82	50	119	169	48	120	168	50	123	173	51	124	175	54	130	184
83	40	100	140	42	107	149	41	108	149	43	111	154	44	111	155
84	35	88	123	34	89	123	36	95	131	35	96	131	36	98	134
80-84	246	588	834	248	600	848	256	617	873	265	633	898	278	651	929
85 and over	127	392	519	128	399	527	129	406	535	130	416	546	131	427	558
All ages	26496	27894	54390	26477	27864	54341	26459	27833	54292	26439	27800	54239	26420	27768	54188

thousands

Age-group	1982			1983			1984			1985			1986		
	Males	Females	Persons	Males	Females	Persons	Males	Females	Persons	Males	Females	Persons	Males	Females	Persons
0	343	324	667	365	345	710	392	371	763	416	393	809	430	407	837
1	328	310	638	341	322	663	363	343	706	390	369	759	414	391	805
2	323	305	628	328	309	637	340	321	661	362	342	704	389	367	756
3	320	302	622	322	304	626	327	308	635	339	320	659	361	341	702
4	318	300	618	319	301	620	321	303	624	326	307	633	338	319	657
0-4	1632	1541	3173	1675	1581	3256	1743	1646	3389	1833	1731	3564	1932	1825	3757
5	315	296	611	317	299	616	319	300	619	321	302	623	325	306	631
6	330	311	641	314	295	609	317	298	615	318	300	618	320	301	621
7	346	325	671	330	310	640	313	294	607	316	297	613	318	299	617
8	359	338	697	345	325	670	329	310	639	313	294	607	316	297	613
9	387	364	751	359	338	697	345	324	669	329	309	638	312	293	605
5-9	1737	1634	3371	1665	1567	3232	1623	1526	3149	1597	1502	3099	1591	1496	3087
10	413	387	800	387	363	750	359	338	697	345	323	668	328	309	637
11	435	412	847	412	386	798	386	363	749	358	337	695	344	323	667
12	425	402	827	435	412	847	412	386	798	386	363	749	358	337	695
13	442	419	861	425	401	826	434	411	845	412	386	798	386	362	748
14	440	415	855	441	419	860	425	401	826	434	411	845	412	385	797
10-14	2155	2035	4190	2100	1981	4081	2016	1899	3915	1935	1820	3755	1828	1716	3544
15	456	433	889	440	415	855	441	419	860	425	401	826	434	411	845
16	458	434	892	457	433	890	441	415	856	442	419	861	425	401	826
17	471	445	916	459	434	893	458	433	891	442	416	858	443	419	862
18	472	448	920	472	447	919	460	436	896	459	435	894	443	418	861
19	464	442	906	474	451	925	474	450	924	462	438	900	461	438	899
15-19	2321	2202	4523	2302	2180	4482	2274	2153	4427	2230	2109	4339	2206	2087	4293
20	458	436	894	466	444	910	476	452	928	475	451	926	464	440	904
21	450	426	876	459	437	896	467	444	911	476	453	929	477	452	929
22	432	410	842	450	426	876	459	437	896	467	444	911	476	453	929
23	426	404	830	432	409	841	449	426	875	459	437	896	466	444	910
24	419	397	816	425	404	829	431	409	840	449	426	875	458	437	895
20-24	2185	2073	4258	2232	2120	4352	2282	2168	4450	2326	2211	4537	2341	2226	4567
25	405	383	788	419	396	815	425	403	828	431	408	839	448	425	873
26	394	370	764	404	382	786	418	395	813	424	402	826	430	407	837
27	381	358	739	393	369	762	403	380	783	416	393	809	423	400	823
28	387	364	751	379	357	736	390	368	758	401	379	780	414	392	806
29	380	365	745	385	363	748	377	356	733	388	367	755	399	378	777
25-29	1947	1840	3787	1980	1867	3847	2013	1902	3915	2060	1949	4009	2114	2002	4116
30	367	356	723	377	364	741	383	362	745	375	355	730	386	366	752
31	365	368	733	365	355	720	375	363	738	381	361	742	373	354	727
32	377	381	758	363	367	730	362	354	716	373	362	735	379	361	740
33	391	387	778	375	380	755	361	366	727	361	354	715	371	361	732
34	416	413	829	389	386	775	373	379	752	359	365	724	359	353	712
30-34	1916	1905	3821	1869	1852	3721	1854	1824	3678	1849	1797	3646	1868	1795	3663
35	458	456	914	414	412	826	387	386	773	371	379	750	357	364	721
36	357	356	713	456	455	911	413	411	824	385	385	770	369	378	747
37	354	348	702	356	355	711	454	454	908	411	410	821	384	383	767
38	360	355	715	353	347	700	355	354	709	453	453	906	410	409	819
39	345	338	683	359	354	713	352	346	698	354	353	707	452	452	904
35-39	1874	1853	3727	1938	1923	3861	1961	1951	3912	1974	1980	3954	1972	1986	3958
40	314	307	621	344	337	681	358	353	711	351	345	696	353	352	705
41	294	291	585	313	306	619	343	337	680	357	352	709	350	344	694
42	316	306	622	293	290	583	312	305	617	341	336	677	355	351	706
43	317	310	627	315	305	620	292	289	581	311	304	615	340	335	675
44	317	308	625	316	310	626	313	304	617	291	288	579	310	304	614
40-44	1558	1522	3080	1581	1548	3129	1618	1588	3206	1651	1625	3276	1708	1686	3394

Figures above the dotted line relate to persons born after mid-1977

Age-group	1982			1983			1984			1985			1986		
	Males	Females	Persons	Males	Females	Persons	Males	Females	Persons	Males	Females	Persons	Males	Females	Persons
45	314	305	619	316	308	624	315	309	624	312	303	615	290	288	578
46	308	301	609	312	303	615	314	307	621	313	308	621	311	302	613
47	299	294	593	306	300	606	311	303	614	313	306	619	312	307	619
48	295	289	584	298	293	591	304	299	603	309	301	610	311	304	615
49	294	292	586	293	288	581	296	291	587	302	298	600	306	300	606
45-49	1510	1481	2991	1525	1492	3017	1540	1509	3049	1549	1516	3065	1530	1501	3031
50	302	303	605	291	291	582	290	286	576	293	290	583	299	296	595
51	308	312	620	300	301	601	289	289	578	288	285	573	291	289	580
52	302	312	614	305	310	615	297	300	597	286	288	574	285	284	569
53	300	309	609	299	311	610	302	309	611	294	298	592	284	286	570
54	296	305	601	297	307	604	296	309	605	299	307	606	291	296	587
50-54	1508	1541	3049	1492	1520	3012	1474	1493	2967	1460	1468	2928	1450	1451	2901
55	300	314	614	292	303	595	294	305	599	292	306	598	295	305	600
56	305	318	623	296	312	608	289	301	590	290	302	592	289	304	593
57	302	318	620	301	315	616	292	309	601	285	299	584	286	300	586
58	300	321	621	297	316	613	296	313	609	287	307	594	280	296	576
59	303	327	630	295	318	613	291	313	604	291	310	601	282	304	586
55-59	1510	1598	3108	1481	1564	3045	1462	1541	3003	1445	1524	2969	1432	1509	2941
60	313	345	658	297	324	621	289	315	604	286	310	596	286	307	593
61	321	358	679	307	341	648	291	320	611	284	311	595	280	306	586
62	334	376	710	313	353	666	299	337	636	284	316	600	277	308	585
63	216	251	467	326	371	697	306	348	654	292	332	624	277	312	589
64	208	243	451	210	248	458	317	366	683	297	344	641	284	328	612
60-64	1392	1573	2965	1453	1637	3090	1502	1686	3188	1443	1613	3056	1404	1561	2965
65	227	269	496	201	239	440	203	244	447	307	361	668	289	338	627
66	233	280	513	219	265	484	194	235	429	197	240	437	297	355	652
67	247	305	552	224	275	499	211	260	471	187	231	418	189	235	424
68	239	300	539	237	299	536	215	269	484	202	254	456	179	226	405
69	228	293	521	228	293	521	227	292	519	205	263	468	193	249	442
65-69	1174	1447	2621	1109	1371	2480	1050	1300	2350	1098	1349	2447	1147	1403	2550
70	213	279	492	217	285	502	217	286	503	216	285	501	196	257	453
71	202	279	481	202	271	473	205	277	482	205	278	483	204	277	481
72	192	271	463	191	271	462	190	263	453	193	269	462	193	270	463
73	181	264	445	179	262	441	178	262	440	177	254	431	181	260	441
74	167	252	419	168	254	422	167	252	419	166	242	418	165	245	410
70-74	955	1345	2300	957	1343	2300	957	1340	2297	957	1338	2295	939	1309	2248
75	151	237	388	154	241	395	155	243	398	154	241	395	153	241	394
76	136	225	361	139	226	365	142	230	372	143	232	375	142	230	372
77	122	212	334	124	213	337	126	214	340	129	218	347	130	220	350
78	109	196	305	110	200	310	112	201	313	114	202	316	117	206	323
79	95	181	276	97	184	281	99	187	286	100	188	288	102	189	291
75-79	613	1051	1664	624	1064	1688	634	1075	1709	640	1081	1721	644	1086	1730
80	81	163	244	85	168	253	86	170	256	88	174	262	89	175	264
81	69	152	221	71	149	220	74	155	229	75	157	232	77	160	237
82	57	134	191	60	138	198	62	136	198	64	141	205	66	143	209
83	46	116	162	48	121	169	52	125	177	53	122	175	55	127	182
84	37	99	136	39	104	143	41	107	148	44	111	155	45	109	154
80-84	290	664	954	303	680	983	315	693	1008	324	705	1029	332	714	1046
85 and over	133	438	571	135	448	583	139	461	600	144	476	620	149	491	640
All ages	26410	27743	54153	26421	27738	54159	26457	27755	54212	26515	27794	54309	26587	27844	54431

thousands

Age-group	1987 Males	1987 Females	1987 Persons	1988 Males	1988 Females	1988 Persons	1989 Males	1989 Females	1989 Persons	1991 Males	1991 Females	1991 Persons	1996 Males	1996 Females	1996 Persons
0	440	416	856	443	419	862	446	421	867	446	421	867	417	394	811
1	428	405	833	438	414	852	441	417	858	444	420	864	423	400	823
2	413	390	803	427	403	830	437	413	850	443	418	861	430	406	836
3	388	366	754	412	389	801	426	402	828	439	415	854	435	410	845
4	360	340	700	387	366	753	411	388	799	435	411	846	438	414	852
0-4	2029	1917	3946	2107	1991	4098	2161	2041	4202	2207	2085	4292	2143	2024	4167
5	338	318	656	360	339	699	387	365	752	425	401	826	440	415	855
6	325	306	631	337	317	654	359	338	697	410	386	796	441	415	856
7	319	301	620	324	305	629	336	317	653	385	363	748	439	414	853
8	317	298	615	319	300	619	324	304	628	358	337	695	436	411	847
9	315	296	611	317	298	615	319	299	618	335	315	650	432	407	839
5-9	1614	1519	3133	1657	1559	3216	1725	1623	3348	1913	1802	3715	2188	2062	4250
10	312	292	604	315	296	611	316	297	613	323	303	626	422	397	819
11	328	308	636	312	292	604	314	295	609	318	299	617	407	383	790
12	344	323	667	328	308	636	312	292	604	316	296	612	384	361	745
13	358	337	695	344	323	667	328	308	636	314	295	609	357	335	692
14	386	362	748	357	336	693	344	322	666	311	292	603	335	314	649
10-14	1728	1622	3350	1656	1555	3211	1614	1514	3128	1582	1485	3067	1905	1790	3695
15	412	385	797	386	362	748	358	336	694	328	307	635	323	302	625
16	435	411	846	412	385	797	386	362	748	344	322	666	318	298	616
17	426	402	828	436	412	848	413	386	799	359	337	696	317	297	614
18	444	421	865	428	403	831	437	414	851	389	365	754	317	297	614
19	445	421	866	446	424	870	430	406	836	417	391	808	317	297	614
15-19	2162	2040	4202	2108	1986	4094	2024	1904	3928	1837	1722	3559	1592	1491	3083
20	462	439	901	446	422	868	448	425	873	441	418	859	334	314	648
21	465	441	906	464	440	904	447	423	870	432	408	840	352	330	682
22	477	452	929	465	441	906	464	440	904	449	426	875	366	344	710
23	476	453	929	476	452	928	464	441	905	447	423	870	393	370	763
24	466	444	910	476	452	928	476	451	927	463	439	902	419	392	811
20-24	2346	2229	4575	2327	2207	4534	2299	2180	4479	2232	2114	4346	1864	1750	3614
25	458	435	893	466	443	909	475	451	926	463	439	902	441	417	858
26	447	424	871	457	434	891	464	442	906	474	449	923	430	406	836
27	428	406	834	446	422	868	455	433	888	473	449	922	445	422	867
28	421	399	820	426	405	831	444	421	865	461	439	900	442	417	859
29	412	391	803	418	398	816	424	403	827	451	431	882	455	434	889
25-29	2166	2055	4221	2213	2102	4315	2262	2150	4412	2322	2207	4529	2213	2096	4309
30	397	377	774	410	390	800	417	397	814	440	419	859	455	434	889
31	384	365	749	394	376	770	408	389	797	420	401	821	464	444	908
32	371	353	724	382	364	746	392	376	768	412	395	807	462	444	906
33	377	360	737	369	353	722	380	363	743	404	388	792	450	434	884
34	369	361	730	375	359	734	367	352	719	388	374	762	440	426	866
30-34	1898	1816	3714	1930	1842	3772	1964	1877	3841	2064	1977	4041	2271	2182	4453
35	357	352	709	368	360	728	373	358	731	376	362	738	429	415	844
36	356	363	719	355	351	706	366	359	725	364	350	714	410	397	807
37	367	377	744	354	362	716	354	350	704	370	356	726	403	391	794
38	383	383	766	366	376	742	353	361	714	363	357	720	396	383	779
39	408	408	816	382	382	764	365	375	740	351	349	700	381	370	751
35-39	1871	1883	3754	1825	1831	3656	1811	1803	3614	1824	1774	3598	2019	1956	3975
40	450	451	901	407	407	814	381	381	762	351	359	710	370	357	727
41	352	351	703	449	450	899	406	406	812	363	373	736	358	346	704
42	349	343	692	351	350	701	448	448	896	378	379	757	364	351	715
43	354	350	704	348	342	690	350	349	699	404	404	808	357	352	709
44	339	334	673	353	349	702	346	342	688	445	446	891	346	344	690
40-44	1844	1829	3673	1908	1898	3806	1931	1926	3857	1941	1961	3902	1795	1750	3545

Figures above the dotted lines relate to persons born after mid-1977

Age-group	1987			1988			1989			1991			1996		
	Males	Females	Persons	Males	Females	Persons	Males	Females	Persons	Males	Females	Persons	Males	Females	Persons
45	308	303	611	338	333	671	352	348	700	347	348	695	345	355	700
46	289	287	576	307	302	609	336	332	668	343	340	683	357	368	725
47	309	301	610	287	286	573	305	301	606	348	346	694	370	373	743
48	310	305	615	307	300	607	285	284	569	332	329	661	394	398	792
49	308	303	611	307	304	611	305	299	604	301	298	599	433	438	871
45-49	1524	1499	3023	1546	1525	3071	1583	1564	3147	1671	1661	3332	1899	1932	3831
50	304	299	603	306	302	608	305	303	608	281	282	563	336	341	677
51	297	295	592	302	297	599	303	300	603	300	296	596	332	333	665
52	288	287	575	294	293	587	299	296	595	300	300	600	335	338	673
53	283	282	565	285	286	571	292	292	584	298	297	595	318	322	640
54	280	284	564	279	280	559	282	284	566	292	292	584	287	290	577
50-54	1452	1447	2899	1466	1458	2924	1481	1475	2956	1471	1467	2938	1608	1624	3232
55	288	294	582	277	282	559	276	278	554	285	288	573	267	274	541
56	292	303	595	284	292	576	274	280	554	275	280	555	284	287	571
57	284	302	586	287	300	587	280	290	570	269	274	543	282	290	572
58	281	298	579	280	300	580	282	298	580	265	276	541	279	286	565
59	275	293	568	276	295	571	275	297	572	271	284	555	272	281	553
55-59	1420	1490	2910	1404	1469	2873	1387	1443	2830	1365	1402	2767	1384	1418	2802
60	277	301	578	270	291	561	271	292	563	272	292	564	263	276	539
61	279	303	582	271	297	568	265	287	552	264	291	555	253	267	520
62	274	303	577	273	300	573	265	294	559	260	285	545	244	261	505
63	270	304	574	267	299	566	266	296	562	252	280	532	239	261	500
64	270	307	577	263	299	562	260	295	555	252	286	538	242	268	510
60-64	1370	1518	2888	1344	1486	2830	1327	1464	2791	1300	1434	2734	1241	1333	2574
65	275	322	597	261	303	564	255	295	550	251	287	538	241	274	515
66	279	333	612	266	317	583	253	298	551	244	285	529	230	271	501
67	286	348	634	269	327	596	256	311	567	237	285	522	223	264	487
68	182	231	413	275	341	616	258	320	578	234	287	521	214	258	472
69	171	221	392	173	225	398	262	334	596	236	299	535	210	261	471
65-69	1193	1455	2648	1244	1513	2757	1284	1558	2842	1202	1443	2645	1118	1328	2446
70	184	243	427	163	216	379	165	220	385	235	306	541	206	260	466
71	185	249	434	174	237	411	154	210	364	237	317	554	196	256	452
72	192	269	461	174	242	416	164	229	393	148	208	356	186	252	438
73	181	261	442	180	260	440	163	234	397	136	197	333	179	250	429
74	168	250	418	168	251	419	168	251	419	143	213	356	176	257	433
70-74	910	1272	2182	859	1206	2065	814	1144	1958	899	1241	2140	943	1275	2218
75	153	235	388	156	240	396	156	241	397	141	217	358	171	259	430
76	141	230	371	140	224	364	143	229	372	143	229	372	167	263	430
77	129	218	347	128	218	346	128	212	340	131	218	349	101	169	270
78	118	208	326	117	206	323	116	206	322	118	205	323	90	156	246
79	104	192	296	106	194	300	105	193	298	104	188	292	91	165	256
75-79	645	1083	1728	647	1082	1729	648	1081	1729	637	1057	1694	620	1012	1632
80	91	175	266	93	179	272	94	181	275	93	180	273	87	162	249
81	78	161	239	80	162	242	82	165	247	82	166	248	84	167	251
82	67	146	213	68	147	215	70	148	218	72	152	224	73	153	226
83	57	129	186	58	131	189	58	132	190	62	136	198	63	137	200
84	47	113	160	48	115	163	49	118	167	51	119	170	53	120	173
80-84	340	724	1064	347	734	1081	353	744	1097	360	753	1113	260	739	1099
85 and over	156	503	659	163	517	680	169	531	700	181	557	738	204	611	815
All ages	26668	27901	54569	26751	27961	54712	26837	28022	54859	27008	28142	55150	27367	28373	55740

thousands

Age-group	2001			2006			2011			2016			2017		
	Males	Females	Persons	Males	Females	Persons	Males	Females	Persons	Males	Females	Persons	Males	Females	Persons
0	372	351	723	364	344	708	396	374	770	419	396	815	419	396	815
1	377	357	734	360	340	700	388	366	754	415	392	807	417	394	811
2	385	364	749	358	338	696	379	358	737	411	388	799	414	391	805
3	394	372	766	359	338	697	371	350	721	405	383	788	410	387	797
4	403	380	783	361	341	702	365	344	709	399	376	775	405	382	787
0- 4	1931	1824	3755	1802	1701	3503	1899	1792	3691	2049	1935	3984	2065	1950	4015
5	412	388	800	367	346	713	359	339	698	392	369	761	398	375	773
6	419	395	814	373	352	725	356	335	691	383	361	744	391	368	759
7	426	402	828	382	359	741	355	334	689	376	354	730	383	360	743
8	432	406	838	391	368	759	355	334	689	368	346	714	375	353	728
9	435	410	845	400	376	776	359	337	696	362	340	702	368	346	714
5- 9	2124	2001	4125	1913	1801	3714	1784	1679	3463	1881	1770	3651	1915	1802	3717
10	438	412	850	409	385	794	364	342	706	357	335	692	361	340	701
11	438	413	851	417	392	809	372	349	721	354	332	686	357	335	692
12	437	411	848	424	399	823	380	357	737	353	331	684	354	332	686
13	435	409	844	430	405	835	390	366	756	354	333	687	353	331	684
14	431	405	836	435	408	843	399	375	774	358	336	694	354	332	686
10-14	2179	2050	4229	2115	1989	4104	1905	1789	3694	1776	1667	3443	1779	1670	3449
15	421	396	817	437	411	848	408	384	792	364	341	705	358	336	694
16	407	383	790	439	412	851	417	392	809	372	348	720	364	341	705
17	385	361	746	438	411	849	426	399	825	381	358	739	373	349	722
18	360	337	697	437	411	848	433	407	840	392	368	760	383	359	742
19	340	319	659	436	410	846	439	413	852	404	380	784	394	371	765
15-19	1913	1796	3709	2187	2055	4242	2123	1995	4118	1913	1795	3708	1872	1756	3628
20	329	309	638	428	403	831	443	418	861	415	390	805	406	382	788
21	326	306	632	414	390	804	445	419	864	424	399	823	416	391	807
22	324	304	628	392	368	760	445	418	863	432	406	838	425	399	824
23	323	302	625	364	342	706	442	416	858	438	412	850	431	406	837
24	319	298	617	342	321	663	438	412	850	441	415	856	437	411	848
20-24	1621	1519	3140	1940	1824	3764	2213	2083	4296	2150	2022	4172	2115	1989	4104
25	335	314	649	329	308	637	428	402	830	443	417	860	441	414	855
26	350	327	677	324	303	627	413	387	800	443	416	859	442	416	858
27	362	340	702	321	300	621	388	364	752	441	414	855	442	415	857
28	388	365	753	317	298	615	359	337	696	436	411	847	439	413	852
29	412	387	799	313	293	606	335	316	651	431	407	838	434	410	844
25-29	1847	1733	3580	1604	1502	3106	1923	1806	3729	2194	2065	4259	2198	2068	4266
30	432	411	843	327	309	636	321	303	624	419	397	816	429	406	835
31	420	400	820	340	322	662	315	298	613	403	382	785	417	396	813
32	435	417	852	352	335	687	311	296	607	378	359	737	401	381	782
33	431	413	844	378	360	738	307	293	600	349	333	682	376	358	734
34	445	430	875	402	383	785	303	289	592	326	312	638	347	332	679
30-34	2163	2071	4234	1799	1709	3508	1557	1479	3036	1875	1783	3658	1970	1873	3843
35	444	429	873	422	407	829	317	305	622	312	300	612	324	311	635
36	454	440	894	411	396	807	331	318	649	306	294	600	310	299	609
37	452	439	891	425	413	838	344	332	676	302	292	594	305	293	598
38	442	430	872	423	409	832	370	356	726	300	289	589	301	291	592
39	433	422	855	437	425	862	394	378	772	296	285	581	299	288	587
35-39	2225	2160	4385	2118	2050	4168	1756	1689	3445	1516	1460	2976	1539	1482	3021
40	422	410	832	437	424	861	415	402	817	312	300	612	296	285	581
41	404	392	796	448	434	882	405	391	796	326	314	640	310	299	609
42	397	386	783	446	434	880	419	408	827	338	327	665	325	313	638
43	390	378	768	435	425	860	417	404	821	364	352	716	337	326	663
44	375	365	740	426	417	843	430	419	849	388	373	761	363	351	714
40-44	1988	1931	3919	2192	2134	4326	2086	2024	4110	1728	1666	3394	1631	1574	3205

Figures above the dotted line relate to persons born after mid-1977.

Age-group	2001 Males	2001 Females	2001 Persons	2006 Males	2006 Females	2006 Persons	2011 Males	2011 Females	2011 Persons	2016 Males	2016 Females	2016 Persons	2017 Males	2017 Females	2017 Persons
45	364	353	717	415	405	820	430	419	849	408	398	806	387	372	759
46	351	341	692	396	387	783	440	429	869	397	386	783	406	396	802
47	357	346	703	389	381	770	437	428	865	411	402	813	395	385	780
48	349	346	695	380	372	752	425	418	843	407	397	804	408	400	808
49	336	338	674	365	358	723	414	409	823	419	412	831	404	396	800
45-49	1757	1724	3481	1945	1903	3848	2146	2103	4249	2042	1995	4037	2000	1949	3949
50	334	348	682	352	346	698	403	397	800	417	411	828	416	411	827
51	344	361	705	339	334	673	383	379	762	424	420	844	413	409	822
52	356	365	721	343	338	681	374	372	746	421	419	840	421	418	839
53	378	388	766	334	338	672	364	364	728	407	408	815	416	416	832
54	414	427	841	321	329	650	348	349	697	396	398	794	403	405	808
50-54	1826	1889	3715	1689	1685	3374	1872	1861	3733	2065	2056	4121	2069	2059	4128
55	320	331	651	318	338	656	335	336	671	383	386	769	391	396	787
56	314	322	636	326	349	675	321	324	645	362	367	729	378	383	761
57	315	327	642	336	353	689	323	327	650	352	360	712	358	365	723
58	298	310	608	354	375	729	314	326	640	342	351	693	347	357	704
59	267	280	547	385	411	796	299	317	616	325	336	661	336	347	683
55-59	1514	1570	3084	1719	1826	3545	1592	1630	3222	1764	1800	3564	1810	1848	3658
60	247	263	510	296	318	614	294	324	618	311	323	634	319	333	652
61	261	274	535	288	308	596	300	334	634	295	309	604	305	319	624
62	257	275	532	288	311	599	307	336	643	296	312	608	289	306	595
63	252	271	523	270	294	564	321	355	676	285	309	594	289	308	597
64	243	265	508	240	263	503	346	388	734	269	299	568	278	305	583
60-64	1260	1348	2608	1382	1494	2876	1568	1737	3305	1456	1552	3008	1480	1571	3051
65	233	259	492	219	246	465	263	299	562	263	305	568	262	295	557
66	221	249	470	229	256	485	254	288	542	264	312	576	255	300	555
67	211	242	453	223	256	479	250	289	539	268	313	581	256	308	564
68	204	240	444	215	250	465	231	271	502	277	328	605	259	307	566
69	202	245	447	205	243	448	203	242	445	294	357	651	266	322	588
65-69	1071	1235	2306	1091	1251	2342	1201	1389	2590	1366	1615	2981	1298	1532	2830
70	198	248	446	193	235	428	182	224	406	220	272	492	282	349	631
71	186	243	429	179	224	403	187	231	418	208	260	468	210	266	476
72	176	235	411	168	215	383	178	228	406	201	259	460	198	253	451
73	165	226	391	158	212	370	168	220	388	182	240	422	190	251	441
74	158	225	383	153	212	365	157	211	368	156	210	366	171	232	403
70-74	883	1177	2060	851	1098	1949	872	1114	1986	967	1241	2208	1051	1351	2402
75	151	221	372	146	212	358	143	201	344	136	192	328	145	203	348
76	139	213	352	133	204	337	129	189	318	136	195	331	127	185	312
77	129	206	335	123	192	315	118	177	295	126	189	315	125	186	311
78	120	199	319	111	181	292	107	170	277	115	178	293	115	179	294
79	113	200	313	103	176	279	101	167	268	104	167	271	105	169	274
75-79	652	1039	1691	616	965	1581	598	904	1502	617	921	1538	617	922	1539
80	106	195	301	94	168	262	93	162	255	91	155	246	93	157	250
81	99	192	291	84	157	241	81	151	232	79	141	220	82	144	226
82	57	119	176	74	146	220	71	138	209	69	128	197	70	130	200
83	49	106	155	65	136	201	61	125	186	60	119	179	60	117	177
84	47	107	154	59	131	190	54	116	170	54	111	165	52	108	160
80-84	358	719	1077	376	738	1114	360	692	1052	353	654	1007	357	656	1013
85 and over	213	634	847	221	646	867	233	672	905	232	665	897	233	662	895
All ages	27525	28420	55945	27560	28371	55931	27688	28438	56126	27944	28662	56606	27999	28714	56713

Appendix Table IVd Projected Total population as at mid-year, by sex, age and marital condition, 1977-2017; mid-1977 based projections

Age	1977	1978	1979	1980	1981	1982	1986	1991	1996	2001	2006	2011	2016	2017
Married males *(thousands)*														
0-14	-	-	-	-	-	-	-	-	-	-	-	-	-	-
15-19	32	32	32	35	36	35	34	30	23	24	32	32	28	28
20-24	607	591	583	589	600	612	660	625	521	430	507	605	589	579
25-29	1356	1289	1251	1225	1217	1222	1298	1415	1326	1095	948	1143	1310	1310
30-34	1563	1602	1604	1599	1584	1490	1400	1517	1652	1554	1290	1120	1350	1419
35-39	1350	1359	1383	1403	1446	1550	1599	1433	1560	1704	1611	1334	1154	1172
40-44	1332	1339	1347	1347	1326	1316	1429	1594	1435	1566	1717	1627	1344	1268
45-49	1346	1329	1310	1295	1283	1283	1293	1403	1568	1416	1551	1703	1612	1578
50-54	1374	1343	1321	1302	1285	1275	1225	1240	1350	1509	1369	1501	1647	1648
55-59	1316	1371	1414	1350	1308	1271	1196	1144	1160	1266	1419	1290	1417	1451
60-64	1164	1098	1038	1082	1126	1168	1164	1071	1029	1046	1146	1285	1172	1188
65-69	1010	1010	1009	1008	988	956	936	969	897	867	887	976	1097	1039
70-74	695	710	721	729	733	734	722	695	721	675	655	676	752	816
75-79	352	370	383	398	408	419	444	441	434	452	428	421	438	438
80-84	132	135	142	147	154	162	189	208	209	211	220	213	212	216
85 and over	48	47	46	45	46	48	55	70	79	83	89	93	92	93
All ages	13677	13625	13584	13554	13540	13541	13644	13855	13964	13898	13869	14019	14214	14243
Other males *(thousands)*														
0-14	6227	6083	5931	5779	5644	5521	5350	5702	6233	6233	5829	5586	5704	5758
15-19	2127	2174	2224	2267	2281	2286	2172	1807	1569	1889	2155	2092	1885	1844
20-24	1357	1406	1448	1490	1533	1573	1681	1607	1344	1191	1433	1608	1561	1536
25-29	606	627	652	673	700	725	816	907	887	752	656	780	884	888
30-34	353	379	401	420	433	426	468	547	619	609	509	437	525	551
35-39	234	247	261	275	290	324	373	391	459	521	507	422	362	367
40-44	211	219	227	236	238	242	279	347	360	422	475	459	384	363
45-49	222	223	223	224	225	227	237	268	331	341	394	443	430	422
50-54	231	231	233	234	236	234	225	231	258	317	321	371	418	421
55-59	217	231	244	242	240	239	236	221	224	248	300	302	348	359
60-64	217	207	197	203	213	224	240	229	213	214	236	283	284	292
65-69	229	229	228	228	224	219	211	233	221	204	204	226	269	259
70-74	220	220	222	222	222	222	217	204	223	209	196	196	216	236
75-79	175	181	187	189	192	194	200	196	186	200	188	177	179	179
80-84	114	114	114	118	124	128	143	152	151	147	156	147	141	141
85 and over	79	81	83	85	85	85	95	111	125	130	132	140	140	140
All ages	12819	12852	12875	12885	12880	12869	12943	13153	13403	13627	13691	13669	13730	13756
Males - *proportions married*														
0-14	-	-	-	-	-	-	-	-	-	-	-	-	-	-
15-19	0.015	0.015	0.014	0.015	0.016	0.015	0.015	0.016	0.014	0.013	0.015	0.015	0.015	0.015
20-24	0.309	0.296	0.287	0.283	0.281	0.280	0.282	0.280	0.279	0.265	0.261	0.273	0.274	0.274
25-29	0.691	0.673	0.657	0.645	0.635	0.628	0.614	0.609	0.599	0.593	0.591	0.594	0.597	0.596
30-34	0.816	0.809	0.800	0.792	0.785	0.778	0.749	0.735	0.727	0.718	0.717	0.719	0.720	0.720
35-39	0.852	0.846	0.841	0.836	0.833	0.827	0.811	0.786	0.773	0.766	0.761	0.760	0.761	0.762
40-44	0.863	0.859	0.856	0.851	0.848	0.845	0.837	0.821	0.799	0.788	0.783	0.780	0.778	0.777
45-49	0.858	0.856	0.855	0.853	0.851	0.850	0.845	0.840	0.826	0.806	0.797	0.794	0.789	0.789
50-54	0.856	0.853	0.850	0.848	0.845	0.845	0.845	0.843	0.840	0.826	0.810	0.802	0.798	0.797
55-59	0.858	0.856	0.853	0.848	0.845	0.842	0.835	0.838	0.838	0.836	0.825	0.810	0.803	0.802
60-64	0.843	0.841	0.840	0.842	0.841	0.839	0.829	0.824	0.829	0.830	0.829	0.820	0.805	0.803
65-69	0.815	0.815	0.816	0.816	0.815	0.814	0.816	0.806	0.802	0.810	0.813	0.812	0.803	0.800
70-74	0.760	0.763	0.765	0.767	0.768	0.768	0.769	0.773	0.764	0.764	0.770	0.775	0.777	0.776
75-79	0.668	0.672	0.672	0.678	0.680	0.684	0.689	0.692	0.700	0.693	0.695	0.704	0.710	0.710
80-84	0.537	0.542	0.555	0.555	0.554	0.559	0.569	0.578	0.581	0.589	0.585	0.592	0.601	0.605
85 and over	0.378	0.367	0.357	0.346	0.351	0.361	0.367	0.387	0.387	0.390	0.403	0.399	0.397	0.399
15 and over	0.675	0.668	0.662	0.656	0.652	0.648	0.642	0.650	0.661	0.653	0.638	0.634	0.639	0.640

Age	1977	1978	1979	1980	1981	1982	1986	1991	1996	2001	2006	2011	2016	2017
Married females *(thousands)*														
0–14	–	–	–	–	–	–	–	–	–	–	–	–	–	–
15–19	134	135	139	143	146	148	144	129	106	119	143	142	131	129
20–24	1010	989	976	981	995	1014	1101	1065	918	790	919	1060	1042	1029
25–29	1559	1490	1445	1414	1399	1401	1484	1645	1586	1330	1148	1364	1565	1570
30–34	1633	1684	1694	1701	1692	1592	1466	1589	1766	1692	1403	1210	1453	1529
35–39	1354	1370	1398	1423	1469	1586	1667	1463	1598	1776	1694	1397	1208	1225
40–44	1309	1314	1323	1323	1303	1299	1425	1634	1441	1578	1750	1665	1373	1298
45–49	1342	1321	1293	1267	1251	1243	1250	1379	1589	1403	1536	1701	1619	1583
50–54	1346	1319	1300	1283	1270	1251	1174	1183	1313	1515	1338	1465	1623	1626
55–59	1252	1304	1344	1285	1243	1210	1144	1065	1078	1201	1384	1225	1344	1380
60–64	1034	979	930	976	1022	1063	1057	976	914	930	1039	1198	1065	1076
65–69	828	828	829	830	812	791	791	819	763	719	736	829	958	908
70–74	526	530	535	537	541	539	534	529	547	518	492	507	578	632
75–79	250	255	259	264	266	270	281	281	287	298	284	273	286	288
80–84	89	88	88	89	90	91	98	104	107	113	117	114	113	115
85 and over	30	26	24	24	23	23	22	26	28	30	32	35	36	35
All ages	13696	13632	13577	13540	13522	13521	13638	13887	14041	14012	14015	14185	14394	14423
Other females *(thousands)*														
0–14	5895	5754	5605	5459	5327	5209	5037	5370	5875	5873	5490	5259	5369	5420
15–19	1912	1957	2002	2041	2053	2054	1943	1593	1385	1677	1912	1853	1664	1627
20–24	847	894	943	986	1026	1059	1125	1049	832	729	905	1023	980	960
25–29	369	386	403	407	420	440	518	562	510	403	354	442	500	498
30–34	240	260	278	301	317	313	329	389	416	379	306	269	330	345
35–39	189	199	212	225	240	267	319	311	358	384	356	292	252	257
40–44	194	201	209	216	221	223	261	327	309	353	384	360	293	276
45–49	235	234	235	235	234	238	251	282	343	321	367	402	376	366
50–54	307	300	294	294	292	290	277	284	311	374	348	396	433	433
55–59	403	419	432	414	400	388	365	338	340	369	442	405	456	468
60–64	535	508	480	484	496	510	504	458	419	419	455	539	487	495
65–69	704	700	695	691	675	656	612	624	565	516	515	560	658	624
70–74	786	796	804	808	809	806	775	712	728	659	606	607	664	719
75–79	721	739	752	763	771	781	805	776	725	742	681	631	635	634
80–84	499	512	530	544	561	573	616	649	632	606	621	578	541	541
85 and over	362	373	382	392	404	415	469	531	584	604	614	637	630	628
All ages	14198	14232	14256	14260	14246	14222	14206	14255	14332	14408	14356	14253	14268	14291
Females – *proportions married*														
0–14	–	–	–	–	–	–	–	–	–	–	–	–	–	–
15–19	0.065	0.065	0.065	0.065	0.066	0.067	0.069	0.075	0.071	0.066	0.070	0.071	0.073	0.073
20–24	0.544	0.525	0.509	0.499	0.492	0.489	0.495	0.504	0.525	0.520	0.504	0.509	0.515	0.517
25–29	0.809	0.794	0.782	0.776	0.769	0.761	0.741	0.745	0.757	0.767	0.764	0.755	0.758	0.759
30–34	0.872	0.866	0.859	0.850	0.842	0.836	0.817	0.803	0.809	0.817	0.821	0.818	0.815	0.816
35–39	0.878	0.873	0.868	0.863	0.860	0.856	0.839	0.825	0.817	0.822	0.826	0.827	0.827	0.827
40–44	0.871	0.867	0.864	0.860	0.855	0.853	0.845	0.833	0.823	0.817	0.820	0.822	0.824	0.825
45–49	0.851	0.850	0.846	0.844	0.842	0.839	0.833	0.830	0.822	0.814	0.807	0.809	0.812	0.812
50–54	0.814	0.815	0.816	0.814	0.813	0.812	0.809	0.806	0.808	0.802	0.794	0.787	0.789	0.790
55–59	0.756	0.757	0.757	0.756	0.757	0.757	0.758	0.759	0.760	0.765	0.758	0.752	0.747	0.747
60–64	0.659	0.658	0.660	0.668	0.673	0.676	0.677	0.681	0.686	0.689	0.695	0.690	0.686	0.685
65–69	0.540	0.542	0.544	0.546	0.546	0.547	0.564	0.568	0.575	0.582	0.588	0.597	0.593	0.593
70–74	0.401	0.400	0.400	0.399	0.401	0.401	0.408	0.426	0.429	0.440	0.448	0.455	0.465	0.468
75–79	0.257	0.257	0.256	0.257	0.257	0.257	0.259	0.266	0.284	0.287	0.294	0.302	0.311	0.312
80–84	0.151	0.147	0.142	0.141	0.138	0.137	0.137	0.138	0.145	0.157	0.159	0.165	0.173	0.175
85 and over	0.077	0.065	0.059	0.058	0.054	0.053	0.045	0.047	0.046	0.047	0.050	0.052	0.054	0.053
15 and over	0.623	0.617	0.611	0.606	0.603	0.600	0.598	0.610	0.624	0.621	0.613	0.612	0.618	0.619

Appendix Table Va Actual and projected Total population as at mid-year by sex and age-groups 1951, 1961, 1971 to 2017; mid-1977 based projections.

Northern Ireland

thousands

Year	Age in years 0-14	15-44		45-64	45-59	65 and over	60 and over	All ages		
	Persons	Males	Females	Males	Females	Males	Females	Males	Females	Persons
1951	379	289	298	128	115	60	105	671	703	1374
1961	413	278	386	146	125	62	119	697	732	1429
1971	457	297	296	152	126	67	138	751	782	1533
1972	457	300	296	151	126	68	139	754	782	1536
1973	455	302	297	150	124	68	140	754	781	1535
1974	452	304	298	149	124	68	141	754	781	1535
1975	445	306	298	148	122	68	142	752	777	1528
1976	440	309	301	147	122	69	140	752	776	1528
1977	433	315	305	145	121	69	141	753	776	1529
1978	425	319	307	145	122	70	141	753	776	1529
1979	417	323	311	144	122	70	142	753	776	1529
1980	411	330	315	142	120	70	142	754	776	1530
1981	405	333	318	142	120	71	143	755	777	1532
1982	398	338	322	142	119	70	144	756	777	1533
1983	395	340	325	142	118	70	145	757	778	1535
1984	392	344	327	142	118	70	145	759	779	1538
1985	391	348	330	141	117	70	144	761	780	1541
1986	389	350	334	140	116	71	145	763	782	1545
1987	388	353	336	140	115	71	145	765	783	1548
1988	389	355	335	140	117	71	145	767	785	1552
1989	394	353	335	142	117	71	145	770	787	1557
1990	398	352	334	143	117	71	145	772	788	1560
1991	403	352	333	142	118	72	145	775	790	1565
1992	408	350	332	146	120	71	143	778	792	1570
1993	412	350	331	145	120	72	144	780	794	1574
1994	417	349	331	146	121	72	142	783	795	1578
1995	422	348	330	148	122	71	141	785	797	1582
1996	423	349	331	149	121	70	142	787	798	1585
1997	425	350	332	149	120	70	142	789	799	1588
1998	425	351	332	150	121	70	142	791	800	1591
1999	425	351	332	153	123	69	141	793	801	1594
2000	424	353	334	152	123	69	141	794	802	1596
2001	421	352	333	155	125	70	141	795	802	1597
2002	417	353	334	157	128	70	140	796	803	1599
2003	416	352	334	159	128	70	141	797	803	1600
2004	412	353	333	162	130	70	141	798	803	1601
2005	407	352	333	165	132	70	142	798	803	1601
2006	404	352	332	169	134	69	142	799	803	1602
2007	401	351	331	172	135	69	144	800	803	1603
2008	396	350	330	174	138	71	145	800	804	1604
2009	395	348	328	176	141	72	145	801	804	1605
2010	390	346	326	181	145	73	145	802	804	1606
2011	388	345	326	183	147	74	145	803	805	1608
2012	388	342	325	186	150	75	144	804	806	1610
2013	386	342	322	187	153	76	145	805	806	1611
2014	387	339	320	190	155	77	145	806	807	1613
2015	386	338	320	192	157	77	145	807	808	1615
2016	388	337	317	193	157	77	148	808	809	1617
2017	390	336	315	193	158	79	149	810	810	1620

Appendix Table Vb Annual changes in projected Total population 1977 to 2017; mid-1977 based projections   **Northern Ireland**

thousands

Mid-year to mid-year	Population at beginning or period	Births	Deaths	Natural increase	Net migration	Total increase
1977-1978	1529	26	17	9	-9	0
1978-1979	1529	27	17	9	-9	0
1979-1980	1529	27	17	10	-9	1
1980-1981	1530	28	17	11	-9	2
1981-1982	1532	28	17	10	-9	1
1982-1983	1533	29	18	11	-9	2
1983-1984	1535	29	18	12	-9	3
1984-1985	1538	30	18	12	-9	3
1985-1986	1541	30	18	13	-9	4
1986-1987	1545	30	18	12	-9	3
1987-1988	1548	31	18	13	-9	4
1988-1989	1552	31	18	14	-9	5
1989-1990	1557	31	18	12	-9	3
1990-1991	1560	31	18	14	-9	5
1991-1992	1565	31	18	14	-9	5
1992-1993	1570	31	18	13	-9	4
1993-1994	1574	31	18	13	-9	4
1994-1995	1578	31	18	13	-9	4
1995-1996	1582	30	18	12	-9	3
1996-1997	1585	30	18	12	-9	3
1997-1998	1588	29	18	12	-9	3
1998-1999	1591	29	17	12	-9	3
1999-2000	1594	28	17	11	-9	2
2000-2001	1596	28	17	10	-9	1
2001-2002	1597	28	17	11	-9	2
2002-2003	1599	27	17	10	-9	1
2003-2004	1600	27	17	10	-9	1
2004-2005	1601	27	17	9	-9	0
2005-2006	1601	27	17	10	-9	1
2006-2007	1602	27	17	10	-9	1
2007-2008	1603	27	17	10	-9	1
2008-2009	1604	27	17	10	-9	1
2009-2010	1605	28	17	10	-9	1
2010-2011	1606	28	17	11	-9	2
2011 2012	1608	28	17	11	-9	2
2012-2013	1610	28	17	10	-9	1
2013-2014	1611	28	18	11	-9	2
2014-2015	1613	29	18	11	-9	2
2015-2016	1615	29	18	11	-9	2
2016-2017	1617	29	18	12	-9	3
2017-2018	1620					

Appendix Table Vc Projected Total population as at mid-year, by sex and single ages 1977 to 1989, 1991-2017; mid-1977 based projections.

thousands

Age-group	1977 Males	Females	Persons	1978 Males	Females	Persons	1979 Males	Females	Persons	1980 Males	Females	Persons	1981 Males	Females	Persons
0	13	12	25	13	12	25	13	12	25	14	13	27	14	13	27
1	13	13	26	12	12	24	13	12	25	13	12	25	14	12	26
2	13	12	25	13	12	25	13	12	25	13	12	25	13	12	25
3	14	13	27	13	12	25	13	12	25	12	12	24	13	12	25
4	14	13	27	14	13	27	13	12	25	13	12	25	12	12	24
0-4	67	63	130	65	61	126	65	60	125	65	61	126	66	61	127
5	15	14	29	14	13	27	13	13	26	13	12	25	13	12	25
6	15	14	29	15	14	29	14	13	27	13	13	26	13	12	25
7	15	14	29	15	14	29	15	13	28	14	13	27	13	12	25
8	15	15	30	15	14	29	15	14	29	15	13	28	14	13	27
9	16	14	30	15	15	30	15	14	29	15	14	29	15	14	29
5-9	76	71	147	74	70	144	72	67	139	70	65	135	68	63	131
10	16	15	31	16	15	31	15	15	30	15	14	29	14	14	28
11	16	15	31	16	15	31	16	14	30	15	15	30	15	14	29
12	17	15	32	16	15	31	16	15	31	15	14	29	15	15	30
13	16	15	31	16	15	31	16	15	31	16	15	31	15	14	29
14	16	15	31	16	15	31	16	15	31	16	15	31	16	15	31
10-14	81	75	156	80	75	155	79	74	153	77	73	150	75	72	147
15	15	15	30	16	15	31	16	15	31	16	15	31	16	15	31
16	15	14	29	15	14	29	16	15	31	16	15	31	16	15	31
17	15	14	29	15	14	29	15	14	29	15	14	29	16	15	31
18	14	13	27	14	14	28	15	14	29	15	14	29	15	14	29
19	14	13	27	14	13	27	14	13	27	15	14	29	14	14	28
15-19	73	69	142	74	70	144	76	71	147	77	72	149	77	73	150
20	13	12	25	13	13	26	14	13	27	14	13	27	15	13	28
21	12	12	24	13	12	25	13	13	26	14	13	27	14	13	27
22	12	11	23	12	12	24	12	12	24	13	12	25	13	12	25
23	11	11	22	11	11	22	12	11	23	12	12	24	13	12	25
24	11	10	21	11	10	21	11	10	21	12	11	23	12	12	24
20-24	59	56	115	60	58	118	62	59	121	65	61	126	67	62	129
25	11	9	20	10	10	20	11	11	22	11	10	21	12	11	23
26	10	9	19	10	9	19	10	10	20	10	10	20	11	10	21
27	10	10	20	10	9	19	10	9	19	10	10	20	10	10	20
28	10	10	20	10	10	20	9	9	18	10	9	19	10	10	20
29	10	10	20	10	9	19	10	9	19	10	9	19	9	9	18
25-29	51	48	99	50	47	97	50	48	98	51	48	99	52	50	102
30	11	10	21	10	10	20	10	9	19	10	9	19	9	9	18
31	10	9	19	11	10	21	10	10	20	10	9	19	10	9	19
32	10	10	20	10	9	19	10	10	20	10	10	20	10	9	19
33	10	10	20	10	10	20	10	9	19	10	10	20	10	10	20
34	10	10	20	10	10	20	10	10	20	10	10	20	10	10	20
30-34	51	49	100	51	49	100	50	48	98	50	48	98	49	47	96
35	9	9	18	10	10	20	10	10	20	10	9	19	10	9	19
36	9	8	17	9	9	18	10	10	20	10	10	20	10	10	20
37	8	8	16	9	8	17	9	8	17	10	10	20	10	9	19
38	8	9	17	8	8	16	8	8	16	9	8	17	10	10	20
39	8	8	16	8	8	16	8	8	16	8	8	16	8	8	16
35-39	42	42	84	44	43	87	45	44	89	47	45	92	48	46	94
40	8	9	17	8	8	16	8	9	17	8	8	16	8	8	16
41	8	8	16	8	8	16	8	8	16	8	9	17	8	8	16
42	8	8	16	8	8	16	8	8	16	8	8	16	8	8	16
43	8	8	16	8	8	16	8	8	16	8	8	16	8	8	16
44	7	8	15	8	8	16	8	8	16	8	8	16	8	8	16
40-44	39	41	80	40	40	80	40	41	81	40	41	81	40	40	80

Figures above the dotted line relate to persons born after mid-1977.

Age-group	1977			1978			1979			1980			1981		
	Males	Females	Persons	Males	Females	Persons	Males	Females	Persons	Males	Females	Persons	Males	Females	Persons
45	8	8	16	7	8	15	8	8	16	8	8	16	8	8	16
46	8	9	17	8	8	16	7	8	15	7	8	15	8	8	16
47	8	8	16	8	9	17	7	8	15	7	8	15	7	8	15
48	7	8	15	8	8	16	8	9	17	7	8	15	7	8	15
49	7	8	15	7	8	15	8	8	16	8	8	16	7	8	15
45–49	38	41	79	38	41	79	38	41	79	37	40	77	37	40	77
50	8	9	17	7	8	15	8	8	16	8	8	16	8	8	16
51	8	8	16	8	9	17	7	8	15	7	8	15	8	8	16
52	7	8	15	8	8	16	8	8	16	7	8	15	7	8	15
53	8	8	16	7	8	15	8	8	16	8	8	16	7	8	15
54	7	8	15	8	8	16	7	8	15	7	8	15	7	8	15
50–54	38	41	79	38	41	79	37	40	77	37	40	77	37	40	77
55	8	9	17	7	8	15	7	8	15	8	8	16	8	8	16
56	8	8	16	8	9	17	7	8	15	7	8	15	7	8	15
57	8	8	16	8	8	16	8	9	17	7	8	15	7	8	15
58	7	7	14	8	8	16	8	8	16	7	8	15	7	8	15
59	6	7	13	7	7	14	8	8	16	8	8	16	7	8	15
55–59	37	39	76	38	40	78	38	41	79	37	40	77	36	40	76
60	6	7	13	7	7	14	7	7	14	7	8	15	7	8	15
61	6	7	13	6	7	13	6	7	13	6	7	13	7	8	15
62	7	8	15	6	7	13	6	7	13	6	6	12	6	7	13
63	6	7	13	6	7	13	6	7	13	6	7	13	6	6	12
64	7	8	15	6	7	13	6	7	13	6	7	13	6	7	13
60–64	32	37	69	31	35	66	31	35	66	31	35	66	32	36	68
65	6	7	13	6	8	14	6	7	13	6	7	13	6	6	12
66	6	8	14	6	7	13	6	8	14	6	7	13	6	7	13
67	6	7	13	6	7	13	6	7	13	6	7	13	5	7	12
68	5	7	12	5	7	12	5	7	12	5	7	12	6	7	13
69	5	7	12	5	7	12	5	7	12	5	7	12	5	7	12
65–69	28	36	64	28	36	64	28	36	64	28	35	63	28	34	62
70	5	6	11	5	7	12	5	6	11	5	7	12	5	7	12
71	4	6	10	4	6	10	4	6	10	4	6	10	4	6	10
72	4	6	10	4	6	10	4	6	10	4	6	10	4	6	10
73	4	6	10	4	6	10	4	6	10	4	6	10	4	6	10
74	3	5	8	4	5	9	4	6	10	4	5	9	4	5	9
70–74	20	29	49	21	30	51	21	30	51	21	30	51	21	30	51
75	3	5	8	3	5	8	3	5	8	3	5	8	3	5	8
76	3	5	8	3	5	8	3	5	8	3	5	8	3	5	8
77	3	4	7	3	5	8	3	4	7	3	4	7	3	4	7
78	2	4	6	2	4	6	2	4	6	2	4	6	2	4	6
79	2	3	5	2	3	5	2	4	6	2	4	6	2	4	6
75–79	13	21	34	13	22	35	13	22	35	13	22	35	13	22	35
80	2	3	5	2	3	5	2	3	5	2	3	5	2	4	6
81	1	3	4	1	3	4	1	3	4	1	3	4	2	3	5
82	1	2	3	1	2	3	1	2	3	1	3	4	1	3	4
83	1	2	3	1	2	3	1	2	3	1	2	3	1	2	3
84	1	2	3	1	2	3	1	2	3	1	2	3	1	2	3
80–84	6	12	18	6	12	18	6	12	18	6	13	19	7	14	21
85 and over	2	6	8	2	6	8	2	7	9	2	7	9	2	7	9
All ages	753	776	1529	753	776	1529	753	776	1529	754	776	1530	755	777	1532

thousands

Age-group	1982			1983			1984			1985			1986		
	Males	Females	Persons	Males	Females	Persons	Males	Females	Persons	Males	Females	Persons	Males	Females	Persons
0	14	13	27	15	13	28	15	14	29	15	14	29	15	14	29
1	14	13	27	14	13	27	14	13	27	15	14	29	15	14	29
2	13	12	25	14	13	27	14	13	27	14	13	27	14	13	27
3	13	12	25	13	12	25	14	13	27	14	13	27	14	13	27
4	13	12	25	13	12	25	13	12	25	13	12	25	14	13	27
0-4	67	62	129	69	63	132	70	65	135	71	66	137	72	67	139
5	12	12	24	13	11	24	13	12	25	13	12	25	14	12	26
6	13	12	25	12	12	24	13	11	24	13	12	25	13	12	25
7	13	11	24	13	12	25	12	11	23	12	11	23	13	12	25
8	13	12	25	12	12	24	13	12	25	12	12	24	12	11	23
9	14	13	27	13	12	25	12	12	24	13	12	25	12	12	24
5-9	65	60	125	63	59	122	63	58	121	63	59	122	64	59	123
10	14	14	28	14	13	27	13	12	25	13	12	25	13	12	25
11	15	14	29	15	13	28	14	13	27	13	12	25	12	11	23
12	15	14	29	14	14	28	14	13	27	14	13	27	13	12	25
13	15	14	29	15	14	29	14	14	28	14	13	27	14	13	27
14	15	14	29	15	14	29	15	14	29	14	14	28	14	13	27
10-14	74	70	144	73	68	141	70	66	136	68	64	132	66	61	127
15	16	15	31	15	14	29	15	14	29	14	14	28	14	13	27
16	16	14	30	15	15	30	15	14	29	15	14	29	15	14	29
17	16	15	31	16	14	30	15	14	29	15	14	29	14	14	28
18	15	15	30	16	15	31	15	14	29	15	14	29	15	14	29
19	15	14	29	15	14	29	16	15	31	15	14	29	15	14	29
15-19	78	73	151	77	72	149	76	71	147	74	70	144	73	69	142
20	14	14	28	15	14	29	15	14	29	15	14	29	15	14	29
21	14	13	27	14	13	27	15	14	29	15	14	29	15	14	29
22	14	13	27	14	13	27	14	13	27	14	13	27	15	14	29
23	13	12	25	13	13	26	14	13	27	14	13	27	14	13	27
24	13	12	25	13	12	25	13	12	25	14	13	27	13	13	26
20-24	68	64	132	69	65	134	71	66	137	72	67	139	72	68	140
25	12	11	23	13	12	25	13	12	25	13	12	25	14	13	27
26	11	11	22	12	11	23	12	12	24	12	12	24	13	12	25
27	11	10	21	11	11	22	12	11	23	12	11	23	12	12	24
28	10	10	20	10	10	20	11	10	21	12	11	23	12	11	23
29	10	10	20	10	10	20	10	10	20	11	11	22	11	11	22
25-29	54	52	106	56	54	110	58	55	113	60	57	117	62	59	121
30	9	9	18	10	9	19	10	10	20	10	10	20	11	10	21
31	9	9	18	9	9	18	10	9	19	10	10	20	10	10	20
32	10	9	19	9	9	18	9	9	18	10	9	19	9	10	19
33	10	9	19	9	9	18	9	8	17	9	9	18	10	9	19
34	10	9	19	10	9	19	9	9	18	9	8	17	9	9	18
30-34	48	45	93	47	45	92	47	45	92	48	46	94	49	48	97
35	10	10	20	10	10	20	10	9	19	9	9	18	9	8	17
36	10	9	19	10	10	20	10	10	20	10	9	19	9	9	18
37	9	9	18	10	9	19	10	10	20	10	9	19	10	9	19
38	10	10	20	9	9	18	10	9	19	10	10	20	10	9	19
39	10	10	20	10	9	19	9	9	18	10	9	19	10	10	20
35-39	49	48	97	49	47	96	49	47	96	49	46	95	48	45	93
40	9	8	17	10	10	20	10	10	20	9	9	18	10	9	19
41	8	8	16	8	8	16	9	9	18	10	9	19	9	9	18
42	8	8	16	8	8	16	8	8	16	10	10	20	10	9	19
43	8	8	16	8	8	16	8	8	16	8	8	16	9	10	19
44	8	8	16	8	8	16	8	8	16	8	8	16	8	8	16
40-44	41	40	81	42	42	84	43	43	86	45	44	89	46	45	91

Figures above the dotted line relate to persons born after mid-1977

Age-group	1982			1983			1984			1985			1986		
	Males	Females	Persons	Males	Females	Persons	Males	Females	Persons	Males	Females	Persons	Males	Females	Persons
45	8	8	16	8	8	16	8	8	16	8	8	16	8	7	15
46	8	8	16	8	8	16	8	8	16	8	8	16	8	8	16
47	7	8	15	8	8	16	8	8	16	8	8	16	8	8	16
48	7	8	15	7	8	15	7	8	15	8	8	16	8	8	16
49	7	8	15	7	7	14	7	8	15	7	8	15	7	8	15
45–49	37	40	77	38	39	77	38	40	78	39	40	79	39	39	78
50	7	8	15	7	8	15	8	7	15	7	8	15	7	8	15
51	8	8	16	7	8	15	7	8	15	7	7	14	7	8	15
52	7	8	15	8	8	16	7	8	15	7	8	15	7	7	14
53	7	8	15	7	8	15	7	8	15	7	7	14	7	8	15
54	7	8	15	7	8	15	7	8	15	7	8	15	7	7	14
50–54	36	40	76	36	40	76	36	39	75	35	38	73	35	38	73
55	8	8	16	7	8	15	7	8	15	7	8	15	7	8	15
56	7	8	15	7	8	15	7	8	15	7	8	15	7	8	15
57	7	8	15	7	8	15	7	8	15	7	8	15	7	8	15
58	7	8	15	7	7	14	7	8	15	7	8	15	6	7	13
59	7	7	14	7	8	15	7	7	14	7	7	14	7	8	15
55–59	36	39	75	35	39	74	35	39	74	35	39	74	34	39	73
60	7	8	15	7	8	15	7	8	15	7	8	15	7	8	15
61	7	8	15	7	8	15	6	7	13	7	8	15	7	8	15
62	7	8	15	7	8	15	7	8	15	6	7	13	6	7	13
63	6	7	13	6	7	13	7	8	15	6	8	14	6	7	13
64	6	6	12	6	7	13	6	7	13	6	7	13	6	7	13
60–64	33	37	70	33	38	71	33	38	71	32	38	70	32	37	69
65	5	6	11	6	6	12	6	7	13	6	7	13	6	7	13
66	5	6	11	5	6	11	5	6	11	5	6	11	6	7	13
67	6	7	13	5	6	11	5	6	11	5	6	11	5	6	11
68	5	7	12	5	7	12	5	6	11	5	6	11	5	6	11
69	6	7	13	5	7	12	5	6	11	5	6	11	5	6	11
65–69	27	33	60	26	32	58	26	31	57	26	31	57	27	32	59
70	5	6	11	5	7	12	5	7	12	5	6	11	4	6	10
71	4	7	11	5	6	11	5	6	11	4	6	10	5	6	11
72	4	6	10	4	6	10	4	6	10	4	6	10	4	6	10
73	4	6	10	4	6	10	4	6	10	4	6	10	4	6	10
74	4	5	9	3	5	8	3	6	9	4	6	10	4	6	10
70–74	21	30	51	21	30	51	21	31	52	21	30	51	21	30	51
75	3	5	8	3	5	8	3	5	8	3	5	8	4	5	9
76	3	5	8	3	5	8	3	5	8	3	5	8	3	5	8
77	3	5	8	3	5	8	3	5	8	3	5	8	3	5	8
78	2	4	6	3	4	7	3	4	7	3	4	7	2	4	6
79	2	4	6	2	4	6	2	4	6	2	4	6	2	4	6
75–79	13	23	36	14	23	37	14	23	37	14	23	37	14	23	37
80	2	4	6	2	3	5	2	3	5	2	4	6	2	4	6
81	2	3	5	2	3	5	2	3	5	2	3	5	2	3	5
82	1	3	4	1	3	4	1	3	4	1	3	4	1	3	4
83	1	2	3	1	3	4	1	3	4	1	2	3	1	2	3
84	1	2	3	1	2	3	1	2	3	1	2	3	1	2	3
80–84	7	14	21	7	14	21	7	14	21	7	14	21	7	14	21
85 and over	2	7	9	2	8	10	2	8	10	2	8	10	2	9	11
All ages	756	777	1533	757	778	1535	759	779	1538	761	780	1541	763	782	1545

Appendix Table Vc *continued*

Age-group	1987			1988			1989			1991			1996		
	Males	Females	Persons	Males	Females	Persons	Males	Females	Persons	Males	Females	Persons	Males	Females	Persons
0	15	14	29	15	15	30	16	15	31	16	15	31	15	14	29
1	15	14	29	15	14	29	15	14	29	16	14	30	15	14	29
2	15	14	29	15	14	29	15	14	29	15	14	29	15	15	30
3	14	13	27	15	13	28	15	14	29	15	14	29	16	14	30
4	14	13	27	14	13	27	14	13	27	15	14	29	15	14	29
0-4	73	68	141	74	69	143	75	70	145	77	71	148	76	71	147
5	14	13	27	14	13	27	14	13	27	15	14	29	15	14	29
6	13	12	25	13	12	25	14	13	27	14	13	27	15	14	29
7	13	12	25	13	12	25	14	13	27	14	13	27	15	14	29
8	13	12	25	13	12	25	13	12	25	14	13	27	15	14	29
9	12	11	23	13	12	25	13	12	25	13	12	25	15	13	28
5-9	65	60	125	66	61	127	68	63	131	70	65	135	75	69	144
10	12	11	23	12	11	23	13	12	25	13	12	25	14	13	27
11	12	12	24	12	12	24	12	11	23	13	12	25	14	13	27
12	12	11	23	12	12	24	12	11	23	12	12	24	14	13	27
13	13	12	25	12	11	23	12	12	24	12	11	23	13	13	26
14	14	13	27	13	12	25	12	11	23	12	11	23	13	12	25
10-14	63	59	122	61	58	119	61	57	118	62	58	120	68	64	132
15	14	13	27	14	12	26	13	12	25	12	11	23	13	12	25
16	14	13	27	14	13	27	13	13	26	12	11	23	12	12	24
17	14	14	28	14	13	27	14	13	27	13	12	25	12	11	23
18	14	14	28	14	14	28	14	13	27	13	12	25	11	11	22
19	15	14	29	14	14	28	14	13	27	13	13	26	11	10	21
15-19	71	68	139	70	66	136	68	64	132	63	59	122	59	56	115
20	15	14	29	14	13	27	14	14	28	13	13	26	11	11	22
21	15	13	28	15	14	29	14	13	27	14	13	27	11	10	21
22	15	14	29	14	13	27	14	13	27	13	13	26	12	11	23
23	14	14	28	15	14	29	14	13	27	14	12	26	12	11	23
24	14	13	27	14	13	27	15	14	29	14	13	27	12	11	23
20-24	73	68	141	72	67	139	71	67	138	68	64	132	58	54	112
25	13	13	26	14	13	27	14	13	27	14	13	27	12	12	24
26	13	13	26	13	13	26	14	13	27	14	13	27	13	12	25
27	13	12	25	13	12	25	13	12	25	14	13	27	12	12	24
28	12	11	23	13	12	25	13	12	25	13	13	26	13	12	25
29	12	11	23	12	11	23	12	12	24	13	12	25	13	12	25
25-29	63	60	123	65	61	126	66	62	128	68	64	132	63	60	123
30	11	11	22	12	11	23	12	11	23	13	12	25	13	12	25
31	11	10	21	11	11	22	12	11	23	12	11	23	14	13	27
32	10	10	20	11	10	21	11	11	22	12	11	23	13	12	25
33	9	10	19	10	10	20	10	10	20	11	11	22	13	12	25
34	10	9	19	9	9	18	10	10	20	11	11	22	12	12	24
30-34	51	50	101	53	51	104	55	53	108	59	56	115	65	61	126
35	9	9	18	10	9	19	9	10	19	11	10	21	12	12	24
36	9	8	17	9	9	18	10	9	19	10	10	20	12	11	23
37	9	9	18	9	8	17	9	8	17	9	9	18	12	11	23
38	10	9	19	9	9	18	9	8	17	9	9	18	11	11	22
39	10	9	19	10	9	19	9	9	18	9	8	17	11	10	21
35-39	47	44	91	47	44	91	46	44	90	48	46	94	58	55	113
40	10	10	20	10	9	19	9	9	18	9	8	17	10	10	20
41	10	9	19	10	10	20	10	9	19	9	9	18	9	9	18
42	9	9	18	10	9	19	10	9	19	9	9	18	9	9	18
43	10	9	19	9	9	18	9	9	18	9	9	18	9	9	18
44	9	9	18	9	9	18	9	9	18	10	9	19	9	8	17
40-44	48	46	94	48	46	94	47	45	92	46	44	90	46	45	91

Figures above the dotted line relate to persons born after mid-1977

Age-group	1987			1988			1989			1991			1996		
	Males	Females	Persons	Males	Females	Persons	Males	Females	Persons	Males	Females	Persons	Males	Females	Persons
45	8	8	16	9	9	18	9	9	18	9	9	18	8	8	16
46	8	7	15	8	8	16	9	9	18	9	9	18	9	9	18
47	8	8	16	8	8	16	8	8	16	9	9	18	9	8	17
48	8	8	16	8	8	16	8	8	16	9	9	18	9	9	18
49	7	8	15	7	8	15	8	8	16	8	8	16	9	9	18
45-49	39	39	78	40	41	81	42	42	84	44	44	88	44	43	87
50	7	8	15	7	8	15	8	8	16	8	8	16	9	8	17
51	7	8	15	8	8	16	7	8	15	7	7	14	8	8	16
52	7	7	14	7	8	15	7	8	15	7	8	15	9	9	18
53	7	7	14	7	7	14	7	7	14	7	7	14	9	9	18
54	7	8	15	7	7	14	7	7	14	7	8	15	7	8	15
50-54	35	38	73	36	38	74	36	38	74	36	38	74	42	42	84
55	7	7	14	7	8	15	7	7	14	7	8	15	7	7	14
56	7	8	15	7	7	14	7	8	15	7	7	14	7	7	14
57	7	8	15	7	8	15	6	7	13	6	7	13	7	8	15
58	7	8	15	6	8	14	7	8	15	6	7	13	7	7	14
59	6	7	13	6	7	13	6	7	13	6	7	13	6	7	13
55-59	34	38	72	33	38	71	33	37	70	32	36	68	34	36	70
60	7	8	15	6	7	13	7	8	15	6	8	14	6	7	13
61	7	8	15	7	8	15	6	7	13	6	7	13	6	7	13
62	6	7	13	6	7	13	6	7	13	6	7	13	6	7	13
63	6	7	13	6	7	13	6	7	13	6	7	13	6	7	13
64	6	7	13	6	7	13	6	7	13	6	7	13	5	6	11
60-64	32	37	69	31	36	67	31	36	67	30	36	66	29	34	63
65	6	7	13	6	7	13	6	7	13	6	7	13	5	7	12
66	6	7	13	6	7	13	6	7	13	6	7	13	5	7	12
67	6	7	13	6	7	13	6	7	13	5	7	12	5	6	11
68	5	6	11	5	7	12	5	7	12	5	6	11	5	6	11
69	5	6	11	5	6	11	5	6	11	5	7	12	5	6	11
65-69	28	33	61	28	34	62	28	34	62	27	34	61	25	32	57
70	4	5	9	4	5	9	4	6	10	5	7	12	4	6	10
71	4	6	10	4	5	9	4	5	9	5	6	11	4	6	10
72	4	6	10	4	6	10	4	5	9	4	5	9	4	6	10
73	4	6	10	4	6	10	4	5	9	4	5	9	4	6	10
74	4	6	10	4	5	9	4	6	10	3	5	8	4	5	9
70-74	20	29	49	20	27	47	20	27	47	21	28	49	20	29	49
75	4	5	9	4	6	10	3	5	8	3	5	8	4	5	9
76	3	5	8	3	5	8	3	5	8	3	5	8	3	5	8
77	3	5	8	3	5	8	3	5	8	3	5	8	3	4	7
78	2	4	6	2	4	6	3	5	8	3	4	7	2	4	6
79	2	4	6	2	4	6	2	4	6	2	4	6	2	4	6
75-79	14	23	37	14	24	38	14	24	38	14	23	37	14	22	36
80	2	4	6	2	4	6	2	4	6	2	4	6	2	4	6
81	2	3	5	2	3	5	2	3	5	2	3	5	2	3	5
82	1	3	4	1	3	4	1	3	4	1	3	4	1	3	4
83	1	3	4	1	3	4	1	3	4	1	3	4	1	3	4
84	1	2	3	1	2	3	1	2	3	1	2	3	1	2	3
80-84	7	15	22	7	15	22	7	15	22	7	15	22	7	15	22
85 and over	2	8	10	2	9	11	2	9	11	3	9	12	4	10	14
All ages	765	783	1548	767	785	1552	770	787	1557	775	790	1565	787	798	1585

Appendix Table Vc *continued*

Age-group	2001 Males	Females	Persons	2006 Males	Females	Persons	2011 Males	Females	Persons	2016 Males	Females	Persons	2017 Males	Females	Persons
0	14	13	27	14	13	27	14	13	27	15	14	29	15	14	29
1	14	13	27	14	13	27	14	13	27	14	13	27	14	13	27
2	14	13	27	13	13	26	14	13	27	14	13	27	14	13	27
3	14	13	27	13	12	25	13	12	25	14	13	27	14	13	27
4	15	14	29	14	12	26	13	12	25	14	13	27	14	13	27
0-4	71	66	137	68	63	131	68	63	131	71	66	137	71	66	137
5	14	13	27	13	12	25	14	12	26	14	13	27	14	13	27
6	15	14	29	14	13	27	13	12	25	13	12	25	14	13	27
7	15	14	29	14	13	27	13	12	25	13	12	25	13	12	25
8	15	14	29	14	13	27	13	12	25	13	12	25	13	12	25
9	15	14	29	14	13	27	13	13	26	13	12	25	13	12	25
5-9	74	69	143	69	64	133	66	61	127	66	61	127	67	62	129
10	15	14	29	14	13	27	13	12	25	13	12	25	13	12	25
11	15	14	29	14	13	27	13	12	25	13	12	25	13	12	25
12	15	14	29	14	14	28	13	13	26	13	12	25	13	12	25
13	14	13	27	15	14	29	14	13	27	13	12	25	13	12	25
14	14	13	27	15	14	29	14	13	27	12	12	24	12	12	24
10-14	73	68	141	72	68	140	67	63	130	64	60	124	64	60	124
15	14	13	27	15	14	29	14	13	27	13	12	25	12	12	24
16	13	13	26	14	13	27	14	13	27	13	12	25	13	12	25
17	13	12	25	14	13	27	14	13	27	13	12	25	13	12	25
18	13	12	25	14	13	27	14	13	27	13	13	26	13	12	25
19	12	11	23	13	13	26	14	13	27	13	12	25	13	12	25
14-19	65	61	126	70	66	136	70	65	135	65	61	126	64	60	124
20	12	11	23	13	12	25	14	13	27	13	13	26	13	12	25
21	11	11	22	13	12	25	13	12	25	13	12	25	13	12	25
22	11	10	21	12	11	23	13	12	25	13	12	25	13	12	25
23	10	10	20	12	11	23	13	12	25	13	12	25	13	12	25
24	10	9	19	11	10	21	12	12	24	13	12	25	12	12	24
20-24	54	51	105	61	56	117	65	61	126	65	61	126	64	60	124
25	10	10	20	11	10	21	12	11	23	13	12	25	13	12	25
26	10	9	19	11	10	21	12	11	23	12	12	24	12	12	24
27	11	10	21	10	9	19	11	11	22	12	11	23	12	11	23
28	11	10	21	9	9	18	11	10	21	12	11	23	12	11	23
29	12	11	23	9	9	18	10	10	20	11	11	22	12	11	23
25-29	54	50	104	50	47	97	56	53	109	60	57	117	61	57	118
30	12	11	23	10	9	19	10	10	20	11	11	22	11	11	22
31	12	11	23	9	9	18	10	9	19	11	10	21	11	10	21
32	12	12	24	10	10	20	9	9	18	11	10	21	11	10	21
33	12	12	24	11	10	21	9	8	17	10	10	20	11	10	21
34	12	12	24	11	10	21	9	9	18	10	9	19	10	10	20
30-34	60	58	118	51	48	99	47	45	92	53	50	103	54	51	105
35	13	12	25	11	11	22	9	9	18	10	9	19	10	9	19
36	13	12	25	12	11	23	9	9	18	10	9	19	10	9	19
37	13	12	25	12	12	24	10	9	19	9	9	18	9	9	18
38	12	12	24	12	11	23	11	10	21	9	8	17	9	9	18
39	12	12	24	12	12	24	11	10	21	8	8	16	9	8	17
35-39	63	60	123	59	57	116	50	47	97	46	43	89	47	44	91
40	12	11	23	12	12	24	11	11	22	9	9	18	9	8	17
41	12	11	23	13	12	25	11	11	22	9	8	17	9	9	18
42	11	11	22	13	12	25	11	11	22	10	9	19	9	8	17
43	11	10	21	12	11	23	12	11	23	10	9	19	9	9	18
44	10	10	20	11	11	22	12	11	23	10	10	20	10	9	19
40-44	56	53	109	61	58	119	57	55	112	48	45	93	46	43	89

Figures above the dotted line relate to persons born after mid-1977.

Age-group	2001			2006			2011			2016			2017		
	Males	Females	Persons	Males	Females	Persons	Males	Females	Persons	Males	Females	Persons	Males	Females	Persons
45	10	10	20	12	11	23	12	11	23	11	10	21	10	10	20
46	9	9	18	11	11	22	12	12	24	11	11	22	10	10	20
47	9	9	18	11	10	21	12	12	24	11	11	22	11	11	22
48	8	8	16	10	10	20	12	11	23	11	11	22	11	11	22
49	8	8	16	10	10	20	11	11	22	11	11	22	11	11	22
45-49	44	44	88	54	52	106	59	57	116	55	54	109	53	53	106
50	8	8	16	9	9	18	11	11	22	12	11	23	11	11	22
51	8	8	16	9	9	18	11	10	21	12	11	23	11	11	22
52	9	8	17	8	9	17	10	10	20	11	11	22	12	12	24
53	8	8	16	8	8	16	10	10	20	11	11	22	11	11	22
54	9	9	18	8	7	15	9	9	18	10	11	21	11	11	22
50-54	42	41	83	42	42	84	51	50	101	56	55	111	56	56	112
55	8	8	16	7	8	15	9	9	18	10	10	20	10	11	21
56	8	8	16	8	8	16	8	8	16	10	10	20	10	10	20
57	8	8	16	8	8	16	8	8	16	9	10	19	10	10	20
58	8	9	17	8	8	16	7	8	15	9	9	18	9	9	18
59	7	7	14	8	8	16	7	7	14	9	9	18	9	9	18
55-59	39	40	79	39	40	79	39	40	79	47	48	95	48	49	97
60	6	7	13	7	8	15	6	7	13	8	9	17	8	9	17
61	6	7	13	7	8	15	7	7	14	7	8	15	8	8	16
62	6	7	13	7	8	15	7	7	14	7	8	15	7	8	15
63	6	6	12	7	8	15	7	8	15	7	7	14	7	8	15
64	6	7	13	6	6	12	7	8	15	6	6	12	6	7	13
60-64	30	34	64	34	38	72	34	37	71	35	38	73	36	40	76
65	5	7	12	5	6	11	6	7	13	6	6	12	6	6	12
66	5	6	11	5	6	11	6	7	13	6	7	13	6	6	12
67	5	6	11	5	6	11	6	7	13	6	7	13	6	7	13
68	5	6	11	5	6	11	6	7	13	5	7	12	6	6	12
69	4	6	10	5	6	11	5	6	11	6	7	13	5	7	12
65-69	24	31	55	25	30	55	29	34	63	29	34	63	29	32	61
70	4	6	10	4	6	10	4	6	10	5	7	12	6	7	13
71	4	6	10	4	6	10	4	5	9	5	6	11	5	6	11
72	4	6	10	4	5	9	4	6	10	5	6	11	5	6	11
73	4	5	9	4	5	9	4	5	9	4	6	10	4	6	10
74	4	5	9	3	5	8	4	5	9	4	5	9	4	6	10
70-74	20	28	48	19	27	46	20	27	47	23	30	53	24	31	55
75	3	5	8	3	5	8	3	5	8	3	5	8	3	5	8
76	3	5	8	3	5	8	3	4	7	3	4	7	3	4	7
77	3	5	8	3	4	7	3	4	7	3	4	7	3	4	7
78	3	4	7	2	4	6	2	4	6	3	4	7	3	4	7
79	2	4	6	2	4	6	2	4	6	2	4	6	2	4	6
75-79	14	23	37	13	22	35	13	21	34	14	21	35	14	21	35
80	2	4	6	2	4	6	2	4	6	2	3	5	2	4	6
81	2	3	5	2	3	5	2	3	5	2	3	5	2	3	5
82	2	3	5	2	3	5	2	3	5	1	3	4	2	3	5
83	1	2	3	1	3	4	1	3	4	1	3	4	1	2	3
84	1	2	3	1	2	3	1	2	3	1	2	3	1	2	3
80-84	8	14	22	8	15	23	8	15	23	7	14	21	8	14	22
85 and over	4	11	15	4	10	14	4	11	15	4	11	15	4	11	15
All ages	795	802	1597	799	803	1602	803	805	1608	808	809	1617	810	810	1620

Appendix Table Ve Mortality rates by sex and single ages,
mid-1977-78 to mid-2011-12

Age last birthday	1977-78		1991-92		2011-12	
	Males	Females	Males	Females	Males	Females
0*	0.02702	0.02833	0.02442	0.02561	0.02113	0.02216
0	0.00323	0.00291	0.00292	0.00263	0.00252	0.00227
1	0.00113	0.00095	0.00102	0.00085	0.00088	0.00074
2	0.00082	0.00064	0.00074	0.00058	0.00064	0.00050
3	0.00068	0.00047	0.00062	0.00042	0.00053	0.00037
4	0.00059	0.00037	0.00054	0.00033	0.00047	0.00029
5	0.00054	0.00030	0.00048	0.00027	0.00042	0.00024
6	0.00049	0.00025	0.00044	0.00023	0.00038	0.00020
7	0.00046	0.00022	0.00041	0.00020	0.00036	0.00018
8	0.00044	0.00020	0.00040	0.00019	0.00034	0.00016
9	0.00045	0.00020	0.00041	0.00018	0.00035	0.00015
10	0.00047	0.00019	0.00042	0.00017	0.00037	0.00014
11	0.00051	0.00019	0.00046	0.00017	0.00040	0.00014
12	0.00056	0.00020	0.00050	0.00018	0.00043	0.00015
13	0.00062	0.00023	0.00056	0.00021	0.00049	0.00018
14	0.00072	0.00029	0.00065	0.00026	0.00056	0.00023
15	0.00091	0.00040	0.00084	0.00037	0.00075	0.00033
16	0.00122	0.00053	0.00118	0.00051	0.00112	0.00048
17	0.00172	0.00060	0.00172	0.00060	0.00172	0.00060
18	0.00214	0.00059	0.00214	0.00059	0.00214	0.00058
19	0.00220	0.00056	0.00218	0.00056	0.00214	0.00055
20	0.00218	0.00054	0.00213	0.00053	0.00207	0.00051
21	0.00213	0.00051	0.00206	0.00049	0.00196	0.00046
22	0.00209	0.00048	0.00199	0.00046	0.00187	0.00042
23	0.00204	0.00046	0.00195	0.00043	0.00181	0.00040
24	0.00200	0.00045	0.00190	0.00042	0.00176	0.00038
25	0.00196	0.00044	0.00185	0.00041	0.00171	0.00036
26	0.00192	0.00044	0.00181	0.00040	0.00166	0.00035
27	0.00188	0.00046	0.00176	0.00041	0.00161	0.00036
28	0.00185	0.00051	0.00174	0.00046	0.00160	0.00040
29	0.00184	0.00058	0.00174	0.00052	0.00160	0.00045
30	0.00186	0.00064	0.00177	0.00058	0.00165	0.00050
31	0.00188	0.00072	0.00181	0.00065	0.00170	0.00056
32	0.00192	0.00081	0.00185	0.00073	0.00176	0.00063
33	0.00198	0.00091	0.00191	0.00083	0.00181	0.00072
34	0.00206	0.00102	0.00199	0.00093	0.00189	0.00082
35	0.00217	0.00114	0.00209	0.00106	0.00199	0.00096
36	0.00230	0.00127	0.00222	0.00121	0.00210	0.00112
37	0.00246	0.00142	0.00237	0.00137	0.00225	0.00130
38	0.00266	0.00156	0.00258	0.00151	0.00248	0.00145
39	0.00289	0.00171	0.00283	0.00168	0.00275	0.00163
40	0.00315	0.00188	0.00311	0.00186	0.00304	0.00182
41	0.00344	0.00208	0.00342	0.00206	0.00339	0.00204
42	0.00380	0.00229	0.00380	0.00228	0.00380	0.00226
43	0.00423	0.00252	0.00423	0.00252	0.00423	0.00252
44	0.00481	0.00278	0.00481	0.00278	0.00481	0.00278

* Probability that a baby born in the year will not survive until the end of the year

Age last birthday	1977–78		1991–92		2011–12	
	Males	Females	Males	Females	Males	Females
45	0.00545	0.00306	0.00545	0.00306	0.00545	0.00306
46	0.00613	0.00337	0.00613	0.00337	0.00613	0.00337
47	0.00685	0.00371	0.00685	0.00371	0.00685	0.00371
48	0.00761	0.00408	0.00761	0.00408	0.00761	0.00408
49	0.00843	0.00448	0.00843	0.00448	0.00843	0.00448
50	0.00931	0.00491	0.00931	0.00491	0.00931	0.00491
51	0.01026	0.00538	0.01026	0.00538	0.01026	0.00538
52	0.01130	0.00590	0.01130	0.00590	0.01130	0.00590
53	0.01244	0.00648	0.01238	0.00648	0.01231	0.00648
54	0.01368	0.00714	0.01358	0.00714	0.01345	0.00714
55	0.01501	0.00784	0.01484	0.00781	0.01461	0.00776
56	0.01646	0.00861	0.01623	0.00855	0.01591	0.00847
57	0.01806	0.00945	0.01769	0.00935	0.01717	0.00920
58	0.01985	0.01036	0.01928	0.01022	0.01848	0.01002
59	0.02190	0.01133	0.02112	0.01112	0.02004	0.01084
60	0.02398	0.01238	0.02293	0.01213	0.02150	0.01177
61	0.02615	0.01355	0.02479	0.01316	0.02297	0.01262
62	0.02859	0.01481	0.02699	0.01428	0.02486	0.01356
63	0.03129	0.01621	0.02946	0.01557	0.02703	0.01469
64	0.03424	0.01776	0.03210	0.01698	0.02927	0.01593
65	0.03738	0.01952	0.03490	0.01858	0.03163	0.01733
66	0.04074	0.02157	0.03781	0.02045	0.03400	0.01895
67	0.04432	0.02394	0.04097	0.02270	0.03662	0.02103
68	0.04824	0.02652	0.04459	0.02503	0.03986	0.02306
69	0.05247	0.02928	0.04870	0.02764	0.04379	0.02546
70	0.05701	0.03243	0.05322	0.03062	0.04824	0.02820
71	0.06193	0.03600	0.05781	0.03390	0.05240	0.03110
72	0.06731	0.04019	0.06310	0.03784	0.05754	0.03471
73	0.07311	0.04492	0.06854	0.04229	0.06250	0.03880
74	0.07959	0.05009	0.07493	0.04695	0.06874	0.04282
75	0.08668	0.05579	0.08161	0.05230	0.07487	0.04770
76	0.09453	0.06199	0.08925	0.05812	0.08221	0.05300
77	0.10301	0.06908	0.09725	0.06476	0.08958	0.05905
78	0.11219	0.07697	0.10637	0.07185	0.09857	0.06513
79	0.12187	0.08591	0.11554	0.08020	0.10707	0.07270
80	0.13246	0.09584	0.12612	0.08947	0.11758	0.08110
81	0.14382	0.10616	0.13693	0.09910	0.12766	0.08983
82	0.15667	0.11697	0.14916	0.10920	0.13906	0.09898
83	0.17138	0.12877	0.16317	0.12021	0.15212	0.10896
84	0.18818	0.14135	0.17916	0.13121	0.16703	0.11798
85	0.20744	0.15509	0.19750	0.14397	0.18413	0.12945
86	0.22868	0.17079	0.21772	0.15855	0.20298	0.14256
87	0.25090	0.18748	0.23888	0.17404	0.22271	0.15649
88	0.27412	0.20417	0.26099	0.18953	0.24331	0.17042
89	0.29832	0.22184	0.28403	0.20593	0.26479	0.18517
90 and over	0.37408	0.30645	0.35616	0.28448	0.33204	0.25579

Appendix Table VIa Actual and projected Total population as at mid-year by sex and age-groups, 1951, 1961, 1971 to 2017; mid-1977 based projections.

United Kingdom

thousands

Year	Age in years									
	0-14	15-44		45-64	45-59	65 and over	60 and over	All ages		
	Persons	Males	Females	Males	Females	Males	Females	Males	Females	Persons
1951	11375	10779	10896	5568	5081	2251	4599	24407	26143	50550
1961	12359	10560	10428	6394	5467	2385	5362	25672	27282	52954
1971	13411	10932	10630	6461	5222	2821	6234	27099	28613	55712
1972	13428	10984	10672	6429	5184	2876	6297	27181	28688	55869
1973	13380	11069	10744	6389	5130	2929	6360	27256	28744	56000
1974	13244	11140	10792	6347	5078	2987	6422	27274	28736	56010
1975	13068	11218	10843	6307	5029	3036	6481	27273	28708	55981
1976	12836	11345	10939	6271	5013	3078	6498	27268	28691	55959
1977	12557	11442	11054	6232	5006	3122	6505	27248	28670	55918
1978	12264	11583	11186	6177	5018	3166	6476	27230	28640	55870
1979	11956	11738	11332	6123	5020	3204	6449	27213	28609	55822
1980	11651	11886	11474	6075	4899	3240	6544	27193	28576	55769
1981	11378	12016	11598	6059	4809	3246	6613	27175	28544	55719
1982	11132	12139	11717	6063	4740	3234	6662	27166	28521	55687
1983	10963	12242	11815	6094	4695	3198	6687	27178	28516	55694
1984	10844	12347	11915	6121	4660	3164	6700	27216	28535	55751
1985	10807	12438	12001	6037	4625	3235	6707	27276	28574	55850
1986	10777	12560	12115	5955	4578	3283	6707	27350	28625	55975
1987	10817	12641	12185	5905	4553	3315	6701	27433	28684	56117
1988	10914	12664	12202	5902	4568	3331	6684	27519	28746	56265
1989	11071	12645	12176	5918	4599	3341	6665	27607	28808	56415
1990	11258	12616	12143	5933	4619	3347	6650	27695	28871	56566
1991	11477	12571	12090	5950	4648	3351	6629	27783	28933	56716
1992	11722	12411	11920	6073	4787	3348	6599	27869	28991	56860
1993	11952	12300	11798	6157	4892	3338	6559	27950	29046	56996
1994	12167	12215	11705	6214	4973	3331	6515	28025	29095	57120
1995	12365	12151	11620	6255	5046	3321	6473	28094	29137	57231
1996	12534	12103	11555	6280	5095	3317	6441	28154	29171	57325
1997	12661	12069	11514	6312	5132	3305	6410	28205	29198	57403
1998	12724	12048	11487	6361	5172	3286	6384	28247	29215	57462
1999	12716	12046	11485	6417	5211	3268	6361	28279	29225	57504
2000	12646	12076	11513	6462	5246	3253	6334	28303	29227	57530
2001	12530	12110	11544	6512	5308	3246	6293	28320	29223	57543
2002	12383	12141	11571	6568	5367	3244	6270	28330	29214	57544
2003	12224	12164	11589	6636	5409	3242	6276	28338	29202	57540
2004	12056	12182	11604	6710	5444	3242	6296	28343	29191	57534
2005	11888	12195	11614	6791	5491	3241	6311	28350	29181	57531
2006	11726	12193	11605	6904	5548	3222	6335	28359	29174	57533
2007	11578	12176	11583	7012	5526	3221	6449	28373	29173	57546
2008	11451	12146	11552	7102	5551	3245	6524	28392	29179	57571
2009	11350	12102	11504	7190	5610	3279	6576	28418	29193	57611
2010	11278	12051	11452	7283	5674	3307	6621	28451	29215	57666
2011	11237	12002	11401	7362	5741	3338	6653	28491	29243	57734
2012	11228	11946	11343	7364	5817	3441	6676	28536	29279	57815
2013	11248	11896	11293	7383	5868	3512	6706	28586	29320	57906
2014	11298	11835	11232	7426	5923	3558	6735	28640	29367	58007
2015	11371	11783	11179	7464	5966	3591	6760	28696	29418	58114
2016	11466	11713	11108	7519	6008	3614	6796	28753	29471	58224
2017	11570	11661	11059	7553	6013	3633	6843	28808	29524	58332

Appendix Table VIb Annual changes in projected Total population 1977 to 2017; mid-1977 based projections

United Kingdom

thousands

Mid-year to mid-year	Population at beginning of period	Births	Deaths	Natural increase	Net migration	Total increase
1977–1978	55918	664	682	− 18	− 30	− 48
1978–1979	55870	668	687	− 18	− 30	− 48
1979–1980	55822	672	691	− 20	− 33	− 53
1980–1981	55769	681	695	− 14	− 36	− 50
1981–1982	55719	707	700	7	− 39	− 32
1982–1983	55687	751	704	47	− 40	7
1983–1984	55694	805	709	97	− 40	57
1984–1985	55751	852	712	139	− 40	99
1985–1986	55850	881	716	165	− 40	125
1986–1987	55975	900	718	182	− 40	142
1987–1988	56117	908	720	188	− 40	148
1988–1989	56265	912	722	190	− 40	150
1989–1990	56415	914	723	191	− 40	151
1990–1991	56566	913	723	190	− 40	150
1991–1992	56716	907	723	184	− 40	144
1992–1993	56860	898	723	176	− 40	136
1993–1994	56996	886	722	164	− 40	124
1994–1995	57120	871	720	151	− 40	111
1995–1996	57231	854	719	134	− 40	94
1996–1997	57325	835	717	118	− 40	78
1997–1998	57403	815	715	99	− 40	59
1998–1999	57462	796	713	82	− 40	42
1999–2000	57504	777	712	66	− 40	26
2000–2001	57530	762	710	53	− 40	13
2001–2002	57543	750	708	41	− 40	1
2002–2003	57544	742	707	36	− 40	− 4
2003–2004	57540	739	705	34	− 40	− 6
2004–2005	57534	741	704	37	− 40	− 3
2005–2006	57531	746	703	42	− 40	2
2006–2007	57533	755	702	53	− 40	13
2007–2008	57546	767	701	65	− 40	25
2008–2009	57571	781	701	80	− 40	40
2009–2010	57611	795	701	95	− 40	55
2010–2011	57666	810	702	108	− 40	68
2011–2012	57734	823	702	121	− 40	81
2012–2013	57815	835	703	131	− 40	91
2013–2014	57906	844	703	141	− 40	101
2014–2015	58007	851	704	147	− 40	107
2015–2016	58114	855	705	150	− 40	110
2016–2017	58224	856	707	148	− 40	108
2017–2018	58332					

Appendix Table VIc Projected Total population as at mid-year, by sex and single ages 1977 to 1989, 1991-2017; mid-1977 based projections.

thousands

Age-group	1977 Males	1977 Females	1977 Persons	1978 Males	1978 Females	1978 Persons	1979 Males	1979 Females	1979 Persons	1980 Males	1980 Females	1980 Persons	1981 Males	1981 Females	1981 Persons
0	332	314	646	335	316	651	337	319	656	339	321	660	344	325	669
1	347	328	675	331	312	643	333	315	648	335	317	652	337	319	656
2	362	341	703	346	327	673	329	310	639	332	313	645	334	316	650
3	376	355	731	361	340	701	346	326	672	328	309	637	331	312	643
4	403	380	783	375	354	729	360	339	699	345	325	670	328	308	636
0-4	1820	1718	3538	1748	1649	3397	1705	1609	3314	1679	1585	3264	1674	1580	3254
5	430	404	834	403	379	782	375	353	728	360	338	698	344	324	668
6	452	429	881	429	403	832	403	379	782	274	353	727	359	337	696
7	442	418	860	451	428	879	429	402	831	402	378	780	373	352	725
8	458	435	893	442	417	859	450	427	877	428	401	829	401	377	778
9	457	431	888	458	435	893	441	417	858	450	427	877	428	401	829
5-9	2239	2117	4356	2183	2062	4245	2098	1978	4076	2014	1897	3911	1905	1791	3696
10	473	449	922	456	431	887	458	434	892	441	417	858	450	426	876
11	474	449	923	472	448	920	456	431	887	457	434	891	441	416	857
12	486	460	946	474	449	923	472	448	920	456	430	886	457	434	891
13	485	461	946	486	460	946	473	448	921	472	448	920	455	430	885
14	475	451	926	485	461	946	486	460	946	473	448	921	472	447	919
10-14	2393	2270	4663	2373	2249	4622	2345	2221	4566	2299	2177	4476	2275	2153	4428
15	466	444	910	475	451	926	485	461	946	486	460	946	473	448	921
16	458	433	891	467	444	911	475	451	926	485	460	945	486	460	946
17	441	417	858	459	434	893	468	444	912	476	452	928	486	461	947
18	436	413	849	442	418	860	460	435	895	469	446	915	478	454	932
19	431	408	839	437	415	852	444	421	865	462	438	900	471	448	919
15-19	2232	2115	4347	2280	2162	4442	2332	2212	4544	2378	2256	4634	2394	2271	4665
20	418	396	814	432	409	841	439	416	855	445	422	867	463	439	902
21	408	385	793	419	396	815	433	410	843	440	417	857	446	423	869
22	397	373	770	408	385	793	419	396	815	433	410	843	440	417	857
23	403	379	782	396	372	768	408	384	792	418	396	814	432	409	841
24	397	380	777	402	379	781	395	372	767	407	383	790	418	395	813
20-24	2023	1913	3936	2057	1941	3998	2094	1978	4072	2143	2028	4171	2199	2083	4282
25	385	371	756	396	379	775	402	378	780	394	371	765	407	383	790
26	385	381	766	384	370	754	396	378	774	401	376	777	394	370	764
27	396	395	791	383	380	763	382	368	750	394	377	771	399	375	774
28	411	401	812	394	394	788	381	379	760	380	367	747	391	375	766
29	436	427	863	409	400	809	392	393	785	379	378	757	378	366	744
25-29	2013	1975	3988	1966	1923	3889	1953	1896	3849	1948	1869	3817	1969	1869	3838
30	479	470	949	434	426	860	407	399	806	390	392	782	377	377	754
31	377	369	746	476	470	946	432	425	857	405	398	803	388	391	779
32	372	362	734	375	368	743	474	468	942	430	424	854	403	397	800
33	377	369	746	371	361	732	373	368	741	473	468	941	428	423	851
34	361	352	713	376	368	744	369	360	729	371	367	738	470	467	937
30-34	1966	1922	3888	2032	1993	4025	2055	2020	4075	2069	2049	4118	2066	2055	4121
35	328	320	648	359	352	711	374	367	741	367	359	726	369	366	735
36	308	303	611	327	319	646	358	351	709	372	366	738	365	359	724
37	329	318	647	306	302	608	326	318	644	357	350	707	371	365	736
38	331	323	654	328	317	645	305	301	606	324	317	641	356	349	705
39	330	321	651	330	322	652	327	317	644	304	300	604	323	316	639
35-39	1626	1585	3211	1650	1612	3262	1690	1654	3344	1724	1692	3416	1784	1755	3539
40	327	317	644	329	320	649	329	321	650	326	316	642	303	299	602
41	321	314	635	326	316	642	328	319	647	328	320	648	325	315	640
42	314	306	620	321	313	634	326	315	641	327	318	645	327	320	647
43	310	302	612	313	305	618	320	312	632	325	315	640	326	317	643
44	310	305	615	309	301	610	311	305	616	318	311	629	323	314	637
40-44	1582	1544	3126	1598	1555	3153	1614	1572	3186	1624	1580	3204	1604	1565	3169

Figures above the dotted line relate to persons born after mid-1977

Age-group	1977			1978			1979			1980			1981		
	Males	Females	Persons	Males	Females	Persons	Males	Females	Persons	Males	Females	Persons	Males	Females	Persons
45	320	316	636	308	305	613	307	300	607	310	304	614	317	310	627
46	326	327	653	318	315	633	307	304	611	306	299	605	309	303	612
47	322	328	650	325	326	651	317	314	631	305	303	608	305	298	603
48	321	325	646	320	327	647	323	325	648	315	313	628	303	301	604
49	317	322	639	319	323	642	317	325	642	320	323	643	312	312	624
45-49	1606	1618	3224	1590	1596	3186	1571	1568	3139	1556	1542	3098	1546	1524	3070
50	323	331	654	315	320	635	316	322	638	315	324	639	318	322	640
51	330	336	666	321	330	651	312	319	631	314	320	634	312	322	634
52	328	338	666	327	335	662	318	328	646	309	317	626	311	319	630
53	329	341	670	324	335	659	324	333	657	315	326	641	306	315	621
54	333	348	681	325	339	664	321	333	654	320	331	651	311	324	635
50-54	1643	1694	3337	1612	1659	3271	1591	1635	3226	1573	1618	3191	1558	1602	3160
55	347	368	715	329	346	675	321	337	658	318	331	649	316	328	644
56	359	383	742	343	365	708	325	343	668	317	334	651	313	329	642
57	376	404	780	354	380	734	338	363	701	320	341	661	313	332	645
58	248	274	522	370	401	771	348	377	725	332	360	692	315	338	653
59	240	265	505	243	271	514	364	397	761	342	373	715	327	356	683
55-59	1570	1694	3264	1639	1763	3402	1696	1817	3513	1629	1739	3368	1584	1683	3267
60	265	295	560	236	263	499	239	268	507	357	393	750	335	369	704
61	276	308	584	259	291	550	230	260	490	234	265	499	350	389	739
62	297	338	635	269	304	573	253	288	541	225	257	482	228	262	490
63	291	335	626	289	334	623	262	300	562	246	284	530	219	253	472
64	284	329	613	283	330	613	281	329	610	255	296	551	239	280	519
60-64	1413	1605	3018	1336	1522	2858	1265	1445	2710	1317	1495	2812	1371	1553	2924
65	270	317	587	275	324	599	273	325	599	272	324	596	247	292	539
66	263	321	584	261	312	573	266	319	585	265	319	584	263	318	581
67	254	315	569	253	315	568	251	306	557	255	312	567	255	313	568
68	246	312	558	244	309	553	242	308	550	241	300	541	245	306	551
69	233	302	535	234	304	538	232	302	534	231	301	532	229	293	522
65-69	1266	1567	2833	1267	1564	2831	1265	1560	2825	1264	1556	2820	1239	1522	2761
70	217	290	507	221	294	515	222	297	519	221	294	515	219	294	513
71	202	280	482	205	281	486	209	286	495	210	289	499	209	286	495
72	187	271	458	189	272	461	193	273	466	197	277	474	198	280	478
73	172	257	429	175	262	437	177	262	439	180	263	443	183	267	450
74	157	243	400	160	247	407	162	251	413	164	252	416	167	253	420
70-74	935	1341	2276	950	1356	2306	963	1369	2332	972	1375	2347	976	1380	2356
75	139	226	365	145	233	378	147	236	383	149	241	390	152	241	393
76	124	219	343	128	215	343	133	222	355	135	225	360	137	229	366
77	107	201	308	113	207	320	116	204	320	121	210	331	123	213	336
78	93	183	276	96	189	285	101	195	296	104	191	295	109	198	307
79	77	164	241	82	171	253	86	176	262	91	182	273	93	179	272
75-79	540	993	1533	564	1015	1579	583	1033	1616	600	1049	1649	614	1060	1674
80	68	151	219	68	152	220	73	158	231	76	164	240	81	169	250
81	56	135	191	59	138	197	60	139	199	64	145	209	67	150	217
82	51	122	173	49	123	172	51	126	177	52	126	178	55	132	187
83	41	102	143	44	109	153	42	110	152	44	113	157	44	114	158
84	35	90	125	34	91	125	37	97	134	35	98	133	37	100	137
80-84	251	600	851	254	613	867	263	630	893	271	646	917	284	665	949
85 and over	130	399	529	131	406	537	130	412	542	133	423	556	133	433	566
All ages	27248	28670	55918	27230	28640	55870	27213	28609	55822	27193	28576	55769	27175	28544	55719

thousands

Age-group	1982			1983			1984			1985			1986		
	Males	Females	Persons	Males	Females	Persons	Males	Females	Persons	Males	Females	Persons	Males	Females	Persons
0	357	337	694	379	359	738	406	385	791	430	407	837	445	421	866
1	342	323	665	355	335	690	377	356	733	405	382	787	428	405	833
2	336	318	654	341	322	663	354	334	688	376	355	731	404	381	785
3	333	314	647	336	316	652	340	321	661	353	333	686	375	354	729
4	331	311	642	332	313	645	335	315	650	339	320	659	352	331	683
0-4	1699	1603	3302	1743	1645	3388	1812	1711	3523	1903	1797	3700	2004	1892	3896
5	327	307	634	330	310	640	332	312	644	334	314	648	339	319	658
6	343	323	666	326	307	633	329	310	639	331	311	642	333	314	647
7	358	337	695	342	322	664	325	306	631	328	309	637	330	310	640
8	373	351	724	358	336	694	342	321	663	325	305	630	328	308	636
9	401	376	777	372	350	722	357	335	692	342	321	663	324	304	628
5-9	1802	1694	3496	1728	1625	3353	1685	1584	3269	1660	1560	3220	1654	1555	3209
10	427	400	827	401	376	777	372	350	722	357	335	692	341	320	661
11	450	426	876	427	400	827	400	376	776	371	350	721	356	335	691
12	440	416	856	449	425	874	426	399	825	400	375	775	371	349	720
13	457	433	890	440	415	855	449	425	874	426	399	825	400	375	775
14	455	430	885	456	433	889	440	415	855	449	425	874	426	399	825
10-14	2229	2105	4334	2173	2049	4222	2087	1965	4052	2003	1884	3887	1894	1778	3672
15	472	447	919	456	430	886	456	433	889	440	415	855	448	425	873
16	474	448	922	472	447	919	456	429	885	457	433	890	440	414	854
17	487	460	947	474	448	922	473	448	921	456	430	886	457	433	890
18	487	463	950	488	462	950	476	450	926	474	450	924	458	432	890
19	479	456	935	489	465	954	489	464	953	477	452	929	476	452	928
15-19	2399	2274	4673	2379	2252	4631	2350	2224	4574	2304	2180	4484	2279	2156	4435
20	472	450	922	481	457	938	491	467	958	491	465	956	479	454	933
21	464	440	904	473	451	924	481	458	939	491	467	958	492	466	958
22	446	422	868	464	439	903	473	450	923	481	458	939	491	467	958
23	439	416	855	445	422	867	463	439	902	472	450	922	481	457	938
24	432	409	841	438	416	854	445	421	866	463	438	901	471	449	920
20-24	2253	2137	4390	2301	2185	4486	2353	2235	4588	2398	2278	4676	2414	2293	4707
25	417	394	811	431	408	839	438	415	853	444	420	864	462	437	899
26	406	382	788	416	393	809	430	406	836	437	413	850	443	419	862
27	392	369	761	404	380	784	414	392	806	428	405	833	435	412	847
28	397	374	771	390	367	757	402	379	781	412	390	802	426	404	830
29	389	374	763	395	373	768	387	366	753	399	378	777	410	389	799
25-29	2001	1893	3894	2036	1921	3957	2071	1958	4029	2120	2006	4126	2176	2061	4237
30	376	365	741	387	373	760	393	372	765	385	365	750	397	377	774
31	375	376	751	374	364	738	385	372	757	390	371	761	383	364	747
32	386	390	776	372	375	747	372	363	735	383	371	754	388	370	758
33	401	396	797	384	390	774	370	374	744	370	362	732	381	370	751
34	426	423	849	399	395	794	382	389	771	369	373	742	368	361	729
30-34	1964	1950	3914	1916	1897	3813	1902	1870	3772	1897	1842	3739	1917	1842	3759
35	468	466	934	424	422	846	397	395	792	380	388	768	367	373	740
36	367	365	732	466	465	931	422	421	843	395	393	788	378	387	765
37	364	357	721	366	364	730	465	464	929	421	420	841	394	393	787
38	370	364	734	363	356	719	365	363	728	463	463	926	419	418	837
39	354	348	702	368	363	731	361	355	716	364	362	726	462	461	923
35-39	1923	1900	3823	1987	1970	3957	2010	1998	4008	2023	2026	4049	2020	2032	4052
40	322	315	637	353	347	700	367	362	729	361	354	715	362	361	723
41	302	298	600	322	314	636	352	346	698	366	361	727	359	354	713
42	324	314	638	301	298	599	320	313	633	351	345	696	365	360	725
43	326	319	645	323	313	636	300	297	597	319	313	632	350	344	694
44	325	317	642	324	318	642	322	312	634	299	296	595	318	312	630
40-44	1599	1563	3162	1623	1590	3213	1661	1630	3291	1696	1669	3365	1754	1731	3485

Figures above the dotted line relate to persons born after mid-1977

Age-group	1982			1983			1984			1985			1986		
	Males	Females	Persons	Males	Females	Persons	Males	Females	Persons	Males	Females	Persons	Males	Females	Persons
45	322	313	635	324	316	640	323	317	640	320	311	631	298	296	594
46	316	309	625	320	312	632	322	314	636	322	316	638	319	310	629
47	307	302	609	314	308	622	318	311	629	320	314	634	319	315	634
48	302	297	599	305	300	605	312	307	619	316	309	625	318	312	630
49	301	300	601	300	295	595	303	299	602	309	306	615	314	308	622
45-49	1548	1521	3069	1563	1531	3094	1578	1548	3126	1587	1556	3143	1568	1541	3109
50	310	310	620	299	299	598	298	294	592	300	298	598	307	304	611
51	315	320	635	307	309	616	296	297	593	295	292	587	298	296	594
52	309	321	630	312	319	631	304	307	611	293	296	589	292	291	583
53	308	317	625	306	318	624	309	317	626	301	305	606	290	294	584
54	303	313	616	305	315	620	303	317	620	306	315	621	298	304	602
50-54	1545	1581	3126	1529	1560	3089	1510	1532	3042	1495	1506	3001	1485	1489	2974
55	307	322	629	299	311	610	301	312	613	299	315	614	302	313	615
56	312	326	638	303	320	623	296	309	605	297	310	607	295	312	607
57	309	326	635	308	323	631	299	317	616	291	306	597	293	308	601
58	307	329	636	304	324	628	303	321	624	294	314	608	287	304	591
59	310	335	645	302	326	628	298	321	619	298	318	616	289	311	600
54-59	1545	1638	3183	1516	1604	3120	1497	1580	3077	1479	1563	3042	1466	1548	3014
60	321	353	674	304	331	635	297	323	620	293	317	610	292	315	607
61	328	366	694	313	349	662	298	327	625	290	319	609	287	314	601
62	341	384	725	320	361	681	306	344	650	291	324	615	284	315	599
63	222	258	480	333	379	712	312	356	668	298	340	638	283	319	602
64	213	249	462	216	254	470	323	374	697	304	351	655	290	335	625
60-64	1425	1610	3035	1486	1674	3160	1536	1724	3260	1476	1651	3127	1436	1598	3034
65	232	276	508	206	245	451	209	251	460	313	368	681	295	346	641
66	238	286	524	224	271	495	199	241	440	202	246	448	303	361	664
67	253	312	565	229	281	510	216	266	482	192	237	429	194	242	436
68	244	307	551	243	306	549	220	275	495	207	260	467	184	232	416
69	234	299	533	233	300	533	232	299	531	210	269	479	197	254	451
65-69	1201	1480	2681	1135	1403	2538	1076	1332	2408	1124	1380	2504	1173	1435	2608
70	218	286	504	222	292	514	222	293	515	220	292	512	200	262	462
71	207	286	493	206	278	484	210	284	494	210	285	495	209	284	493
72	196	277	473	195	277	472	194	269	463	198	275	473	197	276	473
73	185	270	455	183	267	450	182	267	449	182	260	442	185	266	451
74	170	257	427	172	260	432	170	257	427	169	257	426	169	250	419
70-74	976	1376	2352	978	1374	2352	978	1370	2348	979	1369	2348	960	1338	2298
75	154	242	396	157	247	404	159	249	408	158	246	404	157	246	403
76	139	230	369	142	231	373	144	235	379	145	237	382	145	235	380
77	125	217	342	127	218	345	129	218	347	132	223	355	133	225	358
78	111	200	311	112	204	316	114	205	319	117	206	323	119	210	329
79	97	185	282	99	187	286	101	191	292	102	192	294	104	193	297
75-79	626	1074	1700	637	1087	1724	647	1098	1745	654	1104	1758	658	1109	1767
80	83	166	249	86	171	257	88	174	262	89	177	266	91	178	269
81	71	155	226	73	152	225	76	158	234	77	160	237	79	163	242
82	58	136	194	61	141	202	63	139	202	66	144	210	67	146	213
83	47	119	166	50	123	173	52	127	179	54	125	179	56	129	185
84	37	101	138	40	106	146	42	109	151	45	113	158	46	112	158
80-84	296	677	973	310	693	1003	321	707	1028	331	719	1050	339	728	1067
85 and over	135	445	580	138	456	594	142	469	611	147	484	631	153	499	652
All ages	27166	28521	55687	27178	28516	55694	27216	28535	55751	27276	28574	55850	27350	28625	55975

Appendix Table VIc *continued*

Age-group	1987 Males	Females	Persons	1988 Males	Females	Persons	1989 Males	Females	Persons	1991 Males	Females	Persons	1996 Males	Females	Persons
0	455	430	885	458	434	892	461	436	897	461	436	897	432	408	840
1	443	419	862	453	428	881	457	431	888	460	435	895	438	414	852
2	427	403	830	442	417	859	452	427	879	458	433	891	445	420	865
3	403	380	783	426	402	828	441	416	857	455	429	884	450	425	875
4	374	353	727	402	379	781	425	401	826	450	424	874	454	428	882
0-4	2102	1985	4087	2181	2060	4241	2236	2111	4347	2284	2157	4441	2219	2095	4314
5	351	331	682	374	352	726	401	378	779	439	414	853	456	430	886
6	338	318	656	351	330	681	373	351	724	424	399	823	456	429	885
7	333	313	646	337	317	654	350	329	679	399	376	775	454	428	882
8	330	310	640	332	312	644	337	316	653	372	350	722	451	424	875
9	327	307	634	329	309	638	331	312	643	349	328	677	446	420	866
5-9	1679	1579	3258	1723	1620	3343	1792	1686	3478	1983	1867	3850	2263	2131	4394
10	324	304	628	327	307	634	329	309	638	336	315	651	436	411	847
11	341	320	661	324	304	628	327	306	633	331	310	641	421	396	817
12	356	334	690	340	319	659	323	303	626	328	308	636	398	374	772
13	371	349	720	356	334	690	340	319	659	326	306	632	370	347	717
14	399	374	773	371	348	719	356	334	690	323	303	626	347	326	673
10-14	1791	1681	3472	1718	1612	3330	1675	1571	3246	1644	1542	3186	1972	1854	3826
15	426	399	825	399	375	774	371	349	720	340	319	659	335	314	649
16	449	424	873	427	399	826	399	374	773	356	333	689	331	309	640
17	441	415	856	450	425	875	427	399	826	372	349	721	329	308	637
18	459	435	894	442	417	859	451	427	878	402	377	779	329	308	637
19	459	434	893	460	437	897	444	419	863	430	403	833	327	307	634
15-19	2234	2107	4341	2178	2053	4231	2092	1968	4060	1900	1781	3681	1651	1546	3197
20	477	453	930	461	436	897	462	439	901	454	431	885	346	325	671
21	479	454	933	478	454	932	461	436	897	446	421	867	363	340	703
22	492	466	958	479	454	933	478	453	931	462	439	901	378	355	733
23	491	466	957	491	465	956	479	454	933	461	436	897	405	380	785
24	480	457	937	490	466	956	490	465	955	477	452	929	431	404	835
20-24	2419	2296	4715	2399	2275	4674	2370	2247	4617	2300	2179	4479	1923	1804	3727
25	471	448	919	479	455	934	489	465	954	477	452	929	453	429	882
26	461	436	897	470	447	917	478	454	932	489	462	951	443	418	861
27	441	417	858	459	435	894	468	446	914	486	462	948	458	434	892
28	432	411	843	439	416	855	457	433	890	474	452	926	454	430	884
29	424	403	827	430	409	839	437	415	852	463	443	906	468	446	914
25-29	2229	2115	4344	2277	2162	4439	2329	2213	4542	2389	2271	4660	2276	2157	4433
30	408	388	796	422	402	824	428	408	836	452	431	883	467	446	913
31	395	376	771	405	387	792	420	401	821	432	413	845	477	456	933
32	381	363	744	393	375	768	403	386	789	424	406	830	475	456	931
33	386	369	755	379	362	741	391	374	765	415	399	814	463	447	910
34	379	369	748	384	368	752	377	361	738	399	385	784	453	438	891
30-34	1949	1865	3814	1983	1894	3877	2019	1930	3949	2122	2034	4156	2335	2243	4578
35	366	361	727	377	369	746	382	367	749	387	372	759	442	426	868
36	365	372	737	364	359	723	375	368	743	373	360	733	422	408	830
37	377	386	763	363	371	734	363	359	722	379	365	744	414	402	816
38	392	391	783	376	385	761	362	370	732	373	366	739	406	394	800
39	418	417	835	391	390	781	375	383	758	360	357	717	392	380	772
35-39	1918	1927	3845	1871	1874	3745	1857	1847	3704	1872	1820	3692	2076	2010	4086
40	461	460	921	417	416	833	390	389	779	360	367	727	380	367	747
41	361	360	721	460	459	919	416	415	831	372	382	754	367	355	722
42	358	353	711	360	359	719	458	458	916	388	387	775	373	360	733
43	364	359	723	357	352	709	359	358	717	413	413	826	367	361	728
44	348	343	691	362	358	720	355	351	706	455	456	911	355	352	707
40-44	1892	1875	3767	1956	1944	3900	1978	1971	3949	1988	2005	3993	1842	1795	3637

Figures above the dotted line relate to persons born after mid-1977.

Age-group	1987			1988			1989			1991			1996		
	Males	Females	Persons	Males	Females	Persons	Males	Females	Persons	Males	Females	Persons	Males	Females	Persons
45	317	311	628	347	342	689	361	357	718	356	356	712	354	363	717
46	296	294	590	315	310	625	345	341	686	352	348	700	365	376	741
47	317	309	626	295	293	588	313	309	622	357	355	712	379	382	761
48	317	314	631	315	308	623	293	292	585	341	339	680	403	406	809
49	316	311	627	315	312	627	312	307	619	309	306	615	442	448	890
45-49	1563	1539	3102	1587	1565	3152	1624	1606	3230	1715	1704	3419	1943	1975	3918
50	312	307	619	313	310	623	313	311	624	288	289	577	344	350	694
51	304	303	607	309	305	614	310	308	618	307	304	611	340	341	681
52	295	295	590	302	301	603	306	304	610	307	308	615	343	347	690
53	290	289	579	292	293	585	298	299	597	305	304	609	327	330	657
54	287	292	579	286	287	573	289	291	580	300	300	600	295	298	593
50-54	1488	1486	2974	1502	1496	2998	1516	1513	3029	1507	1505	3012	1649	1666	3315
55	294	302	596	284	290	574	283	286	569	292	296	588	274	281	555
56	298	310	608	291	299	590	280	288	568	282	287	569	291	294	585
57	291	310	601	294	308	602	287	297	584	275	281	556	289	297	586
58	288	305	593	286	307	593	289	305	594	271	283	554	285	294	579
59	282	301	583	283	303	586	281	304	585	277	292	569	279	288	567
55-59	1453	1528	2981	1438	1507	2945	1420	1480	2900	1397	1439	2836	1418	1454	2872
60	284	308	592	276	298	574	278	299	577	279	300	579	270	283	553
61	286	311	597	278	305	583	271	295	566	271	298	569	258	274	532
62	280	310	590	279	307	586	271	301	572	266	292	558	250	267	517
63	276	311	587	273	306	579	272	303	575	258	287	545	245	268	513
64	275	315	590	269	307	576	266	302	568	257	293	550	247	275	522
60-64	1401	1555	2956	1375	1523	2898	1358	1500	2858	1331	1470	2801	1270	1367	2637
65	281	330	611	267	310	577	261	302	563	257	294	551	246	281	527
66	285	340	625	272	324	596	258	305	563	249	292	541	236	277	513
67	292	355	647	275	334	609	262	318	580	243	292	535	229	271	500
68	186	237	423	280	348	628	263	327	590	239	293	532	218	264	482
69	176	226	402	178	231	409	268	340	608	241	305	546	215	267	482
65-69	1220	1488	2708	1272	1547	2819	1312	1592	2904	1229	1476	2705	1144	1360	2504
70	188	248	436	167	221	388	170	226	396	240	313	553	210	266	476
71	189	255	444	178	241	419	158	215	373	242	323	565	200	262	462
72	196	275	471	178	248	426	168	235	403	152	213	365	191	258	449
73	185	267	452	184	266	450	167	239	406	140	202	342	183	256	439
74	172	256	428	172	257	429	171	256	427	146	218	364	180	262	442
70-74	930	1301	2231	879	1233	2112	834	1171	2005	920	1269	2189	964	1304	2268
75	156	240	396	159	245	404	159	246	405	144	221	365	174	264	438
76	144	235	379	144	229	373	147	234	381	146	234	380	171	268	439
77	132	223	355	131	223	354	131	217	348	134	223	357	104	173	277
78	120	212	332	119	210	329	119	210	329	121	210	331	92	160	252
79	107	196	303	108	199	307	107	197	304	106	192	298	93	169	262
75-79	659	1106	1765	661	1106	1767	663	1104	1767	651	1080	1731	634	1034	1668
80	93	179	272	95	183	278	96	184	280	95	183	278	88	166	254
81	80	164	244	82	165	247	83	168	251	84	169	253	86	170	256
82	68	149	217	69	150	219	71	151	222	73	155	228	75	155	230
83	58	132	190	59	134	193	60	135	195	63	139	202	64	140	204
84	48	115	163	49	117	166	50	120	170	52	122	174	54	123	177
80-84	347	739	1086	354	749	1103	360	758	1118	367	768	1135	367	754	1121
85 and over	159	512	671	165	526	691	172	540	712	184	566	750	208	622	830
All ages	27433	28684	56117	27519	28746	56265	27607	28808	56415	27783	28933	56716	28154	29171	57325

Appendix Table VIc *continued*

thousands

Age-group	2001			2006			2011			2016			2017		
	Males	Females	Persons	Males	Females	Persons	Males	Females	Persons	Males	Females	Persons	Males	Females	Persons
0	385	364	749	378	357	735	410	388	798	433	409	842	434	410	844
1	392	370	762	373	352	725	401	379	780	430	406	836	432	407	839
2	400	377	777	372	351	723	393	370	763	425	401	826	428	404	832
3	409	385	794	372	351	723	385	363	748	419	396	815	424	400	824
4	417	394	811	375	353	728	378	356	734	413	389	802	419	395	814
0- 4	2003	1890	3893	1870	1764	3634	1967	1856	3823	2120	2001	4121	2137	2016	4153
5	426	402	828	380	358	738	372	351	723	405	381	786	412	388	800
6	434	409	843	388	364	752	369	347	716	397	374	771	405	380	785
7	441	415	856	396	372	768	368	346	714	389	366	755	396	373	769
8	447	420	867	405	381	786	369	346	715	381	358	739	388	365	753
9	450	424	874	414	390	804	372	349	721	375	352	727	381	358	739
5- 9	2198	2070	4268	1983	1865	3848	1850	1739	3589	1947	1831	3778	1982	1864	3846
10	453	426	879	423	398	821	377	355	732	370	347	717	374	351	725
11	453	426	879	432	406	838	385	361	746	367	344	711	370	347	717
12	451	425	876	439	413	852	394	370	764	366	343	709	366	344	710
13	449	422	871	444	418	862	403	379	782	367	345	712	365	343	708
14	445	419	864	449	422	871	413	388	801	370	348	718	367	344	711
10-14	2251	2118	4369	2187	2057	4244	1972	1853	3825	1840	1727	3567	1842	1729	3571
15	436	409	845	452	424	876	422	397	819	377	353	730	371	348	719
16	421	395	816	453	425	878	431	405	836	385	360	745	377	353	730
17	398	373	771	452	425	877	440	412	852	394	370	764	385	361	746
18	372	349	721	451	424	875	447	420	867	405	381	786	396	371	767
19	352	331	683	449	423	872	453	426	879	417	392	809	407	383	790
15-19	1979	1857	3836	2257	2121	4378	2193	2060	4253	1978	1856	3834	1936	1816	3752
20	341	320	661	441	415	856	457	430	887	428	403	831	419	394	813
21	337	316	653	427	402	829	459	432	891	437	411	848	429	403	832
22	335	314	649	404	379	783	458	430	888	445	418	863	437	411	848
23	333	312	645	376	353	729	454	428	882	450	424	874	444	418	862
24	329	308	637	353	331	684	450	423	873	454	427	881	450	423	873
20-24	1675	1570	3245	2001	1880	3881	2278	2143	4421	2214	2083	4297	2179	2049	4228
25	346	323	669	340	318	658	440	413	853	456	429	885	453	426	879
26	360	337	697	335	313	648	424	398	822	456	428	884	455	427	882
27	373	350	723	331	310	641	399	375	774	453	426	879	454	427	881
28	399	375	774	326	306	632	370	348	718	448	422	870	451	425	876
29	423	398	821	322	302	624	346	325	671	442	417	859	446	421	867
25-29	1901	1783	3684	1654	1549	3203	1979	1859	3838	2255	2122	4377	2259	2126	4385
30	443	423	866	336	318	654	331	313	644	430	407	837	440	416	856
31	432	412	844	350	331	681	325	307	632	414	393	807	428	406	834
32	447	429	876	362	345	707	320	304	624	388	369	757	412	392	804
33	443	424	867	389	370	759	316	302	618	360	343	703	386	369	755
34	458	441	899	413	393	806	312	298	610	336	321	657	358	342	700
30-34	2223	2129	4352	1850	1757	3607	1604	1524	3128	1928	1833	3761	2024	1925	3949
35	457	441	898	433	418	851	327	313	640	322	309	631	334	320	654
36	467	452	919	422	408	830	340	327	667	315	303	618	320	308	628
37	465	452	917	437	424	861	353	341	694	312	300	612	314	302	616
38	454	442	896	435	420	855	380	366	746	308	297	605	310	299	609
39	445	433	878	450	436	886	405	388	793	305	294	599	308	297	605
35-39	2288	2220	4508	2177	2106	4283	1805	1735	3540	1562	1503	3065	1586	1526	3112
40	435	421	856	450	436	886	426	413	839	320	309	629	304	293	597
41	416	403	819	460	446	906	416	402	818	335	322	657	319	308	627
42	408	397	805	459	446	905	431	419	850	348	336	684	334	321	655
43	400	389	789	448	436	884	428	415	843	374	361	735	347	335	682
44	385	375	760	437	428	865	442	431	873	399	383	782	373	360	733
40-44	2044	1985	4029	2254	2192	4446	2143	2080	4223	1776	1711	3487	1677	1617	3294

Figures above the dotted line relate to persons born after mid-1977.

Age-group	2001			2006			2011			2016			2017		
	Males	Females	Persons	Males	Females	Persons	Males	Females	Persons	Males	Females	Persons	Males	Females	Persons
45	374	362	736	427	416	843	442	431	873	419	408	827	397	382	779
46	360	350	710	408	398	806	452	440	892	408	397	805	416	407	823
47	365	355	720	399	391	790	449	440	889	421	413	834	406	396	802
48	358	355	713	391	382	773	437	429	866	418	408	826	419	411	830
49	344	346	690	374	368	742	425	420	845	430	423	853	415	406	821
45–49	1801	1768	3569	1999	1955	3954	2205	2160	4365	2096	2049	4145	2053	2002	4055
50	342	356	698	362	356	718	414	408	822	428	422	850	427	422	849
51	352	368	720	347	343	690	393	390	783	436	431	867	425	420	845
52	365	373	738	351	347	698	384	382	766	432	430	862	432	429	861
53	386	397	783	343	346	689	374	373	747	419	419	838	427	427	854
54	423	436	859	329	336	665	358	358	716	406	409	815	414	416	830
50–54	1868	1930	3798	1732	1728	3460	1923	1911	3834	2121	2111	4232	2125	2114	4239
55	328	339	667	326	345	671	344	345	689	393	396	789	402	406	808
56	322	331	653	333	357	690	329	332	661	373	377	750	388	393	781
57	323	335	658	343	361	704	331	336	667	362	370	732	368	375	743
58	306	318	624	362	383	745	321	334	655	351	360	711	356	366	722
59	274	287	561	393	419	812	306	323	629	333	345	678	345	357	702
55–59	1553	1610	3163	1757	1865	3622	1631	1670	3301	1812	1848	3660	1859	1897	3756
60	253	269	522	303	325	628	301	331	632	318	331	649	327	341	668
61	267	281	548	295	316	611	307	341	648	303	317	620	312	328	640
62	263	283	546	295	319	614	314	343	657	302	319	621	297	313	610
63	258	278	536	277	302	579	328	363	691	291	317	608	296	315	611
64	249	271	520	246	270	516	353	396	749	276	305	581	284	313	597
60–64	1290	1382	2672	1416	1532	2948	1603	1774	3377	1490	1589	3079	1516	1610	3126
65	238	265	503	224	253	477	270	306	576	269	311	580	268	301	569
66	226	255	481	234	262	496	260	295	555	270	319	589	261	306	567
67	216	248	464	228	262	490	256	296	552	274	319	593	262	314	576
68	208	247	455	220	256	476	237	278	515	282	336	618	264	314	578
69	207	251	458	210	248	458	208	248	456	300	364	664	272	329	601
65–69	1095	1266	2361	1116	1281	2397	1231	1423	2654	1395	1649	3044	1327	1564	2891
70	203	254	457	197	241	438	186	230	416	225	278	503	288	356	644
71	190	249	439	183	230	413	191	236	427	213	266	479	215	272	487
72	180	240	420	171	220	391	182	234	416	206	265	471	203	259	462
73	169	231	400	162	216	378	172	225	397	187	246	433	194	257	451
74	161	231	392	157	217	374	160	216	376	160	216	376	175	238	413
70–74	903	1205	2108	870	1124	1994	891	1141	2032	991	1271	2262	1075	1382	2457
75	154	226	380	149	217	366	147	206	353	139	197	336	149	208	357
76	142	218	360	137	208	345	132	193	325	139	199	338	129	189	318
77	132	210	342	125	197	322	120	181	301	129	193	322	128	190	318
78	122	204	326	113	185	298	110	174	284	118	183	301	118	184	302
79	116	204	320	105	180	285	103	171	274	106	170	276	107	172	279
75–79	666	1062	1728	629	987	1616	612	925	1537	631	942	1573	631	943	1574
80	108	199	307	96	172	268	94	166	260	94	158	252	95	160	255
81	101	196	297	85	160	245	83	154	237	81	144	225	83	147	230
82	58	122	180	75	150	225	73	141	214	70	131	201	72	133	205
83	50	108	158	67	139	206	62	127	189	61	121	182	61	120	181
84	48	109	157	60	133	193	55	119	174	55	114	169	53	110	163
80–84	365	734	1099	383	754	1137	367	707	1074	361	668	1029	364	670	1034
85 and over	217	644	861	224	657	881	237	683	920	236	677	913	236	674	910
All ages	28320	29223	57543	28359	29174	57533	28491	29243	57734	28753	29471	58224	28808	29524	58332

Appendix Table VId Projected Total population as at mid-year by sex, age and marital condition, 1977-2017; mid-1977 based projections

Age	1977	1978	1979	1980	1981	1982	1986	1991	1996	2001	2006	2011	2016	2017
Married males *(thousands)*														
0-14	-	-	-	-	-	-	-	-	24	-	-	-	-	-
15-19	33	33	33	36	37	36	35	31	24	25	33	33	29	29
20-24	624	608	601	607	619	631	680	644	537	444	523	622	606	596
25-29	1390	1323	1285	1259	1252	1258	1339	1459	1367	1129	980	1178	1348	1348
30-34	1604	1643	1644	1639	1623	1528	1440	1564	1703	1601	1329	1156	1390	1460
35-39	1385	1395	1420	1442	1486	1591	1638	1472	1606	1755	1658	1373	1190	1209
40-44	1364	1372	1380	1380	1359	1350	1467	1632	1472	1610	1765	1672	1382	1304
45-49	1377	1360	1341	1325	1313	1314	1324	1438	1603	1451	1593	1749	1654	1619
50-54	1405	1373	1351	1332	1315	1304	1253	1269	1383	1542	1401	1541	1690	1691
55-59	1346	1401	1444	1379	1337	1299	1223	1170	1186	1296	1449	1320	1453	1488
60-64	1189	1122	1062	1106	1151	1193	1189	1094	1051	1068	1172	1311	1198	1215
65-69	1030	1030	1029	1028	1008	975	955	988	915	884	904	996	1117	1059
70-74	708	724	735	743	747	748	736	708	734	688	667	689	767	831
75-79	359	377	390	406	415	427	452	449	442	460	436	428	446	446
80-84	135	138	145	150	157	165	192	212	213	215	224	217	216	220
85 and over	49	48	47	46	47	49	56	71	80	84	90	94	93	94
All ages	13998	13947	13907	13878	13866	13868	13979	14201	14316	14252	14224	14379	14579	14609
Other males *(thousands)*														
0-14	6451	6302	6147	5991	5853	5727	5552	5911	6452	6451	6038	5787	5905	5959
15-19	2199	2247	2299	2343	2357	2363	2244	1869	1627	1953	2224	2161	1949	1907
20-24	1399	1449	1492	1537	1581	1622	1733	1656	1386	1281	1478	1656	1609	1583
25-29	623	643	668	690	717	743	837	931	909	772	674	801	906	911
30-34	363	389	411	430	443	436	477	559	633	622	521	448	538	564
35-39	241	255	269	283	298	332	382	400	471	533	519	433	372	377
40-44	218	226	234	243	245	249	287	355	369	434	488	471	394	373
45-49	229	230	230	231	232	233	245	277	340	350	406	456	443	435
50-54	238	239	240	241	243	241	232	238	267	326	331	382	431	434
55-59	224	239	252	250	247	247	243	227	232	257	309	311	359	370
60-64	224	214	204	210	220	232	247	236	220	222	244	291	293	301
65-69	237	237	236	236	232	227	219	241	228	211	212	235	278	268
70-74	227	227	229	229	229	229	224	212	230	216	203	203	224	245
75-79	181	187	193	194	198	199	206	202	192	206	193	183	185	185
80-84	117	117	117	121	128	132	147	155	154	151	160	151	144	145
85 and over	80	82	84	86	86	86	96	112	128	133	135	143	143	143
All ages	13251	13283	13305	13315	13309	13298	13371	13581	13838	14068	14135	14112	14173	14200
Males - *proportions married*														
0-14	-	-	-	-	-	-	-	-	-	-	-	-	-	-
15-19	0.015	0.014	0.014	0.015	0.015	0.015	0.015	0.016	0.015	0.013	0.015	0.015	0.015	0.015
20-24	0.308	0.296	0.287	0.283	0.281	0.280	0.282	0.280	0.279	0.265	0.261	0.273	0.274	0.274
25-29	0.691	0.673	0.658	0.646	0.636	0.629	0.615	0.610	0.601	0.594	0.593	0.595	0.598	0.597
30-34	0.815	0.809	0.800	0.792	0.786	0.778	0.751	0.737	0.729	0.720	0.718	0.721	0.721	0.721
35-39	0.852	0.845	0.841	0.836	0.833	0.827	0.811	0.786	0.773	0.767	0.762	0.760	0.762	0.762
40-44	0.862	0.859	0.855	0.850	0.847	0.844	0.836	0.821	0.800	0.788	0.783	0.780	0.778	0.778
45-49	0.857	0.855	0.854	0.852	0.850	0.849	0.844	0.838	0.825	0.806	0.797	0.793	0.789	0.788
50-54	0.855	0.852	0.849	0.847	0.844	0.844	0.844	0.842	0.838	0.825	0.809	0.801	0.797	0.796
55-59	0.857	0.854	0.851	0.847	0.844	0.840	0.834	0.838	0.836	0.835	0.824	0.809	0.802	0.801
60-64	0.841	0.840	0.839	0.840	0.840	0.837	0.828	0.823	0.827	0.828	0.828	0.818	0.803	0.801
65-69	0.813	0.813	0.813	0.813	0.813	0.811	0.813	0.804	0.801	0.807	0.810	0.809	0.801	0.798
70-74	0.757	0.761	0.762	0.764	0.765	0.766	0.767	0.770	0.761	0.761	0.767	0.772	0.774	0.772
75-79	0.665	0.668	0.669	0.677	0.677	0.682	0.687	0.690	0.697	0.691	0.693	0.700	0.707	0.707
80-84	0.536	0.541	0.553	0.554	0.551	0.556	0.566	0.578	0.580	0.587	0.583	0.590	0.600	0.603
85 and over	0.380	0.369	0.359	0.348	0.353	0.363	0.368	0.388	0.385	0.387	0.400	0.397	0.394	0.397
15 and over	0.673	0.666	0.660	0.655	0.650	0.647	0.641	0.649	0.660	0.652	0.637	0.633	0.638	0.639

Age	1977	1978	1979	1980	1981	1982	1986	1991	1996	2001	2006	2011	2016	2017
Married females *(thousands)*														
0-14	-	-	-	-			-	-	-	-	-	-	-	-
15-19	137	138	143	147	150	152	147	132	109	122	146	145	134	132
20-24	1036	1016	1003	1009	1024	1043	1132	1095	943	813	945	1088	1069	1056
25-29	1596	1527	1483	1452	1438	1442	1530	1694	1633	1369	1184	1404	1608	1674
30-34	1675	1725	1735	1741	1732	1630	1506	1636	1817	1741	1443	1247	1495	1572
35-39	1390	1407	1436	1461	1509	1627	1706	1502	1644	1826	1742	1436	1244	1262
40-44	1343	1348	1357	1357	1337	1332	1462	1670	1478	1622	1798	1710	1410	1334
45-49	1375	1354	1325	1299	1282	1274	1281	1414	1623	1438	1577	1746	1662	1625
50-54	1377	1349	1330	1313	1300	1281	1203	1211	1345	1546	1370	1503	1665	1668
55-59	1278	1331	1371	1312	1270	1237	1170	1090	1103	1229	1411	1253	1378	1414
60-64	1055	999	949	996	1042	1084	1078	997	934	950	1061	1220	1088	1100
65-69	844	844	845	846	827	806	805	835	778	734	751	846	975	924
70-74	535	540	545	547	551	549	544	538	557	528	502	517	589	643
75-79	255	260	264	269	271	275	286	286	292	303	289	278	291	293
80-84	91	90	90	91	92	93	100	106	109	115	119	116	115	117
85 and over	30	26	24	24	23	23	23	27	28	30	32	36	36	35
All ages	14017	13954	13900	13864	13848	13848	13973	14233	14393	14366	14370	14545	14759	14789
Other females *(thousands)*														
0-14	6104	5960	5806	5658	5523	5401	5224	5564	6079	6076	5685	5446	5556	5607
15-19	1978	2024	2069	2109	2122	2123	2009	1649	1438	1735	1975	1915	1722	1684
20-24	877	925	975	1019	1059	1094	1162	1083	861	757	935	1056	1014	993
25-29	380	396	413	417	431	451	531	577	523	414	365	455	514	511
30-34	247	268	285	309	324	320	337	398	426	388	314	277	338	353
35-39	195	205	218	232	246	274	325	318	367	394	365	300	259	264
40-44	201	207	216	223	227	230	269	335	317	362	394	370	301	283
45-49	243	242	244	243	243	247	259	291	352	330	378	414	387	377
50-54	317	311	304	304	302	300	286	294	321	384	358	408	446	446
55-59	416	432	446	427	413	400	378	349	351	381	455	417	470	483
60-64	551	523	496	499	512	526	520	473	433	433	471	554	502	511
65-69	724	720	715	710	694	674	630	642	582	532	530	577	675	640
70-74	806	816	824	828	829	826	795	731	747	677	623	624	683	739
75-79	737	756	769	780	788	799	823	794	742	760	698	647	651	650
80-84	509	522	540	555	573	585	628	662	645	618	634	591	553	554
85 and over	368	379	389	399	411	422	477	539	594	615	624	647	641	640
All ages	14653	14686	14709	14712	14697	14672	14653	14699	14778	14856	14804	14698	14712	14735
Females - *proportions married*														
0-14	-	-	-	-	-	-	-	-	-	-	-	-	-	-
15-19	0.065	0.064	0.065	0.065	0.066	0.067	0.068	0.074	0.070	0.066	0.069	0.070	0.072	0.073
20-24	0.542	0.523	0.507	0.498	0.492	0.488	0.493	0.503	0.523	0.518	0.503	0.507	0.513	0.515
25-29	0.808	0.794	0.782	0.777	0.769	0.762	0.742	0.746	0.757	0.768	0.764	0.755	0.758	0.760
30-34	0.871	0.866	0.859	0.849	0.842	0.836	0.817	0.804	0.810	0.818	0.821	0.818	0.816	0.817
35-39	0.877	0.873	0.868	0.863	0.860	0.856	0.840	0.825	0.818	0.823	0.827	0.827	0.828	0.827
40-44	0.870	0.867	0.863	0.859	0.855	0.853	0.845	0.833	0.823	0.818	0.820	0.822	0.824	0.825
45-49	0.850	0.848	0.844	0.842	0.841	0.838	0.832	0.829	0.822	0.813	0.807	0.808	0.811	0.812
50-54	0.813	0.813	0.814	0.812	0.811	0.810	0.808	0.805	0.807	0.801	0.793	0.786	0.789	0.789
55-59	0.754	0.755	0.755	0.754	0.755	0.756	0.756	0.757	0.759	0.763	0.756	0.750	0.746	0.745
60-64	0.657	0.656	0.657	0.666	0.671	0.673	0.675	0.678	0.683	0.687	0.693	0.688	0.684	0.683
65-69	0.538	0.540	0.542	0.544	0.544	0.545	0.561	0.565	0.572	0.580	0.586	0.595	0.591	0.591
70-74	0.399	0.398	0.398	0.398	0.399	0.399	0.406	0.424	0.427	0.438	0.446	0.453	0.463	0.465
75-79	0.257	0.256	0.256	0.256	0.256	0.256	0.258	0.265	0.282	0.285	0.293	0.301	0.309	0.311
80-84	0.152	0.147	0.143	0.141	0.138	0.137	0.137	0.138	0.145	0.157	0.158	0.164	0.172	0.174
85 and over	0.075	0.064	0.058	0.057	0.053	0.052	0.046	0.048	0.045	0.047	0.049	0.053	0.053	0.052
15 and over	0.621	0.615	0.610	0.605	0.602	0.599	0.597	0.609	0.623	0.621	0.612	0.611	0.617	0.618

Printed in England for Her Majesty's Stationery Office by Hobbs the Printers of Southampton
(600) Dd0597311 K13 4/79 G3927